PLAYWRIGHTS' PROGRESS

PLAYWRIGHTS' PROGRESS

Patterns of Postwar British Drama

COLIN CHAMBERS
AND MIKE PRIOR

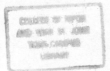

AMBER LANE PRESS

Published in 1987 by
Amber Lane Press Limited
9 Middle Way
Oxford OX2 7LH

Typeset in Ehrhardt by Oxford Computer Typesetting
Printed and bound in Great Britain by Bath Press Limited

Copyright © Colin Chambers and Mike Prior, 1987

ISBN: 0 906399 81 5

Contents

Acknowledgements

Our thanks to Clive Barker, Frances Gray, Katja Hehn, David Holman, Margot Leicester, Ewan MacColl, Genista McIntosh, our typist Kim Montia, Jane Noble, our editor Judith Scott, and Susan Todd.

C.C. & M.P.

Foreword

Playwrights are the prime intermediaries between the theatre and its society. It is their vision of social life that forms the bedrock on which a production rests. It is not necessary to idealize playwrights into the poets of an age but just to acknowledge that they are passionate and intelligent observers who have traced currents in society in a unique way. This is particularly so at moments of change and is certainly the case in the postwar period when playwrights have redefined the concerns of the craft or when one convention has begun to give way to another. It is these points of strain that interest us and have shaped our choices and approach.

The book begins with a chapter on general changes in the theatre, followed by four chapters on themes in postwar drama. The second part is devoted to chapters on individual playwrights. While much of the period has been well charted, though not necessarily from our standpoint, there has been little thematic cross-reference between the generations. The themes that we have chosen to examine in a sense chose themselves; they are important in the life of the society and British playwrights in the period have been preoccupied with them.

There are writers who have produced much well-received material who have little or no mention here, usually because they seemed to us to fit comfortably into existing patterns and to make few challenges to the audience or to theatrical practice. Whatever their individual problems with commercial or subsidized managements, whatever their individual use of techniques pioneered by others, we felt that they did not represent the kinds of tension within the theatre that we have identified as being crucial to its development.

Each reader will have a list of playwrights who could, or should, have been included and/or given more emphasis. At another date our emphasis would be different — some of the plays included have not been tested yet by a second generation. But we are responding in our own way at a given moment to a continuing process of which this book is a small part.

C.C. & M.P.

Note

Dates of plays given in brackets are usually those of first performance. Quotations are generally taken from the first published text. Readers may find variations in different editions.

CHAPTER ONE

Changes in Postwar British Drama

Postwar British drama is marked by two major moments of change that coincided with national and international political events of enormous consequence. The two watershed years of 1956 and 1968 represent the coming together of many factors, both inside and outside the theatre, during which conventional practices have given way under great strain to new ones. The extent and effect of these changes allow the postwar years to be divided usefully into three periods — 1945-56, 1956-68 and 1968-85 (the last full year that could be included in this book) — each precipitating the next through an uneven process of attempted renewal within the overall decline of a traditional drama. It is these conflicts that form the backdrop to this book.

The search for renewal has been dominated by an intense exploration of the relationship between the production and the reception of theatre: new ways of making plays with a new content, scope and purpose allied to an appeal for a new audience. The stimulus to much of the postwar pioneering work has been the effort to win back the working class to the theatre. The rediscovery of popular culture, particularly with music as a vital part of drama, figures prominently in a shift from the private to the public domain. Such a rediscovery is also a means to survive competition from other entertainments, which itself has raised important questions on the nature and role of contemporary theatre. The dilemmas of this reassessment have had various dimensions. Some have been commercial: a pattern of theatre-going which brought a large middle-class audience into the West End has gradually disappeared whilst the expense of maintaining its theatrical venues has soared. The West End has become a tourist theatre, geared to a bland, international taste. Some have been aesthetic: various trends in drama that have paralleled those in music, novels, poetry and painting, seem to have been concerned with forms which have had little engagement with popular taste and are almost incomprehensible to the general public. Yet the theatrical minimalism of, for example, Samuel Beckett or Jerzy Grotowski has been vastly influential in secondary impacts spreading beyond the avant garde theatres. Some dilemmas have been social and political: the apparently stable bourgeois world which had created modern theatre in the late 19th century began to display signs of increasing instability and deep conflict.

The necessary postwar reassessment has taken place within a theatrical culture that at first was still dominated by the values of the market place. These values were modified by the spread of public subsidy but they were not overthrown in the new mixed economy. While value judgements differed in the two sectors of commercial and subsidized theatre, it was a particularly bourgeois system of merit that determined where and to whom Britain's cultural resources should be directed. Such a value system was part of a whole view of society that was born in the heady days of Victorian capitalist expansion which saw society progressing by constant renewal through unrelenting competition. Its most hopeful symbol was the upward spiral, though after the Second World War it could be compared metaphorically to a free-for-all inside a padded cell.

In this system, certain types of theatre are seen as superior to others and, at each level of the hierarchy, only certain subjects are considered appropriate, only certain places are considered as suitable venues and only certain audiences are considered fit to judge. Each generation has to pass a set of tests to be finally judged at a centre of excellence against the past as well as the present, and, by implication, the future too. An actor's pinnacle, for example, might be playing Hamlet on the stages of the Royal Shakespeare Company or the National Theatre.

Such a view paints the past in the colours of the present and sees theatre as a continuous chain of history, a single cultural arena within which the diverse forms of drama engage with universal experience and are judged against a common purpose on a single, hierarchical scale of worth. While this view has rarely been propounded in its purest form during the postwar period, its main ideas have held sway in the bastions of power. This is in stark contrast to the ideas of playgoing in Elizabethan times or even to the type of theatre represented by those 19th-century playbills frequently on display in theatre bars and foyers which advertize what, to modern eyes, is an extraordinary mix of supposedly incompatible and separate forms: drama, ballet, opera, pantomime, concert. Important cultural and social gulfs were acknowledged to exist then, but nevertheless a performance of *Macbeth* reduced largely to its main speeches could be preceded by songs and followed by a dance troupe. The separation that occurred later, which implied that aesthetics existed in a social and political vacuum unrelated to the material conditions of creation, led to the erection of neat cultural categories — drama as opposed to dance, serious tragedy as opposed to light comedy — with less neat social divisions, music hall for example, being considered appropriate for one class, opera for another.

The development of this system has not necessarily been a recipe for complacent or easy theatre; the tradition of the classical humanist repertoire, and in particular the battle it has provoked between naturalism and anti-naturalism in the 20th century, is a monument to its creative potential. There are many examples, too, of imaginative, effective drama that are also politically and culturally subversive of the status quo. But, equally, the system has not offered a recipe for popular theatre; the process was designed to protect theatre from the consensus of popular judgement which was believed to induce artistic stagnation. Yet in 1945, for example, wartime experience provided evidence for the opposite argument — the 'cultural gap' had temporarily disappeared and a new, popular enthusiasm for the arts had opened up tremendous possibilities.

1945-56

In the immediate postwar period the arts and the theatre came well down on the list of political priorities. Life was austere, even though Britain had not been reduced to the conditions of Germany or Japan. Women were forced back into the home, nursery places were cut, food was still rationed (in the case of meat until 1956) and coal shortages caused power cuts and domestic heating difficulties. Housing was a major problem and many cities with large areas of bomb sites often took years to clear and redevelop them.

Radicals and reformers of many different kinds operated throughout the arts yet there was little determined attempt to join together to use the new Labour Government for change. By the end of the 1950s such administrative options as had been opened up had been firmly gathered in by the cultural establishment.

The Labour Government did achieve something, however: it began to secure a future for the arts through state support. The 1948 Local Government Act granted local authorities the right to spend annually up to the product of a 6d (2½p) rate on leisure activities. But this was not made into a statutory obligation and very few local councils had any idea of what to do with the money. Most did virtually nothing. The London-based mandarins at the newly established Arts Council shelved proposals for greater democracy and regional initiatives. They ran an arts policy of 'Few But Roses'. This contrasts with the slogan 'The Best for Most' that CEMA (the Council for the Encouragement of Music and the Arts) had adopted in wartime.

Various projects were set up in the late 1940s but their implementation seemed to drag on for ever. The National Theatre Act of 1949, for example, authorized the Treasury to cooperate with the London County Council to finance, build and equip a new theatre as part of Labour's nationalization programme. It was 1963 before a company of

actors was formed and 1976 by the time the theatre on the South Bank
was opened to the public. Similarly, Labour's Chancellor of the Ex-
chequer attended a theatre conference in 1948 (chaired by J.B. Priestley but boycotted by commercial managers). The conference called for
the setting up of a public authority to control rents and take charge of
theatre buildings. It took until 1962 for all sections of the profession to
come together in the Theatres Advisory Council to consider such
matters and it was only in 1977 that the Theatres Trust was established to protect theatre buildings. Civic theatre building did not
develop on a large scale until the 1960s and Britain had never had a
Minister for the Arts until the Labour Government created the post in
1964.

The immediate postwar period did see some exciting developments.
The Glasgow Citizens' Theatre was reopened in 1945, and in 1946
the Bristol Old Vic was launched. Groups like the Midlands Theatre
Company, which toured the region around its base in Coventry, were
among the pioneers to lay the foundation for the new civic theatre
movement that was to follow. While Sir Barry Jackson was overhauling
the Memorial Theatre in Stratford-upon-Avon where he was director
(1945-48), Laurence Olivier and Ralph Richardson were leading the
Old Vic Company at the New Theatre in London and Tyrone Guthrie
was presenting his experimental Company of Four at the Lyric.

A few explorers of new theatrical territory were beginning to
emerge. Some were social pioneers and some came from a self-
conscious intellectual elite. All were under-financed. George Devine
and Michel Saint-Denis, for instance, wanted to create a theatrical
centre at the Old Vic that would combine productions of classical
drama with a school and a young people's touring theatre. They did
succeed in setting up a new performance circuit for the Young Vic
(1946-51) but with little encouragement from educationalists in the
provinces. (More than one hundred Chief Education Officers were
notified of the scheme and not one responded positively. Liverpool
Local Education Authority went so far as to declare itself thoroughly
fed up with such ventures — a mere two years after the 1944 Education Act had opened the door for them.) Although the Young Vic
survived for such a short time — its companion school was also
short-lived and was closed in 1952 — it did manage to spread its
influence through the individuals who had been associated with it.

Meanwhile, in the commercial theatre, both in the West End and
out of London, the status quo was quickly re-established. One fifth of
London's theatres had been destroyed during the War but the same
handful of big chains continued to run those that were left. In spite of
the entertainment tax, and massive increases in rents and rates, all of
which pushed ticket prices up, it was business as usual. The regional
reps were replaying West End hits while the West End waited for the

next star vehicle to come along in between the staples of musicals, thrillers, revues and drawing-room comedies. William Douglas Home scored a hit with his play *The Chiltern Hundreds* (1947) in which a socialist peer is defeated in an election by his Tory butler, and Agatha Christie's *The Mousetrap* started its world-record-breaking run (1952).

For playwrights it was not a propitious time. George Bernard Shaw still towered as a monumental cultural institution (he died in 1950, aged 94), while fellow Irishman Sean O'Casey, who had settled permanently in England, carried with him a reputation but exerted much less influence than he deserved. He had trouble getting *Red Roses for Me* into the West End in 1946 and continued to have similar difficulties. Although Terence Rattigan, Noël Coward, J.B. Priestley, Emlyn Williams, James Bridie, Ben Travers and Benn Levy were still active, new playwriting talent was decidedly thin on the ground. The only writing with a distinct presence was verse drama. The chief practitioners were Ronald Duncan, Christopher Fry and T.S. Eliot but the genre was guaranteed to have limited appeal. Much of this and other new work took place in the proliferating private clubs, away from commercial pressures and the threat of censorship. It is arguable, however, that these clubs merely served to widen the culture gap even further.

In the absence of home-grown theatrical excitement attention turned abroad. Peter Daubeny began to bring foreign companies to Britain in 1951 (long before his successful World Theatre Seasons at the Aldwych of the 1960s and 70s), and London saw a good deal of Jean Anouilh's work before 1956. Arthur Miller and Tennessee Williams caused shock-waves but were not as influential as they might have been. Their plays were regarded as exotic and therefore without any real bearing on the British sensibility.

All in all, the first postwar decade was a period of stagnation for new drama and a time of missed opportunities, characterized by a steady pulling away of artistic function from social and political attitudes. But by the mid-1950s something of a cultural revolution had begun, with a whole new range of outside influences. Jazz, rock 'n' roll, television, American cinema, youth as an important social category and working-class style were beginning to transform the social scene.

1956-68

It is common to see 1956 as the beginning of a new theatrical wave, mainly associated with the era inaugurated at the Royal Court by the English Stage Company, with John Osborne's *Look Back in Anger* as the catalyst. Certainly 1956 is the year that the theatre picked up from the interruption of the War, but the great changes that crystallized in that landmark year did not concern only — or mainly — the Royal Court.

In a small but important way 1956 also means the successful challenge to convention and censorship represented by the opening of the New Watergate theatre club at the West End's Comedy Theatre to stage plays related to gay themes; it means the launch of the impressive theatre magazine *Encore*; it means the influence of the Europeans and the absurdists — Samuel Beckett's *Waiting for Godot* was first seen in London at the Arts Club in August 1955; it means more significantly the wider recognition of Joan Littlewood's Theatre Workshop; and, most importantly, it means the Berliner Ensemble under Bertolt Brecht, which first visited London in 1956.

Elements of Brecht's stagecraft have become so much taken for granted, even if his theory and practice are rarely applied in full, that it is necessary to note again the impact of this visit and to underscore the enormous importance of the work that he and his collaborators created. Much of Brecht's work is still little known in Britain, though his innovations have become common currency, despite continual critical attempts to separate his art from his politics and to downgrade his standing. Ironically, there is evidence to suggest that the 1956 uprising against Soviet domination in Hungary helped kill Brecht's *The Good Woman of Setzuan* at the Royal Court whilst the British military intervention that year in Suez gave added life to *Look Back in Anger*.

The period 1956-68 transformed the social landscape of Britain. It was the most sustained period of economic growth in the country's history and, although the growth was hardly meteoric by international standards, this opened up cultural activity in many ways. Some of these are obvious — higher living standards caused leisure industries of all kinds to boom. But other factors were also at work. There was an expansion in higher education which provided various employment niches for budding writers and also provided a new audience. For the first time, in some cities, students could form the backbone audience for experimental theatre. State funding was the key motif of the period and the drive to reconstruct war-damaged city centres meant a surge of new, municipal theatres and associated local backing, as well as increased central government subsidy.

These years were dominated artistically by the achievements of those who were attempting to sustain the identity of four companies in London — Theatre Workshop, the English Stage Company, the Royal Shakespeare Company and the National Theatre. Each company was striving to develop an ensemble feeling with a recognizable style of performance that was expressed through all the elements of a production. In 1956 the scandalously underfunded Theatre Workshop made the first of seven transfers to the West End with an adaptation by Ewan MacColl of Jaroslav Hašek's novel *The Good Soldier Schweik*, which was followed by, among others, *The Quare Fellow* and *The Hostage* by Brendan Behan, *A Taste of Honey* by Shelagh Delaney and *Oh, What a*

Lovely War! in 1963. (The last two were also made into successful films.) This kind of breakthrough, which was crucial to the company's survival, led to its effective demise as new and inexperienced casts had to be assembled at the home base.

At the Royal Court, George Devine wanted initially to win back to the theatre writers who had preferred the novel, poetry or even journalism to the stage. The birth of the English Stage Company was the result of accident and compromise. Yet before either of the national companies existed, Devine and his associate Tony Richardson created an environment in which playwrights could develop. This policy was continued with as much conviction and perhaps even more single-mindedness under William Gaskill, Devine's successor in 1965. All the playwrights considered in the individual chapters in this book owe a great deal to the Royal Court's championship of new writing.

The Royal Shakespeare Company was formed in 1960 under Peter Hall with a strong directorial team that included Peter Brook and Michel Saint-Denis. Apart from directly challenging the star system that had operated in Stratford-upon-Avon as a microcosm of the commercial theatre, Hall took his new company into the heartland of the West End by acquiring the Aldwych Theatre as a London outlet. Having won substantial state subsidy, he not only changed the shape of British theatre but provided the first prolonged incursion from the public sector into the competitive market place.

Following the RSC's footsteps, the National Theatre Company was formed in 1963 after more than a century of debate. The National Theatre was based initially at the Old Vic before a permanent theatre was built on the South Bank in London. Laurence Olivier became the National's first artistic director, with a core of actors from the Chichester Festival Theatre which he also led. There were close links at first between the National Theatre and the Royal Court and much talk at different times of a merger between the NT and the RSC. Each company has retained its independence, although there has been considerable exchange of personnel, and the two larger companies have grown increasingly similar. Both, inevitably, were to play an important role in the fate of new writing.

Against this London weighting came a strong push from relatively isolated theatre workers in the rest of Britain. While the old commercial rep system was dying, with television dealing the final blow, civic programmes were getting under way; the first new regional theatre to be built entirely with local authority money was the Belgrade in Coventry, which opened in 1958. It was there that the three plays making up Arnold Wesker's Trilogy were first seen (1958-60). It was also at the Belgrade that Britain's Theatre-in-Education movement took off, with the formation in 1965 of a project devised by the artistic director and some local teachers.

Out-of-London initiatives proved extremely important — from the likes of the new Nottingham Playhouse to the smaller Liverpool Everyman, the Library Theatre, Manchester or the Traverse, Edinburgh. Stephen Joseph's touring Studio Theatre, which he founded in 1955 based in Scarborough, pioneered much theatre-in-the-round work and presented new plays by James Saunders, David Campton and Alan Ayckbourn. The company came to rest in 1962 at the Victoria, Stoke-on-Trent and, under Peter Cheeseman, has developed into a leading community theatre which has influenced British drama far beyond its own locale. The Citizens' Theatre in Glasgow continued to break new ground. In 1967 they premiered Peter Nichols' *A Day in the Death of Joe Egg*, a daring, funny play about a spastic child that changed many notions of what was acceptable on stage.

While the 1956-68 period was a fruitful one for director/playwright teams — John Osborne with both Tony Richardson and Anthony Page, Arnold Wesker with John Dexter, Harold Pinter with Peter Hall, Edward Bond with William Gaskill — it did not see any widespread acceptance of the collective methods used by Theatre Workshop. There was no sustained examination of the body politic but there was a general democratic shift that affected content, acting styles, design and appeal. The theatre became broader and more social, its stages more open and its buildings more municipal. The trade union movement became involved, briefly, through a project called Centre 42, led by Arnold Wesker. It was a time of John Arden's *The Workhouse Donkey* at Chichester, *The Wars of the Roses* at Stratford-upon-Avon and *Oh, What a Lovely War!* at Stratford East — all 1963 — but it was also a time of closer experiment, of Jean Genet and Antonin Artaud, of radical, smaller-scale explorations that can be summed up in Peter Brook's manifesto to theatrical rediscovery, *The Empty Space*, which appeared in 1968.

Brook's production of *US* (1966) at the Aldwych had marked a dividing point. Collectively written by the RSC cast and outside writers and drawing freely on a range of dramatic techniques, it was the first full-scale excursion by a major, nationally subsidized company into an explicit and contemporary political theme — the Vietnam War. Both politically and dramatically, a new era was beginning.

1968-85

Those who had grown up since the Second World War were not only critical of consumer capitalist society dominated by US imperialism; they also rejected the socialism of the Soviet Union — 1968 was the year of the Soviet invasion of Czechoslovakia. A rhetoric concerning public politics emerged that was centred on the individual, fostered through the continued expansion of higher education with new universities and the upgrading of polytechnics.

Most of those who entered the theatre in the late 1960s were fuelled by a desire for change both inside and outside the auditorium. The post-1956 writers had generally held radical political views in the sense of supporting unilateral nuclear disarmament or voting Labour but they still tended to work within the given system. Although Theatre Workshop had broken down some conventions, it had collapsed under the effort, and whatever their merits, the English Stage Company (ESC), RSC and NT remained rigidly hierarchical bodies which, in many respects, would have been easily recognizable to Harley Granville-Barker from the Edwardian Royal Court era.

Around 1968 a moral and political curtain dropped in the theatre, with the alternative movement on one side, feeding off its own energies and motivated by a common ideology of being separate from and rejecting all that lay on the other side. Older theatre workers who were dissatisfied with the way that their profession was organized joined with younger enthusiasts to mount a thorough-going challenge to all aspects of theatre and beyond. The American counter-culture was central, particularly through the visits in 1967 of companies like Café La Mama and the Open Theatre, through an influx of Americans to the British theatre and through greater travel and communication opportunities.

It was now the era of instant theatre, on any issue, created by anyone, in any style, performed anywhere. A radical, flamboyant, egalitarian edge to the work permeated the whole process: workshops and collectives replaced traditionally atomized ways of working; old hierarchies and divisions were broken down. Censorship in the shape of the Lord Chamberlain's office was abolished in 1968 and no subject was taboo. There was a new and invigorating sense of belonging to a movement, nationally and internationally, that embraced everyone, not just the playwrights. The fringe had become the alternative theatre. Groups ranging from Broadside Mobile Workers' Theatre to Monstrous Regiment, from Welfare State to Inter-Action, created a new audience from among its own generation and developed a network of arts centres and small theatres out of buildings such as warehouses and old churches. Big repertory theatres and the national companies opened their own small auditoria and studio spaces. In the early 1970s, with public money forthcoming, the alternative theatre could say that it had arrived. Many groups with specific aims fulfilled a much-needed service, in communities, in pubs and clubs, in sexual politics, in education for old and young people, for black people, for disabled people. When the National Theatre opened on the South Bank in 1976 it was met by protests from the alternative theatre movement which claimed to be the *other* national theatre. One cost £16 million to build, received £2 million subsidy a year and would employ 500 staff and just over 100 actors, claimed the protesters, while the other, using existing buildings often many years old, received £700,000 subsidy, employed over 1,000 people and was still expanding.

Despite the impact of the alternative, especially outside London, there was less of an audience breakthrough in sociological terms than had been hoped for. Overtly politically conscious groups like 7:84, CAST, Belt and Braces and Foco Novo emerged along with a new trade union militancy in the early 1970s but were often cut off through attitude, life-style and organization from the very people they were trying to reach. Strenuous efforts were made to connect the new political culture with the unions and there were some notable successes, but in general these were short-lived.

Nevertheless, the middle classes were changing rapidly and represented important strata that any political culture would ignore at its peril. The alternative groups kept theatre alive for many thousands of people, and gave new life to the bastions of the establishment — the subsidized theatres that had been the vanguard of the 1950s and early 1960s. There was an extraordinary mushrooming of playwrights and some, like Trevor Griffiths, Howard Brenton, David Hare and David Edgar, moved from one world to the other with apparent ease while regional theatres like Nottingham, Sheffield and Birmingham became much stronger, presenting more new writing and making a real challenge to the dominance of London.

During the post-1968 period the system made its accommodations, although the processes of democracy and devolution proved to be slow. Alan Ayckbourn emerged as the most successful and experimental new playwright to be staged in the West End, and his plays, like much else that sustained Shaftesbury Avenue, arrived via the subsidized theatre. The alternative movement made little impression on the commercial sector until the 1980s, when Dario Fo's *Accidental Death of an Anarchist*, which had been toured by the revolutionary socialist group Belt and Braces, appeared in the West End for a long run, later to be broadcast on television.

As ever, star names helped the commercial and larger regional theatres, and these were provided by television and occasionally the world of popular music, particularly at Christmas-time. Musicals retained their hold, and with composer Andrew Lloyd Webber and lyricist Tim Rice came the embryo of a new British contribution to that form.

The climate changed in the late 1970s and more so in the early 1980s as the economic squeeze saw a string of West End theatres go 'dark' and change owners. But Shaftesbury Avenue could still rely on the old staples — musicals, thrillers and comedies. Not all gains were lost, although the original motor of the alternative theatre had burnt out when a radical right-wing government was elected in 1979 and shattered the welfare state consensus. Following some severe but limited cuts, the Arts Council came under right-wing leadership and introduced a new slogan in 1984: 'The Glory of the Garden'. This seemed a grim throwback to its previous horticultural metaphor of 'Few But Roses'. Once again theatre and the arts in general were under great threat. The government imposed punitive financial limits on local authorities and announced its intention to abolish six metro-politan councils that were responsible for a great bulk of Britain's arts, spending together a sum that equalled one third of the total Arts Council budget. The responsibility for expansion in the arts was placed in the uncertain hands of private patronage.

For a generation that now had four television channels and the prospect of cable and satellite to come, the map had been redrawn. The beginnings of a pluralistic, multi-cultural theatre had begun to emerge, but with the return of mass unemployment and the prospect of Britain as a front line nuclear target, it became clear that another era had ended.

Theatrical Structure

While the changes in postwar theatre are to be considered in this book mainly through the work of playwrights, there are three important areas that need to be emphasized first: one is funding, the second is professional organization, and the third is technical change.

1. **Funding**. The economic and organizational underpinning to the great postwar changes has been the establishment and growth of state subsidy. This became necessary for the survival of theatre which, as a labour-intensive, craft-based industry, could not otherwise have developed in an era of mass production, automation and rapid techno-logical change. The first theatre to be financed by the state was the Theatre Royal, Bristol, the country's oldest working theatre. The Arts Council's predecessor CEMA rescued it from destruction during the Second World War and helped visiting companies play there until it became stable under a group from the Old Vic.

Little of the Arts Council's funding goes directly to playwrights, although a limited number of bursaries has been provided by the Arts Council and other bodies. But the implicit knowledge in the subsidized theatre that the source of finance for a play is not dependent simply on the box office has altered theatre workers' attitudes. What is of interest is how the Arts Council — the very existence of which represents a shift towards proper state support — has confirmed the dominant system of values that shaped postwar developments.

Funding for British theatres is three-fold: most importantly, by the

Arts Council, which receives annually a grant from Parliament, and by the fifteen regional arts associations, which receive roughly two-thirds of their income from the Arts Council and one third from local government, local education authorities, and local industries and organizations; secondly, by local government direct; and thirdly, by private sponsorship and backing.

The Arts Council's budget has grown from a little over £¼ million with some 300 clients just after the War to about £105 million for around 1,200 clients in 1985. A breakthrough came in the mid-1960s when Jennie Lee became the first Minister for the Arts. Increased funding was made available for housing the arts, for companies to occupy such buildings and, at a later stage, for fringe and alternative theatre activities. The main principle behind the funding is one of laissez faire, with the major drama portion going to the two national 'centres of excellence', the RSC and NT. The funding is carried out at arm's length from government, the Arts Council being an independent, autonomous body appointed by a Minister. Its dealings are notoriously labyrinthine, secretive and undemocratic and are not, therefore, subject to proper public scrutiny. This does not mean that it is entirely narrow-minded, although it has never produced an adequate and coherent statement of how it pursues its obligations under the Royal Charter, particularly when faced with major new demands on its purse. The phrase 'accessible excellence' aptly describes the thrust of its thinking, which accommodates the twin impulses of the postwar period — the parallel pursuit of the social and the artistic.

While not underestimating the mainstream developments of the 1960s, which laid the ground for much that came later, the most crucial change in attitude came under the impact of the alternative theatre. This forced the Arts Council to recognize new areas of work and to introduce a multi-faceted view of theatre. It became possible to answer the question, 'What is the aim of your theatre/group/show/ project?' in a variety of acceptable ways, not all of which had anything to do with the central cultural norms; in some cases even, in order to secure funding, the answer had to embrace a non-artistic policy (such as playing to a 'disadvantaged' group).

The process of requiring and providing an answer is both discrete and bureaucratic — something which, in political terms, has cut both ways. Groups with an explicit left-wing vision have never had to write in the appropriate part of their Arts Council application that their purpose was to bring a socialist message to the working class and to challenge bourgeois cultural aesthetics. Yet when the 7:84 company, for example, found itself funded on a project grant instead of an annual revenue grant as expected — following a libel action against the company concerning *The Ballygombeen Bequest* by John Arden and Margaretta D'Arcy — there was no way of proving that a political

decision had been taken. Clearly the group was being penalized despite having produced excellent work.

Subsidy has helped to reinstate a variety of purposes in the theatre
which require different forms and working practices for their achievement. An unusually clear-cut example of this is Theatre-in-Education
(TIE) which, since the formation of the original Coventry group, has
blossomed in all parts of Britain. This work obviously exists within the
area defined by theatre and it also involves technical skills which are as
highly developed as in any other part of the theatre. It is not a
cut-down version of larger stage-shows presented in a suitable form
for children; it is a different type of work with its own particular aims
and marks of success. Though often less clear-cut, the same is true of
other types of theatre; for instance, particular kinds of regional or local
theatre provided by such companies as Medium Fair in Devon or the
Combination at London's Albany Empire; feminist or gay theatre;
drama with particular ethnic emphases or committed to a particular
group such as disabled people; or drama that concentrates on the
development of some specific form, such as in performance art, which
may move sharply away from conventional theatre.

The contradictory and undefined status of subsidy has had several
effects on British playwriting. It has certainly opened up new areas of
work for which there continues to be great demand, from the conven-
tionally written play texts to those created collectively. Although the
exact numbers are unknown, it is probably true that more new plays
were produced during the 1970s than in any preceding decade, including the great heights of Edwardian theatre. Much of this work was
aimed at new audiences which, successfully or not, the alternative
theatre was trying to reach. But the indirect and uncertain nature of
subsidy has continued to make a playwright's life both meagre and
precarious. The role of 'house-writer' working with some kind of
long-term security has not been adequately tried. Ironically, it is only
foreign royalties from the massively subsidized theatres of continental
Europe, particularly Germany and Scandinavia, that has enabled some
of Britain's most celebrated playwrights to survive when they have
failed to gain access to London's commercial stages or have chosen not
to write for television.

2. Professional Organization. The problem of funding is related to
the second factor — the growing importance of professional organization — which can be seen in the establishment of the Theatre Writers'
Union in 1976 or, more generally, in the changing status of Actors'
Equity. Actors are now better trained than before and have increased
their purchase on conditions of work, a situation unusual in a grossly
exploited and often seasonal profession. One of the most remarkable
facts of the theatre has been how this section of workers, who suffer as

great a level of unemployment as any in Britain, has carried through a difficult and wide-ranging reappraisal of its profession to a degree that has transformed it. However, there is still enormous room for improvement for actors, not just over pay and accommodation, or in sexual equality — including the crucial matters of childcare, training and retraining — but also on issues such as the bias in casting against non-white performers, and the isolation of drama schools from the state system.

Changes in material standards and in the general quality of work are the most important overall results of professional organization, whether among actors, playwrights, musicians or production staff. But there has also been another important change — in the shifting pattern of power and control within the theatre. Although the degree and form has varied widely, control has become a central issue. Some of the democratic impulse has been absorbed into normal rehearsal practice, but where new theatrical territory is being explored, or where there are scant human and financial resources, there is a persistent tendency for the issue of control to arise as a central and often overriding concern. For the playwright, this has been double-edged. The Theatre Writers' Union was formed to correct the appalling treatment of the dramatist as the idealized artist with little or no influence over production and very small commission fees. Along with the Writers' Guild of Great Britain (formed in 1959 to negotiate primarily in the world of film and television), the Union's success has been limited but significant in this material sphere. There has been great improvement for the writer on access to rehearsals, on casting decisions and in some cases on appointing the director and designer, but virtually nothing on power within a company, which, as a general rule, is automatically invested in a director even at that most well-known writers' theatre, the Royal Court.

On the issue of control over work the outcome has been ambiguous. Many playwrights have found a collaborative process, including the extensive revision of material during rehearsal and even the effective creation of texts on the rehearsal floor, a very fruitful way of working. Perhaps the best example of this has been the way the Joint Stock touring company has produced work with playwrights such as Howard Brenton, David Hare, Stephen Lowe, Barrie Keeffe and Caryl Churchill. For others it is anathema. But clearly the area has remained one of unresolved tension, in which the role and status of playwrights has been fluctuating — a situation as true of playwrights within small collective theatre groups as of those who work with the big national companies. It is significant just how many playwrights have left the traditional British stage or feel excluded from it over issues that essentially come down to control of their own work.

It is difficult not to conclude that some kind of artistic crisis exists within British theatre, particularly in how it allows its playwrights to develop. A lot of talent has bubbled up which never quite fulfils early promise. A lot of fine playwrights have been abandoned, have drifted grumpily away or have taken easier and financially more rewarding options in other media. In the end it is not a cheerful note that has to be sounded, although there have been fewer casualties from the playwrights of the 1970s than might have been expected.

3. Technical Change. Within the third area, that of technical developments, the internal changes appear at first sight to be small but they are of great significance. At the centre of the dominant theatrical tradition is its technical definition, that of well-lit and, to some extent, realistic sets, mainly indoors, placed before an audience in a darkened auditorium. Realistic costumes, sound-effects and variable lighting are accompanying requirements.

The technical problems of providing this in the period before the late-Victorian era were vast and required a great concentration of various kinds of technical talent. Lighting problems alone were critical, not just because of frequent fires but because of the great clumsiness and constraints of any kind of combusted light-source. Electricity solved this, transforming the technical possibilities of the theatre and making possible a genuine naturalism. But it also finally tied theatre down to a fixed and cumbersome building requiring heavy and permanently sited lights and complex control systems. Similarly, the technical solutions found for design or sound problems required the use of very specialized technicians and, often, of unwieldy apparatus. Theatre had to be big to make it pay.

Since the 1950s, technological advance and the increased availability of its products has swept away most of these constraints; lightweight alloys, spray paints, plastic, new fibres, sophisticated sound-systems, microchip lighting boards and video have all improved the flexibility and range of possibilities. Hundreds of innovations from non-iron fabrics and artificial smoke to the Ford Motor Company's great gift to the theatre, the Transit van, have made the gargantuan hives of specialized enterprise redundant. In general, smaller and cheaper venues can provide nearly all the technical and dramatic requirements for modern theatre. This is not to say that touring groups or small makeshift theatres consistently match the technical quality of the larger theatres; problems of wage levels, ability to plan, training, continuity and access to financial resources have to be taken into account as well. The best equipment is expensive, but nevertheless the range of technical achievement in the British theatre by the 1970s was much more uniform than at any time in the century.

The 'all-singing-and-dancing' mechanical stages under central computer control that so fascinated both the RSC and NT managements soon seemed like the last of the dinosaurs. For example, the complex machinery installed for the mammoth 'Roman' season in 1972 at Stratford-upon-Avon marked not the beginning of a technical expansion but the last frantic gasps of a whole style. Artistically, the energy of the company flowed into its tin-hut theatre, The Other Place, a replica of the alternative theatre in almost every way, down to inadequate funding, uncomfortable seating and, in compensation, absolutely committed acting, directing, design and production work. In the 1980s, reliance on technical spectacle returned as artistic inspiration waned, in common with a similar shift in the theatre generally.

There has been a constant lament for the slow ruin of the commercial London theatres and their few provincial counterparts since the rise of the subsidized network. Such lament has usually concentrated on the collapse of their cultural values but the root cause is much simpler. They are economic and technical whales stranded on the beach, too expensive, too limited and lacking their earlier social function.

Something of the same process has been at work in the large provincial theatres built on a wave of municipal enthusiasm in the late 1950s and 1960s. These do retain a social and civic purpose, however, even though this has often remained obscure or ambiguous. Their open or thrust stages, instead of the earlier proscenium designs, along with the use of studio theatres, has frequently meant greater flexibility of repertoire than in the West End.

External Change

Outside the theatre, the general challenge presented by other media has contributed to the loss of the theatre's unique and well-defined cultural role. Immediately after the Second World War, dramatic writing was a clear-cut artistic category with its main links extended to the novel. For example, in 1956, Devine's initial approach towards getting new plays was to bring in established novelists. In Britain, unlike the USA, playwrights were not heavily engaged in the cinema.

In the succeeding decades, this categorization has become less and less obvious as cinema and television have provided a direct cultural alternative to the theatre, creating within it all kinds of difficulties and ambiguities. Some of these were concerned with financial viability, though these should not be over-emphasized. The theatre shed old forms like the commercial reps and revived both artistically and financially during the period when television had its greatest purchase. It was the cinema, not the theatre, which collapsed under television's impact, although many plays still seem to be unduly influenced by the naturalism and structure of small-screen drama. However, because neither television nor film is capable of theatre's dynamic live reproduction, writers in those media have been removed from the central position. A remake of a film at best preserves the plot outline, and in television little material is ever shown more than once. What may be reproduced is a general style, a set of characters, a particular plot framework. The tendency is to devalue the writers, even to the point of reducing them to an almost anonymous state as in those conglomerate film scripts which pass through the traditional rewrite process of several hands or in the factory line production of scripts for a well established TV serial.

While new technologies open up extraordinary possibilities, there are dangers for political definition and control of future leisure time. Television has already proved more sensitive in terms of censorship than the more remote medium of theatre where, in most cases, overt censorship has been replaced by a discreet system of consensus. Nevertheless, the other media competing with live theatre have created a greater range of work within the general sphere of drama, and here the dominant cultural view of theatre has worked in its favour. To write exclusively, or mainly, for television, regardless of the numbers of audience you are reaching, can keep you relatively unknown, as in the case of playwrights like John Hopkins or Jim Allen. By contrast, David Hare, who has written much less for television, has acquired a much greater prestige because of his stage plays. The paraphernalia of status maintains this unjustifiable disparity and, while there is a steady exchange between the two media, there are relatively few established and noted playwrights who prefer to move into television. (An obvious exception is Trevor Griffiths.)

The exchange with radio has been more complementary, both media sharing an emphasis on the imagination and words. Radio can boast an impressive list of practitioners from Dylan Thomas, whose *Under Milk Wood* was first broadcast in 1954, and Giles Cooper, who made the medium his own, to playwrights like John Arden or Peter Barnes who were finding it impossible to work on the stage; BBC radio, it should be noted, presents more new plays than theatre or television.

Under all these different pressures, the theatre has had to make many adjustments, though the results are far from negative. Stage plays have tended to move away from traditional concerns of plot and character to a greater embracing of ideas, with important shifts in the use of language and moral tone. This has sometimes led to a new role for the audience — from passive if critical spectators of the proscenium style to active agents in a social process. At times the audience is cast as both judge and defendant, incriminated as representatives of a sick society but urged to go forth and change it.

While the social and political shifts of the postwar period form the background to these theatrical changes, their impact is much more complex and ambiguous than a simple politicization towards the Left. There has always been a very strong and often dominant strain of social radicalism amongst dramatists and theatre workers as a whole, not necessarily in any highly political or analytical way but as a part of their commitment to working in a social art form. Although many socialists have been active in the theatre, the number interested professionally in developing a recognizable 'socialist' theatre has always been relatively limited. However, there has been an enormous interest in creating a *popular* theatre, a much less precise idea, stretching on the one hand from groups like Belt and Braces, aiming to combine the popular with a socialist orientation, to many provincial theatres and touring groups for whom popularity has the most straightforward of definitions — of searching out new local audiences who would never have dreamt of entering a traditional theatre. An extraordinary example is the Glasgow Citizens' Company, which presented the boldest repertory in Britain in the 1970s and early 1980s in its own distinct style, attracting full houses on a cheap ticket policy and winning accolades at home and abroad.

The root of many such successes in getting new audiences has not been political but a straight appeal to local sentiment over a specific event. Such a local or regional commitment is a major element in British postwar theatre, both in terms of subject matter and in the loyalty of playwrights, like Alan Ayckbourn, Alan Plater, Willy Russell, C.P. Taylor or Peter Terson, to name a few. It is no longer true that metropolitan theatre automatically dominates, although the procedures of newspaper theatre critics might belie this, when every West End show, however limping, gets into national editions whilst regional plays, if reviewed, often only make the regional editions.

Critical attention and financial security continue to be important to playwrights as to all other artists and it remains true for live drama that only by being performed in a London theatre for a considerable run can a playwright gain access to wider acclaim. It is the continuing critical and financial hold of established London theatre, with all its conventional rigidities, that makes the partial shift of artistic power away from the capital and its dominant values all the more remarkable. It also makes the threat in the 1980s to this development all the more serious.

CHAPTER TWO

Images of the Working Class

By the beginning of the Second World War certain kinds of drama had been given an exclusive definition as theatre; they had become a key to middle-class culture — the bourgeoisie watching enactments of bourgeois life in conditions which guaranteed a self-conscious homogeneity of both content and form. The argument has been presented too often to need lengthy repetition but it is clear that the conventions of this theatre-going, many of which remain strong, from the manner of booking tickets to the times of performance, helped to guarantee a middle-class audience or required a working-class audience to mimic its behaviour. This theatre acquired an aura of respectability that imposed itself as soon as one walked through its doors. One of the main factors inhibiting working people from going to the theatre was simple intimidation; they were made to feel that they did not belong, as indeed they did not. Other kinds of live entertainment, such as music hall, were separated out as distinct and inferior forms, suitable for the vulgarity of the lower classes. On the metropolitan stage this situation intensified rather than diminished during the 1920s and 1930s, with the conventions both of play-going and what was regarded as suitable content for plays reaching self-parodying limits.

The situation was different outside London where the repertory movement had grown up to challenge the Shaftesbury Avenue orientation of 'proper' theatre. As with all such innovations, the inspiration came partly from the audiences and partly from the profession. The demand was for a new approach to the classics and for new, socially based writing — very much the cry of the later subsidized theatres. Trade provided the backing. Annie Horniman used her tea profits in 1908 to champion a new theatre, the Gaiety in Manchester, having already financed the Abbey Theatre in Dublin. Basil Dean, a member of her company, set up the Liverpool Playhouse in 1911, and in 1913, Barry Jackson used his grocery profits to set up the Birmingham Rep. But despite a strong regional emphasis, the pressure of the London stage held sway and the reps degenerated.

This was not a simple or uniform process, as the struggles within the repertory movement or the efforts of Lilian Baylis at the Old Vic show. As the process occurred the exclusion of the working class both as subject and audience from the 'proper' theatre had a serious effect on playwrights. The radical drama movement at the turn of the century, which was focused on writers like Ibsen, did not concern itself with popular appeal. The socialist Bernard Shaw was creating an intellectual drama that was almost devoid of working-class characters save as servants or stereotypes of the Pygmalion kind. Portrayal of the manufacturing trades and the world of the skilled artisan were acceptable, and that was a great jump forward for the Edwardian stage. Such were the limits of progressive liberalism or Fabianism, and they were shared with whatever degree of different emphasis or content by the writers of the old Royal Court, like John Galsworthy or Harley Granville-Barker, and by the Manchester school of Stanley Houghton or Harold Brighouse — two trends that came together later in the work of J.B. Priestley.

It is a measure of the pre-First World War era that one of the greatest periods of trade union activity threw up so little of direct relevance to it on the stage. Galsworthy's *Strife* (1909), which tells the story of a strike at a tin plate works, does present the strikers as characters in their own right. But the dramatist uses the model of a balanced debate to express the class conflict, which tidies up the dispute to an argument between two leaders and imparts a strong plea for justice within the bounds of class consensus.

Even up to the Second World War, theatrical pioneers were generally circumscribed by the middle-class world in which they operated, however radical their views. This was obviously true for aesthetic innovators, such as William Poel or Michel Saint-Denis, and also for the experimenters in clubs and small theatres (always a hidden strength of British theatre) whether it was the Group Theatre presenting Auden and Isherwood or the flowering of amateur groups at universities and in towns under the auspices of bodies like the British Drama League. But it was also true for those involved in more political activities, such as the drama associated with women's rights and the suffragette movement, for example.

The linked questions of who is represented on stage and to whom took on increasing prominence to become the central issue after the Second World War. The political catalyst came from the post-general strike upheavals of the 1930s and the great struggles against unemployment and fascism that produced for the first time a national theatre movement from within the working class going beyond the earlier activities of organizations like the Clarion Clubs.

Many agitational amateur theatre groups, mostly associated with the Communist Party or Independent Labour Party, had come together in the late 1920s as the Workers' Theatre Movement. It had a distinct theatrical philosophy on venue, style of speaking, construction of a play, and use of props, gesture and characters; this was thoroughly anti-bourgeois and anti-illusion. Its chief slogan was 'a propertyless theatre for a propertyless class'. There was enormous interest in the revolutionary theatre of the Soviet Union, Germany and the USA.

With the development of the popular front strategy in the mid-1930s the emphasis shifted to a broader appeal. Unity Theatre was set up in north London in 1936, bringing into the amateur workers' theatre leading socialist professionals, some of whom had been working in the small theatres and clubs on radical new plays. Unity remains the only theatre to have been sustained by the Labour movement; it is remembered, among other things, for Clifford Odets' *Waiting for Lefty* (1936); for introducing the drama of Brecht to Britain through *Señora Carrar's Rifles* (1938); for Ben Bengal's *Plant in the Sun* (1938), which had Paul Robeson in the original cast; for the world premiere of Sean O'Casey's *The Star Turns Red* (1940); and for developing the working-class history play, the techniques of the living newspaper and — its greatest contribution — political satire, most notably the anti-Munich panto *Babes in the Wood* (1938), which played for six months to nearly 50,000 people.

By 1939 individual membership of London Unity had risen to 7,000 and affiliated membership through Labour movement organizations to over a quarter of a million. As part of the Left Book Club Theatre Guild, which was set up in 1937 by the Book Club and Unity, the movement could boast some 250 theatre groups all over Britain. The book club also had a 300-strong professional actors' group. After the War the Unity movement had fifty branches (two of them professional) and two million members. It was one of the organizing bodies of the 1948 Theatre Conference.

The success of the Unity theatres was linked to the existence of a Left culture on a country-wide and international scale; it included film, poetry, music, art, novels, dance and criticism, as well as a drama that embraced agitprop, journalism, expressionism, social realism, revue, mass declamation and mass pageants which could involve several thousand people. Paradoxically, this produced no British stage playwrights who have left any mark. The most exciting plays displaying any kind of social conscience came from America — from Howard Lawson, John Wexley, Albert Maltz, Ben Bengal, Irwin Shaw, Marc Blitzstein, Albert Bein and Clifford Odets — though few are remembered today. This state of affairs was finally changed by the development of the other important theatre company to come out of the Workers' Theatre Movement — the group that became Theatre Workshop. Its founder, Ewan MacColl, had helped to start the Red Megaphones in Manchester in 1931, taking the name from a German street theatre group. He was joined by Joan Littlewood in 1934 and the group changed its name to Theatre of Action.

Theatre of Action became Theatre Union and was reconstituted as Theatre Workshop in 1945. Like Unity it was at first a touring group but was more experimental in a self-conscious way. It moved to a permanent base in London at the Theatre Royal, Stratford East, in 1953 and lost the support of MacColl for so doing, though his work stayed in the repertoire until 1955. This was just when the company was beginning to gain a solid reputation, strengthened by the success of plays by Brendan Behan and Shelagh Delaney, and culminating in *Oh, What a Lovely War!* (1963).

If one were to add to the Theatre Workshop participants the names of the indigenous writers presented by Unity theatres and the many unnamed creators of their group-devised pieces, then a picture would begin to emerge of a tradition of theatre rooted in the working class, however local or specific, that has yet to be given its due weight in the history of Britain's cultural development. The lack of any production or organizational network that could sustain this alternative drama around the country, and the fact that many of its innovations were absorbed into the general theatrical world, helps explain why 1956 is heralded as the start of a new revolution rather that being the fruit of previous pioneering.

Ewan MacColl

Immediately after the Second World War, the nearest one could get to popular, working-class theatre in the West End (apart from the brief Glasgow Unity visit at the Garrick) were the comedies and farces presented at the Whitehall Theatre. Compare *While the Sun Shines* by Terence Rattigan with *Worm's Eye View* by R.F. Delderfield. The Rattigan ran from 1943-46 at the Globe and concerned the marital problems of aristocrats, with rival allied officers thrown into the middle-brow mix. The Delderfield transferred from the Embassy after two weeks to the Whitehall and ran with a short break from 1945-47. In *Worm's Eye View* it is possible to see the loosening of social attitudes, which perhaps was inevitable in a play about ordinary soldiers billeted in a small town during the War. Even so, the central character is clearly a man of good education and middle-class background. His working-class comrades are the ones who provide the laughs.

Reluctant Heroes (1950), a farce by Colin Morris, and the first of Brian Rix's long-running Whitehall productions, is much more clearly class-based with its stereotypes of working-class spiv, rural innocent and public-schoolboy. It would be difficult to see in *Reluctant Heroes* anything other than a hugely popular farce written to a formula. But it does provide a genuine link with writers such as Henry Livings a decade after and to the later Theatre Workshop comedies, with their anarchic working-class or lumpen heroes and a constant subversion of petty authority.

Ewan MacColl, on the other hand, was opening up a different tradition of popular drama with Theatre Workshop. As well as original plays, such as *Rogues' Gallery* (1949) or *Landscape with Chimneys* (1951), his work spanned the living newspaper format, dramatizations of working-class history, and modern versions of the classics, such as *The Flying Doctor* (1945) adapted from Molière, *Operation Olive Branch* (1947) based on *Lysistrata*, and *The Good Soldier Schweik* (1954) from the novel by Jaroslav Hašek.

MacColl wanted to devise a new style of drama embracing all the disciplines of theatre, both physical and technical, that drew on older cultural forms as diverse as ballads, folk dance, expressionism, and Greek and Elizabethan stagecraft. Three poetic philosophical plays — *Uranium 235* (1946), *The Other Animals* (1948) and *The Travellers* (1952) — sum up his ideas at the time. *Uranium 235* must count as one of the first anti-nuclear war plays; it was performed within a year of the bombing of Hiroshima and Nagasaki, and tells the story of atomic energy, with famous scientists explaining their theories like music-hall comics. Science has been hijacked and must be won back to the service of humanity. Knowledge and commitment also figure in *The Other Animals*, which shows a political prisoner in solitary confinement examining the contradictions of society through his own recollections and through the creatures of his imagination that are materialized on stage. In *The Travellers*, a train symbolizing Europe is going on a journey to an unknown destination; the actors use movement with sound and light to make the audience feel as if they are making the same trip, rushing headlong to war.

The first production of Theatre Workshop in 1945 was MacColl's ballad opera *Johnny Noble*, a simple but affecting story of a sailor who leaves his sweetheart to find work away from the sea; in the years of the 1930s' depression he can find none. Eventually, in desperation, he takes a job as a deckhand on a ship running supplies to a beleaguered Spain. This experience, together with other, ill-defined voyages, politicizes him and he returns to marry his patient, waiting 'girl'. Later he goes off to war in the Arctic convoys and comes back determined to build a new world.

Johnny Noble is written in a formal and non-naturalistic way, incorporating poetry, song, dancing, lights and sound to conform to MacColl's concept of dramatic aesthetics. One scene is set on a ship undergoing a bomber attack and relies almost wholly on lighting, sound and the actors miming the loading and firing of an anti-aircraft gun to achieve its effect. It is followed immediately by the narrator singing:

And back in the homeland,
Where time passes slow,
There Mary sits waiting
For Johnny, her Jo.

Her trust has not faded,
Though they are apart,
And the love has not withered
That grows in her heart.

[*Full lighting. Johnny and a woman neighbour enter from opposite directions, dancing.*]

NEIGHBOUR [*singing*]: O Johnny, O Johnny, O Johnny,
And is it yourself that I see?
I thought you were on the Atlantic.
JOHNNY [*singing*]: I've been up through the cold northern sea.
[*Two girls enter, dancing.*]
TWO GIRLS [*singing*]: It's Johnny, it's Johnny, Johnny Noble's come home.
He left his love, Mary, the wide world to roam;
But now he's come back from the ocean.
You're a welcome sight, Johnny, to me.
[*Two youths enter, dancing.*]

In the final scene the voice of a man in the audience (a characteristic device in this area of dramatic theory) reminds Johnny of the dead he has left in the War and the duty he has to make a better world for their memory.

MAN: It's time you remembered why the war was fought. There's a
    job to be done, Johnny.
JOHNNY: But what can I do?
MAN: You've two hands and a brain and there's plenty of you. Take
    the world in your hands, Johnny, and wipe it clean. It's up to
    you, Johnny.
JOHNNY: Do you hear that? It's our world. It's up to us. We can do it,
    can't we?
CHORUS: Yes!
JOHNNY: Thanks, pal, for reminding me.
MAN: That's all right.

There is no attempt at characterization; Johnny Noble is the representative working-class man who sets out on a voyage of exploration which results in his change of consciousness. The technique of a picaresque journey through society and through history is a convenient one repeated again and again in subsequent plays of this kind. They demonstrate the politicization of the individual but fail to say very much about the social and political change that is its background. In fact, *Johnny Noble* shows a crucial internal contradiction which has never been surmounted in the later work of such left-wing groups as

7:84 or Red Ladder. On the one hand there is an idealized individual who achieves political consciousness through learning from immediate experience. On the other hand the point of this individual experience is that it is also the experience of the mass of the working class; yet this background, except for a few impressionistic events, remains, in general, unpolitical and inert. It is not so much the problem of reducing the complexities of social change to a simple pattern, but the difficulty of preventing a degree of contempt for the mass of the working class from creeping in. MacColl is quite open about this. Popular music and dancing are the contemporary opiates used throughout *Johnny Noble* to indicate how men and women are seduced away from the reality of their situation. This corrupting culture is set in odd and unexplained contrast with traditional folk song and dancing which implicitly represent an older and genuine culture that is supposed to deal with reality rather than displace it.

Later groups, following in MacColl's tradition, would have different views about the status and value of contemporary popular culture. Such shifts within the political theatre tradition do not necessarily matter; they provide a constant reflux of ideas about presentation and content. But the incorporation of any such assumption about the current values of one's audience inevitably limits the scope of what can be presented and to whom. It becomes difficult to do more than construct a form of presentation within which can be placed the simplest of uncorrupted messages. Often the value is reduced to the very act of saying the message at all. For example, dramatic elements of *Johnny Noble* can be found in a play like *Strike While the Iron is Hot*, presented by the socialist Red Ladder Theatre group as a touring show in 1974-76. It reveals less of an imperative to follow formal dramatic rules, although it is the product of much theoretical debate among the members of the group who wrote it collectively. Even so, in its use of song and music, and the rejection of naturalism, it follows closely the Theatre Workshop pattern. Certainly Red Ladder studied the same forebears of Soviet and German theatre, and the play is consciously modelled on Brecht's *The Mother*, showing the journey of a working-class woman to political consciousness. At the end of *Strike While the Iron is Hot* there is a similar appeal to that used by MacColl:

> We fight against all these things and what we've achieved is a beginning. But the fight won't end while we keep asking for crumbs. We've got to fight for something different. A world where children can grow up under decent conditions, where women can choose when to have kids, where we can have free contraception, and, when we need it, abortion. Where women can choose not to have kids and that's just as natural as having them. A world where women really are men's equals, not just with equal pay — and that's just equal exploitation — but a world with no exploitation. This means big

> changes and only you and I can make them. But if they are needed,
> can you say we're asking too much.

The message has become more sophisticated and it introduces a new
element: the linking of socialism and feminism. But it relies upon
much the same emphasis as *Johnny Noble*: that by joining together,
men and women can build a better world.

The issue is as much political as aesthetic: is there a political
statement which, if put over with sufficient power and repetition, will
eventually win the day? Or should the message be as complex as the
medium? Attempts to find an answer always involve the issue of
audience and venue because the question cannot be asked without
knowing the context. In the case of both *Johnny Noble* and *Strike While
the Iron is Hot* the plays were toured to places where a non-theatre-
going audience might turn up, even if also joined by regular attenders
seeking the new and the radical. Red Ladder made every effort to
arrange their bookings through Labour movement organizations, and
Strike While the Iron is Hot was first performed at a weekend school of
the engineering union's TASS section.

In contrast, the power of the classic literary tradition to embrace a
wider class than its natural constituency can be seen in a near-
contemporary piece of *Johnny Noble*, Ena Lamont Stewart's *Men
Should Weep* (1947). (Both plays were revived in 1982 by 7:84 as part of
a 'Clydebuilt' season, which also included *In Time of Strife* by Joe
Corrie (1927) and *Gold in His Boots* (1947) by George Munro.) Ena
Lamont Stewart had worked as a receptionist in a children's hospital in
Glasgow and used this experience to write her first full-length play,
Starched Aprons, about the lives of nurses; it became Glasgow Unity's
big success of 1945. *Men Should Weep* followed as a women's version of
another Unity hit, *The Gorbals Story* by Robert McLeish.

Men Should Weep has none of the theatrical experiment of *Johnny
Noble;* instead it uses powerfully the conventions of classic European
theatre and extends them into a type of social setting — a working-
class tenement in the 1930s — that was unfamiliar in the tradition,
except in the work of writers like O'Casey and O'Neill. The play
portrays a family in a situation of mass unemployment and of almost
absolute male domination. It is remarkable for the complexity of
relationships which it allows. It is a strong and emotional play that
makes no particular political appeal. Put alongside it, *Johnny Noble* has
an almost saccharine quality in its idealization of working-class life,
especially in its attitude to the women, who are shown as perfectly
content to wait for years before their male heroes return to whisk them
to the altar.

MacColl's importance should be recognized though not overstated.
His work is highly mannered and depends for its success upon a fusion
of poetic vision and complex theatrical technique which is often un-

even. Despite his pre-occupation with popular culture there is something forced about his plays, as if they are grafted onto rather than emerging out of any existing tradition, perhaps as a result of a rather self-conscious application to the British stage of European innovations. But he remained a key influence, through the developments of Theatre Workshop, and contributed to the folk song revival, particularly with the influential *Radio Ballads* (1958-64) with Charles Parker, and through the annual political entertainment from 1965-71 of the Festival of Fools, which were among the earliest examples of pub theatre. MacColl has had a lasting impact on all those playwrights and groups — too numerous to list — who have since attempted to introduce elements of popular music into their plays and to work within a new theatrical context.

After Osborne

A certain postwar stability, a gradual expansion of education and the beginnings of civic policies form the broad backdrop to the theatrical changes of the mid-1950s. Politically, the peace movement and the emergence of the New Left were instrumental in the formation of a new cultural climate. One important project was Centre 42, which was set up by Arnold Wesker to mobilize the trades union movement as a promoter of culture. Centre 42 took its name from the number of a resolution on the arts at the Trades Union Congress in 1960. Within two years six arts festivals had been organized in industrial towns at the invitation of the local trades councils. The festivals included plays, jazz, poetry, folk and exhibitions and they took place in factory canteens and pubs as well as in arts centres. Although they were well received by many union members, the general response was poor. The regional commitment had to be abandoned and somehow recreated in a permanent home in London. But by 1968, when the Roundhouse was ready, union co-operation had waned and the original project failed for lack of funds. (Ironically, the Roundhouse venue was to become instead the centre for American-inspired counter-culture.)

Although left-wing groups in the 1970s made contact with individual unions, nothing appeared on the scale of Centre 42 or the earlier Unity. The alternative theatre movement turned mainly to the state for its funding and catered largely for another generation of middle-class theatre-goers, often in ignorance, and sometimes contempt, of its predecessors from the earlier period.

Nevertheless, from the mid-1950s onwards there was a re-evaluation of theatre's popular role, which was bound up with a new type of representation on stage. So-called 'kitchen sink' drama became the vogue and working-class characters were no longer portrayed as aliens to be treated only as comic relief or criminals. Arnold Wesker's

Chicken Soup with Barley, first performed in 1958 at the Belgrade Theatre, Coventry, was by no means the first play to be set in a working-class milieu and to treat its characters seriously, but it signalled a wider acceptance of a new realism that proved to be historic. With *Roots* (1959) and *I'm Talking About Jerusalem* (1960), Wesker's treatment of two working-class families and their political ideas became a new benchmark for future writers and audiences alike.

The traditional progenitor of it all, John Osborne's *Look Back in Anger* (1956), has no real place in any discussion on the working class. Lines suggesting that Jimmy Porter was a genuine working-class lad because he arrived at a party dressed in a dinner jacket stained with oil from his bike or that he went with 'his Poplar cronies' to break up Conservative Party meetings, let alone the extraordinary suggestion that his working-class father, back from the Spanish Civil War, was kept by a regular monthly cheque from his estranged family, all indicate that Osborne had not the slightest knowledge of working-class life. Nor on the evidence of his later work is there any evidence that he had any real interest in class except as a topic for mockery. But two aspects of *Look Back in Anger* are significant.

Firstly, Osborne must have found it necessary because of external factors to include working-class references as a guarantee of the credentials of his anti-hero; there is no obvious reason to require this, either in Osborne's background or in Jimmy Porter's. Osborne's theatrical antennae must have told him that there was a desire for a new tone of realism and, after the dominance of foreign writers like Jean Anouilh, also a desire for a homegrown product that had guts — a feature that was being associated with the working class. Britain was entering into a period when new working-class heroes were emerging to challenge (at least in appearance) the effete and enervated middle class. Working-class style was becoming dominant and would stay so for twenty years and more.

Secondly, it appears to have been the presentation of a brief excerpt of *Look Back in Anger* on TV that sparked off the acceleration in public awareness of this new kind of play. It not only filled the seats at the Royal Court, it made the drama into something newsworthy and a fit subject for public interest.

The English Stage Company at the Royal Court never had specific pretensions to present either popular or, even less, working-class theatre. Its initial aim was to break the isolation of the theatre from the great social issues of the day by bringing the intelligentsia back into the arena. Moreover, belief in the importance of the writer in this process did not oust the director from his prime position. The ESC acquired a reputation for using working-class authors more by accident than design, which was reinforced by successful plays like Willis Hall's *The Long and the Short and the Tall* (1959). There was an eclectic attitude towards new work rather than any conscious search for a new class orientation. Peter Gill's magnificent and influential productions in the late 1960s of D.H. Lawrence's three plays set in a Nottinghamshire mining community were the exception rather than the rule, and these had been written, of course, before the First World War.

While the 'revolution' at the Royal Court was getting under way, crucial changes were taking place under Joan Littlewood at the Theatre Royal, Stratford East. Writers played an ambiguous and often awkward role in this; several felt abused by the Theatre Workshop method — Sean O'Casey refused point-blank to work with Joan Littlewood and her group productions because he felt a play had to be the product of a playwright and not that of a director or the actors. Certainly the culminating success of Littlewood's work, if it can be encapsulated in a single production, is *Oh, What a Lovely War!*, which is credited to 'Theatre Workshop, Charles Chilton and the members of the original cast.'

Two of Joan Littlewood's key productions at the time of the Royal Court's breakthrough were Brendan Behan's *The Quare Fellow* (1956) and Shelagh Delaney's *A Taste of Honey* (1958), both of which were re-written through improvisation and both of which marked a departure as much from the world of Jimmy Porter as from that of Noël Coward.

The Quare Fellow had originally been presented in Dublin but Littlewood and the cast cut it and reshaped it in London. The author said on the first night: "Miss Littlewood's company has performed a better play than I wrote." Behan, with his IRA connections and liking for drink, was taken up, as Osborne was, by the media; the theatre was news again. Behan's next stage play, *The Hostage*, did not come until 1958 and was first performed as *An Giall* in Dublin. It was translated and adapted through hours of improvised work based on his stories and songs as he performed them to the company. This method of production has since become an accepted theatre practice but at the time it marked a major assault on traditional procedures. Behan's success helped to dissolve the old categories that had separated the 'theatre' and 'live entertainment'.

Littlewood's technique also worked well for Shelagh Delaney, a nineteen-year-old from Lancashire who had worked in an engineering factory, as an usherette and as a sales assistant. With Behan, the strength of the production method lay in bringing to life the rich characters, the vigour and humour of the dialogue and the earthy resilience imparted by the plays. For Delaney, its strength was to combine her teenage viewpoint and fresh dialogue with the assurance of a mature presentation.

A Taste of Honey feels spontaneous but it is also ingenuous and inconclusive, with some dreadfully artificial lines. However, it is very haunting, in parts beautifully written, and with a deceptive structural toughness that goes beyond the use of music-hall technique, the direct address to the audience, and the episodic form of a variety act. It is easy to see why the play has become one of the staples of secondary school English classes; engaging and easy to read, it remains exactly what it was — a play written by a young person about a world in which adults are suspicious and grasping and the young are self-absorbed and looking for independence. The cult of youth was in the ascendant as well as the cult of working-class style.

The unsatisfied need for cultural representation of the working class did not prevent (and may even have encouraged) the descent of Theatre Workshop into the narrow pit of 'loveable' Cockney low-life with shows like *Sparrers Can't Sing* (1960) by Stephen Lewis and *Fings Ain't Wot They Used T'be* (1959) by Frank Norman and Lionel Bart. This may seem a harsh judgement on such transient confections but it needs to be set against the company's original aspirations; by this standard, MacColl's thesis of the corrupting effects of contemporary culture is more than justified. But they were good fun and popular, and they provided more training for the most important play of the early 1960s, *Oh, What a Lovely War!*, whose influence continues to reverberate in British theatre. It is not a play about the working classes as such, although it deeply concerns them and draws on their culture for its savage impact by self-consciously using a marginalized form of live entertainment, the seaside pierrot show, to transcend triumphantly the boundaries of conventional theatre.

The contrast between *Oh, What a Lovely War!* and those plays of the period which attempt to deal with the contemporary working class is very striking. The latter are imbued, if not always with optimism, then at least with a degree of light-heartedness, as opposed to the grim madness of the former. This is as true for Theatre Workshop productions, such as Alun Owen's Liverpool-based *Progress to the Park* (1961), as for the work of other working-class playwrights like Bernard Kops in *The Hamlet of Stepney Green* (1956) or *Enter Solly Gold* (1962).

The early stage plays of Henry Livings, like *Stop It, Whoever You Are* (1961), *Nil Carborundum* (1962) and *Eh?* (1964), are in some ways the most interesting of this period when the theatre was unsure of its new purpose. They all present an array of manic working-class characters who spreadeagle the forces of authority with their anarchic yet logical behaviour. They are short on conventional plot and structure and are placed in what were then startling settings for the 'proper' theatre (though not for the world of seaside postcards or the music hall) — a boiler-house in *Eh?* or the latrines of a northern factory in *Stop It, Whoever You Are.*

Despite such precise settings the plays are an escape from contemporary reality. Maybe Livings' formative experience as an actor with Theatre Workshop also set certain limits. His plays are possessed of that kind of English humour which can be endlessly transferred from place to place, adjusted in tone but still portraying the same kind of contained challenge to authority. *Nil Carborundum* is very close, on one side, to Colin Morris's farce *Reluctant Heroes* and, on the other, to Arnold Wesker's much more seriously intended *Chips with Everything* (1962). In the latter it is very difficult to believe that the solemnly presented singing of an old rebellious folk song amounts to more than the resolutely non-serious micky-taking of *Reluctant Heroes* (though, of course, Wesker intended it to carry much more weight). In the 1950s, the widespread male experience of National Service provided a common subculture of more or less open resentment at its strictures. Livings' characters, such as Perkin Warbeck in *Stop It, Whoever You Are* or Valentine in *Eh?*, have been compared with Schweik, though more appropriate models exist closer to home; comedian Norman Wisdom, for example, portrayed an endless series of such characters in films of the 1950s and early 1960s — anarchic and cheerful destroyers of pomposity as represented by a council official, a factory foreman or an army sergeant. Stand-up comics like Frank Randle, Arthur English or Max Miller had such random rebelliousness as part of their normal patter.

What Livings does is to transfer a stock figure from other forms of popular entertainment to the 'proper' theatre of, for example, the Royal Shakespeare Company, which presented *Nil Carborundum* and *Eh?* This allowed the eminent critics to say high-blown things that they would never have dreamed of addressing to Norman Wisdom. Thus Harold Hobson:

> This is what I mean when I say that Mr. Livings has an answer to man's present involvement with dangerous and interfering forces that are greater than himself. Through all the bustle and confusion, thieving, shouting, and folly which make up the action of this uproariously funny yet tragic play, Neville Harrison [the 'hero' of *Nil Carborundum*] moves in and out of his kitchen, resolutely and separate from everything that is going on around him. He is uninvolved, uncompromised, uncommitted, and alone. He is, in Mr. Livings's opinion, a wise man.

All that Hobson has witnessed is a change of social milieu from the usual theatrical fare, and he gives a definition of that milieu himself:

> Neville Harrison is not a complex character. One cannot imagine him singing madrigals, examining the theoretical bases of the *nouveau roman*, arguing the merits of Sartre against those of Camus as a revolutionary writer … He is simple and uncultivated. He may have heard of Winterbottom and Real Madrid, but not of Marguerite

Duras. He can therefore cut himself off from society, with all its risks
and madnesses, without personal deprivation.*

In other words, despite his wisdom, the working-class character does
not really *feel* anything at all, he is not part of *real* society.

The same kind of critical numbness followed by extravagant non-
sense greeted two other plays that could be said to belong to this
period: Harold Pinter's *The Caretaker* (1960) and Edward Bond's
Saved (1965). Although totally different from the Livings plays, they
also put on the stage characters from social backgrounds that were
foreign to the traditions of the conventional theatre. Both playwrights
take over and slightly exaggerate the rhythms and patterns of working-
class speech to create an accumulating sense of shock or disturbance.
As with *Nil Carborundum*, it seemed necessary for many critics to build
up a complex response to *The Caretaker* and *Saved* that did everything
but say the obvious, that this was how non-middle-class sections of
British society lived and talked. Other important aspects of Pinter and
Bond helped to obscure this — even for later critics — but in any case
it was clear that anyone who could identify with their characters was
unlikely to be in the theatre to do so. This was not a problem for
Pinter, who soon moved on to parody more affluent classes, but it was
a difficulty for a playwright like Livings who never achieved the
popular success that he needed for his own development.

David Mercer

Popular appeal was more readily available through other media, notably television. Whatever were the shifts in the class content of live
drama they were nothing to the changes here, and this had a huge
impact on the theatre and its audiences. Television became a voracious
devourer of material, always seeking products with which the audience
at home could identify. New forms of drama were explored, frequently
drawing on working-class lives, the most important being the single
play and the series, in which the same central characters are presented
regularly in a succession of separate stories; *Z Cars* was one of the best
written and most influential examples of this format which was first
pioneered on radio. A related form is the serial, in which each episode
leaves the audience wanting to know what happens next — a format
embracing the working-class 'soap opera' such as *Coronation Street*.
These new forms offered work and money to writers. But more than
that was the chance to reach a vast audience, potentially the bulk of the
population, and therefore one that might be significantly or even
overwhelmingly working-class.

---

* H. Hobson: *Introduction to New English Dramatists — 6* (Penguin, 1963).

The early 1960s saw the breakthrough of the television single play and the creation of a new drama that was also very influential in the theatre. This new drama was not centred necessarily on working-class characters, which was more the province of the series, but for the first time on any scale and in front of a large audience it examined the nature and consequences of class society and treated the historical challenge posed by the working class as a central subject for debate.

The most important of these new television dramatists was David Mercer, who was born to a working-class family, left school at fourteen and took various jobs including a stint in the navy. He turned to writing while working as a supply teacher after attending Durham University. Throughout his prolific writing life he examined, in a variety of styles, the effects on the individual of living in a class society. He came to feel that the theatre world had rejected him for being a television writer, despite the boldness, humour and curiosity of his stage work and his relatively early exploration of themes that were only later to become more familiar. These themes can be seen in his pioneering television trilogy, *The Generations*, a landmark in the history of broadcasting.

The first play of the trilogy, *Where the Difference Begins* (1961), is a much less complex piece than the other two, being little more than an extended fight between two 'de-classed' brothers returning to their working-class home as their mother is dying. Above them both stands their father, a railwayman nearing retirement, who understands neither of his sons nor why they are fighting. Around them are grouped various women — wives, (estranged or otherwise) and a friend — whose function is to do little more than express various forms of irritation with the men who dominate their lives.

The generations referred to in the title of the trilogy have a greater significance than that of the individuals depicted. They are meant as pictures of an entire country. The first generation, born at the turn of the century, is manual working-class, socialist and deeply rooted geographically and culturally; the second, upwardly mobile, is either smug or guilty and dissatisfied but unable to explain why; the third generation, supporting CND in their twenties, hates modern society, is nihilistic and has no hopes about the future. All three are largely male-centred.

The task of holding together this heroic endeavour within the frame of a realistic television drama places great strain on Mercer. The first generation is buried a little too conveniently whilst the third topples into improbable and symbolic retreats from Britain. Only the second generation is left, somewhat forgotten, vaguely worrying about academic advancement and dandruff.

All of this allows Mercer to be seen as the first in a long line of writers who have written about Britain as being irretrievably over the edge, a class-ridden country which has driven its children to madness or flight. He abandons his second generation, the troubled middle-aged liberals, with no attempt to resolve dramatically their situations.

The centre of the three plays is, however, the starting point: the generation of working-class socialists from which all the other characters have developed. Without their continual and brooding presence little else of the plays makes any kind of sense. These characters provide both the sense of potential and of subsequent loss which is the essence of all three pieces. It is thus possible to consider the plays as constituting a working-class frame even when most of their characters are middle-class.

Mercer's view of the working class is at heart a defeated one as shown in the set of younger working-class characters, who are inserted as a deliberate and symptomatic counterpoint to the older workers. He sees the basic corruption of society as resting within the inability of the working class to reproduce itself in the mould of its forebears and to have learnt from them. The lorry drivers in the third play, *Birth of a Private Man* (1963), ridiculing the ideas of workers supporting CND; Linda, a working-class woman in the same play, who walks out on the self-destructing son; the Newcastle man who shares his cell in *A Climate of Fear* (1962) — all are gentle portraits of people who are largely peripheral, who mock at the pretensions of the middle-class characters but nevertheless hold out no hope for their own class. George sums it up in *A Climate of Fear*:

> What we want now is strikes, man. Industrial action. But the workin' man today — an' I'm a workin' man meself — he doesn't give a damn aboot nothing. Not even obliteration. You see? You educated fellers that's workin' for the cause, you'll get nowhere wi' the workin' man.

The main point concerns simplicity: that the generation gone before were simple people who worked, and whose lives grew out of that work. Simple responses, simple loves, simple issues — a socialism which was a consequence of the conditions of their lives. As Tom explains in *A Climate of Fear* when chided for his failure to join the Communist Party:

> Being a communist or not being a communist had nowt to do with it for fellers like me. All I know is, there come a time in 1917 when soldiers looked at the people marching on — and lowered their rifles.

Loyal, faithful, strong — the virtues are piled on so thick that it becomes impossible to recognize any real human being under the gloss, only men like giants. In a sense, that is precisely what they were, for what becomes clear is that Mercer is mourning not the loss of particular men but the loss of childhood when such men did indeed seem like giants. All the simplicities that Mercer gropes for become focused on the simplicity of a working-class childhood, clear and uncomplicated, as expressed by Peter in *Birth of a Private Man:*

> My mother was just a huge warm bundle that smelled of carbolic and new bread. I didn't experience these complex middle-class responses.

The snag to this long-lost simplicity is that Mercer cannot give to his working-class characters any degree of complexity; when faced with difficult situations, they are required to react with various degrees of bewilderment, resignation or humour. In *A Climate of Fear* the miner father of one of the central characters is given a set of gags and throw-away catch-phrases but then exits just as the serious arguments are beginning. An initial assumption of a state of innocence removed such characters from any possibility of contributing to the arguments in which their children engage; and they are arguments which are not negligible debates to be resolved by an appeal to times past.

Mercer acknowledges this in the end by removing the entire debate from its initial setting and transplanting it into Poland where he is able to set a character whose past contains sufficient complexity, combined with honour, to allow him to stand up to the ideas of the young in a way that the older characters in Britain cannot. He seems to find it impossible to conceive of any older Britons whose past experience does not necessarily consign them either to morbid self-loathing or wistful romanticism.

The critical failure is that by abandoning all his British characters to their fate Mercer denies the existence of the very virtues that he sets out to hold on to. By denying the working-class characters any intellectual statement, placing them either as mythic heroes or superficial materialists, he attacks them as much as the despised middle classes who, whatever their defects, can at least put up a show of trying to cope with difficult reality. The choice appears to be either to refuse education and stay simple but dumb or to take up the burden of knowledge and become suicidal. Mercer never resolved this problem; he deflected it by looking instead at those who had acquired knowledge, in particular those who considered themselves Marxists like himself, and exploring how they could bear to live.

This desperate cycle is reproduced in the stage work. Mercer's first full-length play, *Ride a Cock Horse* (1965), which has affinities with the television play *Morgan, A Suitable Case for Treatment* (1962), shows a working-class intellectual retreating into infantilism to escape the problems of the world. In *After Haggerty* (1970) the retreat of the Marxist critic brings full circle the relationship of father and son as seen in *Where the Difference Begins.* Virtually the same working-class father appears, but this time as a reactionary bigot — no longer even a hero of the past. His son, a drama critic who is running away from his political and emotional inertia, tries to return to his roots through memory — as if Mercer is acknowledging that the model of the earlier work is hopelessly idealized. The critic is confronted by the wife of the previous occupant of his new home; she is looking for her husband Haggerty, a black activist who, it is learnt, has been killed as a guerrilla in Africa. It is *his* unseen presence, through telegrams, messages and his wife, and not that of the father, that now dominates Mercer's world; the British working class has been robbed even of its mythical past.

Mercer's most generous view of the betrayal of the working class comes in *Belcher's Luck* (1966), a Chaucerian parable of the old aristocracy being superseded by a new ruling class which is derived from a combination of the lower orders (in the form of a child of his servant, Belcher) and the landowner's niece. Belcher is a kindred spirit of the vicar in *Flint* (1970) whose agnostic ideas and boundless sexual passion for anyone other than his wheelchair-ridden wife underlines Mercer's continual celebration of a person's uniqueness — that individuals exist separately from the organizations to which they give themselves and to which they inevitably surrender. Flint could just as easily have been a communist at odds with the parties that profess his beliefs. This is a recurring theme in Mercer's continuing attempts to write himself out of his own dilemma of being what he called a theoretical communist in a world where existing communism to him was anathema, of trying to reconcile the insights of Marxism and the inexorable drift to madness that those insights must cause. This is the substance of his second television trilogy — *On the Eve of Publication* (1968), *The Cellar and the Almond Tree* (1970) and *Emma's Time* (1970) — which look forward to such plays as Howard Brenton's *Weapons of Happiness* (1976) in contrasting the political experiences of 'East' and 'West'.

Mercer, always an internationalist, nevertheless propounds a depressing and despairing analogy between all '-isms', whether Nazism or communism, regardless of history, particularly in *The Cellar and the Almond Tree*. It is relieved somewhat at the end of the stage play *Cousin Vladimir* (1978), which challenges the hypocrisies in the Western fad of self-congratulatory support for Soviet dissidents. While dismissing the pretensions of both the capitalist and socialist societies, he allows the dissidents to choose between the two — and they opt for the Soviet Union with all its problems.

Mercer's plays are inhabited by those who have lost their way while trying to bring ideas of political and personal liberation to fulfilment; most have become disillusioned with the task itself, and many have explicitly abandoned it. But however much he explores the roots of intellectual frailty with the emancipation of the working class in the background, he is never able to give up the assumption that only within the middle class does one find anguish, real insight or even profound concern over moral issues.

The struggle that Mercer has in order to come to terms with the class from which he is derived and yet alienated is paradoxical and stems from a belief that it is the working class alone which carries a special kind of virtue, with its origins in manual labour. This is a view that he shared with other playwrights who also moved out of their class. David Storey's *The Contractor* (1969), for example, received wide acclaim for showing the process of work on stage — this coming, apparently, as a revelation to most critics. Yet its major function is ambiguous except as a dramatic exercise, which received from Lindsay Anderson the kind of production usually described as 'meticulous'. A huge marquee is erected for the wedding-party of the daughter of a tenting contractor. In the final act the marquee, now torn and dishevelled by the revels, is dismantled. Nothing else actually happens except that a set of working-class misfits, whilst putting on various ropes and laying planks, muse on the vagaries of life. What is presented is an elaborate ballet masquerading as work and satisfying middle-class views about its worth and sanctity. The audience is left to construct its own meanings from this metaphoric display, and each meaning is equally valid — something which is true also of other Storey plays, such as *The Changing Room* (1971) and *Home* (1970).

In Celebration (1969) is a much more serious exploration of class by Storey. In structure it is very much like Mercer's *Where the Difference Begins*, and it too focuses on the male members of the family. Three sons assemble at their parents' house to celebrate their fortieth wedding anniversary. All three have left their class, to become a teacher, a personnel manager and a solicitor turned artist respectively. All are in some way alienated within their professions. They have arguments, stretching into rows, and then they separate with nothing solved. Dominating everything is the past; its power derives from the assumption that manual labour ennobles — at least that which is associated with men — and that the harsher it is, the more noble it must be. The father is not only a miner but also a face worker in a 13 inch seam — something which was a comparative rarity even in the 1960s. The background of such work is crucial to the play. Consider the dramatic impact if the father had been a manual worker on a car production line. What is never explored is why this matters. The play uses rather than analyses a slightly sentimental popular attitude. But despite the nobility conferred by his work, the father emerges as quite unable to understand or participate in the complex wrangles of his sons. Is *he* actually satisfied with his life? The question is never really asked let alone answered. Yet it is the central one. At the very end of the play, the sons leave and the mother turns to the father:

MRS. SHAW: What was all that about then?
MR. SHAW: Nay, search me, love...

Just like Mercer, Storey presents manual work and mental complexity as incompatible.

Storey does not idealize the working class. The plays are strongly metaphorical and invite an individual response to a general statement that is frequently ironic. The overall feeling is one of being dispossessed, like his early hero in *The Restoration of Arnold Middleton* (1966), or as in *The Farm* (1973), which is peopled by dull workers and a drunken farmer resentful of his son who has gone south to be a poet.

Storey's dyspeptic view of class is summed up in *Mother's Day* (1976) and *Sisters* (1978). Both are set in council houses and use sexual metaphor to pronounce through grim humour on thorough-going alienation and loss of moral direction. Storey's work forms a link between the world of Mercer and his generation of playwrights who through education were the first to lose their class, and the world of playwrights like Barrie Keeffe in the 1970s for whom social mobility is a subject in history books. It is a shift that reflects major changes in postwar society, in the composition, aspirations and geographical location of the working class, and which in the theatre accompanies the rise of the national subsidized companies. Much of Storey's work was presented at the Royal Court and Mercer's main stage plays were performed by the Royal Shakespeare Company. Even the budding National Theatre in its second season at Chichester played John Arden's *The Workhouse Donkey* (1963), a Jonsonian comedy of misrule exposing among other things the corruption of a working-class town.

Between the worlds of Mercer and Keeffe lies another group of playwrights — C.P. Taylor, Alan Plater, Peter Terson, Willy Russell, for example — who have pursued as an explicit goal the broadening of the class basis of theatre, using mainly social realist plays about the working class and concentrating their work on regional theatres. Their plays frequently carry a good humour and even an optimism that have been abandoned by Mercer and Storey and which in Keeffe's work are often overshadowed by intense anger and an acute sense of political frustration and powerlessness.

The commitment with which these regional writers have followed their aim can be judged from Alan Plater's commentary on the opening of his play *Close the Coalhouse Door* (1967), when it was first produced at Newcastle:

> When 'Close The Coalhouse Door' was running in Newcastle it is recorded history that strong men, only able to obtain tickets for the Saturday matinee, voluntarily missed football matches to see the show: in the North East greater love hath no man. This reponse, *among the folk for whom it was created,* [our stress] was hardly anticipated...
>
> We set off with inbuilt attitudes towards the subject and the stated aim of creating 'an unqualified hymn of praise to the miners, who

created a revolutionary weapon without having a revolutionary intention'. We selected those areas of history which confirmed our attitudes — though, as it happens, there were plenty to choose from.*

Close the Coalhouse Door, if judged as a play which tries to understand the problems and tensions of working-class life in a declining mining area, has little merit; it is grossly over-sentimental, its politics are simplified to the point of caricature and it is crudely sexist. Yet it did succeed in bringing people to the theatre who otherwise might not have gone, to see a celebration of *their* life rather than the equally slanted views of middle-class life which still form the staple diet of theatres in dominantly working-class towns. It was a joyous occasion using the familiar music-hall techniques of local entertainers.

The work at regional theatres has been impressive and varied, as has that of community theatres in London like the Half Moon. By its nature much of it is of purely local interest but that does not mean that it cannot have wider appeal or significance. As well as producing a proliferation of working-class documentary drama and encouraging local writers, these theatres under directors like Alan Dossor at the Liverpool Everyman have helped provide a focus for the likes of the nationally known Alan Bleasdale, John McGrath, Bill Morrison, Mike Stott, Chris Bond, Ted Whitehead, Sarah Daniels and Debbie Horsfield. Yet steelworkers helping Peter Cheeseman at Stoke to produce *Fight for Shelton Bar* (1974), which took its honourable place in their campaign to defend the local steel plant, is as important a landmark as Nottingham Playhouse launching a play like *Touched* (1977) by a new local playwright, Stephen Lowe. Nottingham is a good example of a regional theatre that offered for a time a bold policy, including plays such as *The Ruling Class* (1968) by Peter Barnes, *Brassneck* (1973) by Howard Brenton and David Hare and *Comedians* (1975) by Trevor Griffiths, without the use of a second, studio space. Other theatres, for instance Sheffield Crucible, sometimes found their most exciting work, often by new working-class writers such as Ron Hutchinson, taking place in the studio but to very small audiences. It would have been interesting to have seen a play with direct working-class appeal like Stephen Bill's *The Old Order* (1979), which is set in an engineering works, performed in the large auditorium of the Birmingham Rep instead of its studio. The studios, however, did take their place in the network of small venues around the country for groups like Hull Truck or CVI to tour their plays, many of which were concerned with or rooted in working-class life, for example, Paines Plough's productions of *Rise of the Old Cloud* (1980), Mike Dorrell's play about a South Wales mining community, or *Welcome Home* (1983), Tony Marchant's commentary on young soldiers returning from the Falklands War.

---

* Alan Plater: Introduction to *Close the Coalhouse Door* (Methuen Playscripts, 1969).

Related to this is another important strand of regional commitment —
the work of political touring groups like North-West Spanner or Red
Ladder in creating analytical plays about the working class and its
history.

C.P. Taylor

There are many reasons why most of the work in the smaller venues
was not seen in larger auditoria — for one, graphic colloquial language
is acceptable in the factory but not in a public place like a civic theatre.
The plays also generally took a critical view of their subject and were
not the celebration of working-class life that Alan Plater, Peter Terson
or C.P. Taylor often created. Take, for instance, one of Taylor's most
successful plays, *And a Nightingale Sang...* first performed in 1977 by
the Live Theatre Company, a Newcastle community theatre group
with whom Taylor was involved for many years. The play later opened
in the West End. It is about a family in Newcastle-on-Tyne during the
Second World War. Mum is an obsessive Catholic given to falling in
love with the local priest. Grandad buries dead whippets in the local
park. Dad does little other than play popular music and, as if on a
whim, join the Communist Party. The crippled daughter has an affair
with a married man who eventually goes back to his wife. The younger
daughter marries badly and has an affair with a serviceman whilst her
husband is away. The play is very funny, and as a comedy there are
implicit signs all over it saying, 'Don't take me too seriously'. As the
Daily Express review put it: 'It's a pleasure to welcome a comedy to the
West End that doesn't consist of a number of middle-class citizens
standing around trying to sort out their sexual and social problems over
cocktails in Hampstead'. (Instead we have a group of working-class
citizens sorting out their social and sexual problems over beer in
Newcastle.)

There is no reason why one should not combine religious obsession,
politics and old age and treat them as comedy. But only by making the
characters working class is it possible to suggest that this is also a slice
of life, a warm-hearted streak of humanity as it really is lived. Working-class people have their ups and downs but come through it smiling
and can always relax at a good knees-up. On cue at the end of *And a
Nightingale Sang...* the crippled sister has such a problem; her lover
has gone back to his wife and child.

> HELEN: [*to audience*] ... Too many things had happened to us ... that
> day ... I was still drained inside us ... whenever I thought of
> Norman ... It was like a real pain in my body ... It stabbed us ...
> Every time I thought of him ...
> ... They all went back into the house ... I stood on the pave-
> ment taking everything in ... The whole of Welbeck Road was a

> string of lights ... People making their way to the Park for the
> bonfire ... Eric called out to us ...
>
> ERIC: Eh, Helen, man. Come and dance with us.
>
> HELEN: [*to audience*] ... I was going to say to him ... 'Eric ... I can't
> dance' ... Then I remembered I did ... I *could* ... now ... And I
> let him put his arms round us ... And dance us away ...
>
> [*They all sing 'Roll Out the Barrel'.*] The End.

In his next major play, *Good* (1980), Taylor takes on a big theme: the
Nazis and acquiescence in the extermination of the Jews. The main
character, Halder, like Dad in *And a Nightingale Sang...*, is obsessed
with popular tunes which move through his head in counterpoint to the
reality of his life. Yet, as if to signal the serious theme, Halder is
specifically defined as a member of the middle class, an academic and
author. Taylor wants the audience to identify with Halder and thereby
to consider the possibility of its own implication in a contemporary
drift to reactionary politics. His choice is to ignore the working-class
majority of those who put on SS uniforms, except in the minor figure
of the brutish beer-drinking Bok, and concentrate his attack on middle-class liberalism.

Taylor is also capable of being hard-headed about his own people.
This is true of *Bread and Butter* (1966), set in the Glasgow Jewish-
Marxist milieu of his upbringing, and in a political way it can be seen in
Bandits (1976). Here he has come a long way from *Blaydon Races*
(1962), a passionate account of a Tyneside miners' strike in the 19th
century that he wrote to open the Flora Robson Theatre in Newcastle.
Bandits is an unromantic look at the jungle of Newcastle's gangland in
the 1960s; the play issues a stark warning that in the underbelly of the
'swinging sixties' life could be harsh and cruel.

This represents a shift away from plays of the traditional working
class based on men who work as miners, dockers or engineers, and
which tend to present the class in terms of its men as either victims or
heroes. It is not surprising that writers who have been committed, in a
loose sense, to the virtues of the working class have generally concentrated on the occupations that have contained a high proportion of
skilled manual workers and that have nurtured the finest aspects of the
British Labour movement — cohesion, solidarity, strength, continuity.

The direction of the shift is towards the dispossessed urban working
class who are unskilled, inarticulate and usually young. Edward Bond's
Saved or, more tenuously, Harold Pinter's *The Caretaker* and even Ann
Jellicoe's *The Sport of My Mad Mother* (1958) might be considered as
early examples. Certainly Peter Terson's football play *Zigger Zagger*
(1967) is about such a set of characters. But Terson evades the play's
central tension when at the end, and against the grain of all that has
been presented, the working-class lad opts for a quiet life and an
apprenticeship (then still a real possibility).

Barrie Keeffe

Barrie Keeffe's break with the view of the working class as shown by Terson or Plater is very sharp. There is a direct comparison invited, for example, between *Zigger Zagger* and Keeffe's *Abide With Me* (1976), the story of three football fans on Cup Final day outside Wembley Stadium without tickets to get in. It ends in anticipation of the post-match riot:

> They'll barricade the windows, the pubs'll lock their doors, the lights will go off in the shops and the police will line the pavements, white with fear... cops' hats'll bobble like decorations on a windy promenade... the air will be heavy with shouts and yells and the smashing of glass... No one will ignore us. We will not be ignored. They'll talk about us, write about us, hate us. Hate us. Hate us. Animals, call us animals... not ignore me... won't be ignored... not ignore me... not... ignore... me.
>
> [*The lights go to black. More roars. Rolling Stones' 'Sympathy for the Devil'.*]

The society being described is no longer one based upon relatively stable working-class life, however hard, and a community centred around obviously useful work; here we see a disintegrating social fabric in which work either does not exist or is marginal and unproductive. It is a society in which any sense of community has been obliterated by the bulldozer; the alienation of the class has become an alienation within the class.

There is a lot that is obvious about Keeffe's work; in many ways that is its greatest strength. At its best, it is clear, direct and precise, charted down to the very particular use of the appropriate rock song, and using powerful colloquial language. Keeffe is highly aware of the subtlety and power of class barriers and the near-impossibility of communication across them. In the *Gimme Shelter* trilogy (1975-77) the rebel schoolboy cannot communicate with the semi-rebel clerks, who in turn cannot communicate with the university student. Each group has particular parameters, their lives within those limits being a mystery to outsiders. A key difference between Keeffe and the older generation of playwrights is this stress on being trapped. Education is no longer the channel of escape from the working class; the danger is not alienation from one's roots and the prospect of class betrayal which it brings. For Keeffe, education is just another means of control — it might offer the chance of becoming a clerk in an insurance office but for most it is a few years of head-banging boredom, a pointless ritual in which both teachers and pupils collude. The difference in these two perspectives is a genuine reflection of social change.

The problem with Keeffe's work is the dilemma of resistance, of how to break the circle of despair that his view inevitably invokes. In his longer plays, in particular *Frozen Assets* (1978) and *Bastard Angel* (1980), the treadmill of life tends to overwhelm where in the shorter pieces it only emphasizes. The oppressed express rebellion and dissent, but to what extent are they in control of their fight-back? It is the old tramp Sammy who has the last word in *Frozen Assets* and not Buddy, the Borstal boy whose story the play tells. Sammy says to Buddy:

> I've seen deprivation and poverty and seen rats chewing babies in slum rooms. But I ain't a pessimist. Smash down the manor, rip it up, smash it down, fuck up decent people's lives but — the tribe lives on … Can't destroy that heart. It's in the blood. Never kill that. Never. Bon voyage kiddo, bon voyage.
>
> [*Boomtown Rats' 'Joey's on the Street Again'.*]

As a vivid and sharp chronicler of his class, Keeffe is unparalleled, but where the earlier generation had education, Keeffe's had music as an avenue for escape or change; that too led to disillusionment as shown in the disturbing play *Bastard Angel*, which concerns the destruction of a female rock singer. The failure of rock music as a liberating force, standing for the decay of an entire generation, is undeniably a powerful image. But it is a closed circle, winding back upon itself to the point of flickering extinction, not able to find a place from where it could even perceive its own past with any clear memory. In the one moment of tenderness in *Bastard Angel* the singer, Shelley, is unable even to remember whether or not she had gone to bed with the woman whose consolation she wants. The only targets attacked with any purpose are two servants, and it is clear that it is they, having remained subaltern, who are the object of a vindictive pursuit and not any wider class system.

Just as in *Teeth 'n' Smiles* (1975), David Hare's play about the decline of a rock singer, the final emphasis in *Bastard Angel* suggests that the true 'heroes' are those who did not make it to stardom but who dropped out somewhere along the way. In effect there *are* no more heroes — as individuals we lack the moral heart to survive with our own individuality intact:

> SHELLEY: Dylan sang: Shouldn't let other people get your kicks for you. But I don't feel the big things anymore. I get destroyed by the small things. The trivial. Nothing more trivial than a seven-inch band of black vinyl —

Keeffe's core of resilience survives, however attenuated and however grim the reality, and the same resilience can be found right across this particular spectrum of post-1968 dramatic writing, from John Byrne's *The Slab Boys* trilogy (1978-82) to Peter Flannery's chilling *Savage Amusement* (1978). At one of the dramatic extremes there is the work of Steven Berkoff, notably *Decadence* (1980), which dramatizes the corrupted state of the two classes that make up British society, and *East* (1975), a scabrous hymn to the waste that is the working-class East End of London. Against projected images of this location and to the accompaniment of an offstage piano, five Cockneys tell of everyday occurrences in heightened, allusive language that contains aggressive and destructive power. Sylv, typically, dreams a macho dream:

> I for once would like to be a fella, unwholesome both in deed and word and lounge around one leg cocked up and car keys tinkling on my pinky... such things are known when passion's smarting angels are defied and I may die in loathsome sickness here upon this plastic and formica divan...

At the other pole is the naturalistic work of Stephen Poliakoff, whose young dispossessed are a suburban generation, nervous and disturbed, shaped by an impersonal pop culture of commercial radio, shopping precincts and the Wimpy Bar; they are symbolized by the self-loathing Midlands disc jockey of *City Sugar* (1975). It is extraordinary how such plays precisely register the differences of period, taste and fashion. The Bradford teenage girls in Andrea Dunbar's *The Arbor* (1980) share a distinct though overlapping world with those from Birmingham and Sheffield in Poliakoff's *American Days* (1979).

Poliakoff tends to present society more in terms of the emptiness of consumerism and its problems of alienation than in terms of class division, unlike Nigel Williams who stands between him and Berkoff with his linguistic torrents that give plays like *Class Enemy* (1978) or *Sugar and Spice* (1980) their distinctive edge. In Williams' *Line 'Em* (1980), a classic confrontation of class society is examined with a characteristic emotional rather than realistic thoroughness. Soldiers try to break a picket line and almost succeed until the most volatile and individualistic young worker stands firm and turns the tide:

> Shoot us if you're so fuckin' keen... I tell you there's a few more back there an' woch yoo gonner do when you've shot 'em all eh? Shoot their sons an' their fuckin' sons oh lissen ter me I reckon iss well past the shootin' stage... We've arrived.

This is perhaps the closest that this type of play comes to a positive political statement; gestures recur as in Peter Flannery's *Our Friends in the North* (1982), which encapsulates the hopelessness that these playwrights feel: all societies, East and West, have failed; political parties and trades unions have failed. The only flicker in *Our Friends in the North* (ironically the same as in Mercer's *After Haggerty*) is the liberation movement in Africa which inspires an ex-mercenary Geordie lad, who has passed through Britain's corrupt society in *Johnny Noble* fashion, to bomb a Soho club. Gathered inside are the top politicians, policemen and pornographers who work together to keep the majority of the people ignorant and impoverished.

Trevor Griffiths

For the progressive playwright who feels pessimistic about the working class there has always been a tension between a truthful expression of that perception and a desire to help improve the situation. A further complication is the difficulty of reflecting accurately but not destructively such a critical view in a form and a venue that might gain popularity with the very people whose predicament is being represented on stage. The turn to political cabaret in the late 1970s and early 1980s was a response to this problem but for some playwrights the medium of television has offered a more productive solution, despite its evident limitations. Playwrights have continued to struggle within the confines of production and scheduling and in the ever-looming shadow of censorship to try and harness television's enormous power — and none more so than Trevor Griffiths who, like David Mercer before him, uses television to dramatize the effects of living in a class society from the standpoint of the working class. Without entirely abandoning the stage, which he considers to be the better forum for serious political debate, Griffiths has switched his energies to television because of its large audience.

In Griffiths' stage plays the problem of social mobility that obsessed one generation of playwrights can be found in *Sam, Sam* (1972) in the conflict between two brothers; the rejection of Stalinism can be seen in *Thermidor* (1971); the debate on political strategy and the source of the revolution can be seen in *Occupations* (1970) in the clash between the Italian Communist workers' leader Gramsci and a Comintern agent Kabak over the future of the Turin factory councils; and this can also be seen in the arguments among representatives of sections of the British Left in *The Party* (1973). It culminates in *Comedians* (1975) in a classic confrontation between the old, humanist virtues of the traditional working class and the hatred that mobilizes the new.

Comedians is a play that brings together the different images of the working class that have held sway since the Second World War and finds them irrevocably in conflict. Griffiths chooses the terrain of comedy for this political battle — in itself a daring gambit. Comedy, which in contemporary terms is overwhelmingly sexist, racist and anti-working-class, reproduces the values that help to subjugate the working class. That it can also form an anarchic break with those same values is the firm belief of the play's central character, Eddie Waters, a retired professional comic who runs an evening class in Manchester for aspiring comedians. Eddie is preparing his six students for their adjudication in the 'real' world of a working men's club at the hands of a London agent, Bert Challenor, himself an ex-comic and an old adversary of Eddie's. Challenor is also an organizer of a Managers' Federation and Eddie is outspoken in his contempt:

> I didn't like what they stood for. I've been a union man all my life...
> They wanted to control entry into the game. I told 'em no comedian
> worth his salt could ever 'federate' with a manager. And as far as I'm
> concerned no comedian ever did... A real comedian — that's a
> daring man. He *dares* to see what his listeners shy away from, fear to
> express. And what he sees is a sort of truth, about people, about their
> situation, about what hurts or terrifies them... above all, about what
> they *want*... A true joke, a comedian's joke... has to *liberate* the will
> and the desire, it has to *change the situation.*

Challenor's rule of thumb is equally clear:

> Don't try to be deep. Keep it simple. I'm not looking for philo-
> sophers. I'm looking for comics... We're servants, that's all. They
> demand, we supply. Any good comedian can lead an audience by the
> nose. But only in the direction they're going. And that direction is,
> quite simply ... escape. We're not missionaries, we're suppliers of
> laughter.

The students each perform their act at the club in 'a *brief* interval in
the bingo'. They are a cross-section: Jewish, Protestant, Catholic and
atheist, a shady businessman, insurance salesman, docker, milkman,
building worker and British Rail delivery van driver. The only one to
offer a truly original act is Eddie's favourite pupil, Gethin, the van
driver. In a gruesome and deliberately unfunny performance he presents an expressionistic ritual, dressed as a soccer skinhead. He carries
a violin and gets rid of a thread of gut hanging from the bow by setting
light to it. As the bow smoulders the violin plays an intricate piece of
Bach unaided. Gethin crushes the violin under his bovver boot and
proceeds with a Kung Fu routine. A spotlight picks out two dummies
in elegant evening dress. Gethin tries unsuccessfully to engage them in
conversation then pins a marigold between the female dummy's
breasts. A red stain appears on her white dress. The spotlight focuses
then snaps out. Gethin confronts his audience.

> I made them laugh, though. [*Depressed*] Who needs them? Hunh...
> we manage. [*Chanting*] U-n-i-t-e-d. Uni-ted. You won't keep us
> down there for long, don't worry. We're coming up *there where* we
> can gerrat yer... I shoulda smashed him. They alus mek you feel
> sorry for 'em, out in the open... [*Pause. He looks after them. Calling.*]
> National Unity? Up yours, sunshine. [*Pause. He picks up a tiny violin,
> i.e. another, switched, uncrushed, and a bow. Addresses it. Plays 'The Red
> Flag' — very simple and direct.*] Still, I made the buggers laugh.

Both Eddie and Challenor find Gethin's act repulsive but it is
Eddie's response that matters:

> EDDIE: ...It was ugly... It was drowning in hate. You can't change
> today into tomorrow on that basis. You forget a thing called...
> the truth.

GETHIN: The truth... You think the truth is *beautiful?* You've forgotten what it's *like*. You knew it when you started off... Because you were still in touch with what made you... hunger, diphtheria, filth, unemployment, penny clubs, means tests, bed bugs, head lice... Was all *that* truth beautiful?... Truth was a fist you hit with. Now it's like cow-flop, a day old, hard until it's underfoot and then it's... green, soft. Shitten. [*Pause*.] Nothing's changed Mr. Waters, is what I'm saying... We're still caged, exploited, prodded and pulled at, milked, fattened, slaughtered, cut up, fed out. We still don't belong to ourselves. Nothing's changed. You've just forgotten, that's all.

Eddie replies with a memory of a visit he made to a concentration camp: 'I discovered ... there were no jokes left. Every joke was a... final solution.' Gethin, before telling Eddie that his wife and children have left him, declares: 'I stand in no line. I refuse my consent.' The play ends with Eddie offering a Mr. Patel a place on his next course after hearing him tell a Jewish joke.

In *Comedians* Griffiths offers a much less comforting view of the working class than MacColl, who idealized it, Mercer, who lamented its passing, or Taylor, who lovingly poked fun at it. It would be misleading, however, to see the play as a clash between reformist and revolutionary politics as Griffiths himself described it. Gethin's angry but isolated rebellion has neither a tradition nor a manifesto and Griffiths, not surprisingly, is unable to point the way forward in denouncing the failures of labourism and the Left. In his portrayal of Gethin there is a sense of the demand for autonomous organization that has been vociferously proclaimed by the women's and black movements; Gethin is not one of the led but a force in his own right, refusing to compromise or consent.

Comedians has proved to be Griffiths' most successful and accessible work for the stage (although the television version lacked the tension provided by a live audience) and it transferred from the Nottingham Playhouse to the Old Vic en route for the West End and Broadway, by which time his declared policy of 'strategic penetration of the cultural establishment' was more than justified.

Whereas George Devine decided to subvert the cultural establishment from inside and John McGrath decided to leave it and set up in opposition, Griffiths chose to build a base in the mass medium of television although his first attempt — *Such Impossibilities* (1971) which deals with transport workers' leader Tom Mann and the Liverpool seamen's strike of 1911 — was not broadcast despite being commissioned by the BBC. He won his footing in television in 1974 with *All Good Men*, which puts a retiring renegade Labour MP under the microscope, and *Absolute Beginners*, set in 1903 when Lenin, Trotsky and others began the revolutionary Bolshevik Party.

The success of the Griffiths' strategy is considerable. An estimated eleven million people watched the first broadcast of *Through the Night* (1975) and saw the young working-class woman who went into hospital thinking she was going to have a routine cancer test wake up to find that she has had a breast removed. Analogies were clear — not just with the way institutions like the NHS force people to submit to their own interests but with the way the state manipulates too. 1976 marked the culmination of his popular appeal, with the eleven-part series *Bill Brand*, which took up the theme of strategy and commitment, focusing on a young working-class radical in the Parliamentary Labour Party.

Griffiths remains one of the foremost writers about class on television — not necessarily in the naturalistic sense of representing to a working-class audience of viewers a range of working-class characters, as he does in his adaptation of *Sons and Lovers* (1981) or *Oi for England* (1982), but in dramatizing class interest and how it is negotiated privately and publicly. He applied this approach to his version of *The Cherry Orchard* (1977) and, as with *Occupations* and *Comedians*, had the stage version broadcast. But it can be more clearly seen in the television play *Country: 'A Tory Story'*, (1981), set in 1945 against the backdrop of the Labour election landslide. A wealthy brewing family, the Carlions, sort out their feuds to decide which member will best pursue the strategy that their class interests require in the changed political situation following the death in action of the natural heir. Classically shaped, with a country-house focus, the play shows that the workers are at the gates but not centre stage. As in a Gorky play, they are present as a force of the future, but they are not yet the controllers of society's history. Carlion, the old beer baron, now in a wheelchair, with Philip, his chosen business heir, watch the workers celebrate around a bonfire the end of the War — dancing, drinking, happy, energetic; they burn an effigy dressed in a top hat and mock Eton collar, but it is only the symbols of past rule that disappear in the flames.

> CARLION: What is it? Is it a funeral?
> PHILIP: I rather think it is, Father. [*pause*] They have not yet noticed that the grave is empty.

The play ends with the singing of 'Roll Out the Barrel' and a close-up of a barrel from which the drink is being poured that has stamped on it the name Carlion; there is no doubt who has succeeded best in the wider struggle for class power.

Griffiths constantly returns to the central issue of power: how it is maintained by the ruling class and how it is to be achieved by the working class. His main focus is the role of human agency in this fight and, within that frame, the process of individual choice and change. In *Real Dreams* (1983) he offers his clearest statement of hope for the future of collective political action. A group of white, middle-class students come to a poor neighbourhood in Cleveland, Ohio. Griffiths shows all their weaknesses as they search for a theory, for a personal and political practice and for ways of being accepted by the local community. They bungle an attack on a supermarket and are put under siege by the angry Puerto Ricans who had ordered the action. One of the students, Sandler, offers a defence:

> ...Maybe they're doin' us a big favour, teachin' us what it feels like to play for keeps... We've gotta take it as it comes... But there *is* a revolution goin' on out there, and there's not a part of the world that can't feel it. We didn't start it, we're not gonna finish it, and we're not gonna have a lot to say about what happens in between. But we know what it's for and what it's against. And we know who's gonna win. All we can do is push. In whatever direction looks like the right one. Hard, and as long as we can. And we are, man. We are... no one's gonna tell me there's anything better to *be* in this pig world than what we're tryin' to become. After we're all dead, maybe someone will know if any of us were worth anything... What we've gotta worry about now is *not* doin' it. All the shit that holds us back and fucks us up — the personal, the comfortable, the safe, the neurotic, the racist — you know, everything that feels natural — well, that shit's there, it's gonna fuck us up, but we gotta make sure it doesn't stop us, man... I know what *I'm* workin' on... It's a list as long as your arm, man... But we're only gonna get as far as we get, man.

The Puerto Ricans leave and Sandler tells the audience that later he dropped out of the struggle. 'But,' he says, 'these are dreams that will not go away. These are real dreams.' The actors then perform as a single unit a graceful, disciplined Tai Chi sequence in bright, unreal light, wearing judo clothes and red head-sashes. The play ends with a prison poem by Ho Chi Minh.

Over the last decade or so playwrights have vigorously debated their strategy for survival, with the relative merits of television and live drama being fully aired. Television's need continually to win and re-win its audience has led to a more fluent treatment of working-class life on the small screen than can be found in the theatre. The most provocative and potent class image of the early 1980s came on television in the shape of Yosser Hughes created by Alan Bleasdale in *Boys from the Blackstuff* (1982). Bleasdale's stage work is by comparison simplistic, yet the devastating effect of Yosser and the other characters in the television series derives from their enormous theatricality.

For all the politically conscious theatre that has been presented, there has been nothing exploring contemporary working-class struggle to match the impact of the plays on television that are associated with Jim Allen, Colin Welland, Ken Loach and Tony Garnett. One of the problems for the theatre is the much greater self-consciousness of its efforts to become more popular. The problem is also linked to television's deployment of naturalistic techniques, particularly in terms of location, costume and precise social detail. But perhaps the theatre's biggest problem has been the inability to depict working-class characters with a sufficient degree of complexity while, nevertheless, confronting ideas with a candour and consistency usually lacking in television. Playwright after playwright has thrown the burden of serious thought onto middle-class men or has abandoned it altogether, leaving their working-class figures as marginal stereotypes or romanticized ideals, whether as victims or heroes in an oppressive class system.

In most of the larger theatres, the Whitehall farce formula, local variations of Theatre Workshop's Cockney capers and fantasies like *Billy Liar*, have held sway for working-class audiences, with Willy Russell emerging in plays like *Breezeblock Park* (1975), *Educating Rita* (1980) and *Blood Brothers* (1983) as the most serious of the popular entertainers writing about class. Arnold Wesker's early work marked a breakthrough but his reference point has moved away from a notion of the working class as a class. On the other hand, John McGrath has increasingly moved away from the representation of character in favour of stressing class structure. Most of the alternative and challenging images of the class has come from the political touring groups. Several have worked with shop stewards and rank-and-file activists; for example, Broadside with building workers (*The Big Lump*, 1975) and aerospace workers (*The Participation Waltz*, 1975), Belt and Braces with Vickers stewards (*The Front Line*, 1974), or Community Theatre with Ford, Dagenham, workers (*The Motor Show*) using playwrights Steve Gooch and Paul Thompson. Thompson had written plays showing the struggles of the agricultural workers' union and Gooch throughout the 1970s presented working-class history on its terms and not those of a restrictive bourgeois perspective.

The Women's Theatre Group worked with equal pay strikers at a windscreen wiper factory to produce *Out! On the Costa del Trico* (1976) and North-West Spanner, one of the most consistent groups performing at factories, pubs and clubs, dramatized several local struggles and issues of industrial concern, from health and safety at work (*Safety First and Last*, 1975), unemployment (*Dig for Victory*, 1976) and nuclear power (*Out of Control*, 1977) to the textile industry (*Winding Up*, 1975), the fight for trade union recognition (*Just a Cog*, 1976) and the occupation of a multi-national car works (*Partisans*, 1978).

Yet despite such work, including a clutch of general strike anniversary plays in the mid-1970s, different versions of the socialist classic novel *The Ragged-Trousered Philanthropists* (from Unity's to Stephen Lowe's), and the internationalist plays of companies like Foco Novo (*A Seventh Man*, 1976) or Bite Theatre Group (*Gast*, 1976,

Grunwicks, 1977), it has made little impression on the national consciousness. Much of it was local, ran briefly and was barely recorded. It was often agitational and supportive and lay outside of the communications apparatus that forms what is — and is not — considered part of the national cultural arena. For those playwrights who have managed to break into this arena, the working class has remained strong as an idea but elusive as a reality. The philosophy that socialist playwrights drew from their political culture, especially in the 1970s with its union militancy but lack of a mass revolutionary party, did not generally equip them to resolve this dilemma. Workers were rarely shown at all and those that were, like the strikers in Edward Bond's *The Worlds* (1979) or the young workers in *Weapons of Happiness* (1976) by Howard Brenton, were much less convincing than the bourgeois characters. If the Left was present, it was a far Left separate from the main current of working-class activity and not the Left that was bound up with it, even when such activity, like the miners forcing a general election, was still being invoked as a positive index of what the class could achieve, as in *Maydays* (1983) by David Edgar. This lack of appreciation of or connection with the organized working class — despite the rhetoric — resulted in plays about other people's revolutionary moments — Robert Bolt's *State of Revolution* (1977), David Hare's *Fanshen* (1975) — but a vacuum on the British front.

Whatever the limitations have been of the many attempts to win back the working class to live theatre both as audience and subject-matter, they have stimulated experiment and imagination on an impressive scale. The theatrical map has been redrawn since the War, which is a precondition of any further advances, even if some of the dynamism has gone out of the regional and touring theatre's efforts to gain a wider audience. Ironically it could be claimed with some justification that a political touring group like Belt and Braces reached more working-class people when it played one Dario Fo farce in the West End for a long run than during all its years of touring plays about working-class struggle, but by that time the political content had been largely neutralized.

By the early 1980s there had been a clear retrenchment, much of which had come about under the understandable pressures of diminished economic possibilities. But there was some internal failure of nerve too, coinciding with a social and political tide flowing against the desire to radicalize and broaden cultural life. Politics has been redefined in the postwar period and certainly the nature of the working class has changed even if its exploitation has stayed much the same. Imperialism, feminism, ecology, nuclear power have all challenged traditional assumptions; the theatre has reflected this but the political edge has gone and the old problem of the class culture gap remains.

CHAPTER THREE

Problems of Political Theatre: The Culture Gap

Political theatre to most people means left-wing theatre. Within a relatively stable bourgeois country those on the right or in the centre have little need for a distinct drama of their own as their stake within the established traditions and practices of theatre is as secure as their stake in society.

Before the Second World War a political theatre movement sprang up in Britain as part of a wider development across Europe and in the USA. It pioneered both new form and new content, and was unambiguously left-wing. A thin but crucial line connects this movement with postwar British drama via the Unity theatres and Theatre Workshop.

Although the influence of Brecht altered perceptions of political theatre in Britain and some writers such as John Arden did tackle political themes, it was not until the late 1960s that a radical break came. Changes were widespread and theatre began to respond to the times, fighting for its own survival against external challenges. Even conventional theatre, both subsidized and commercial, took on board political plays; theatre-in-education, community theatre, women's theatre, ethnic theatre, tribal theatre, agitprop, performance art, gay theatre — all were considered in one degree or another to be political. This represented both an advance and a diversion. It opened up vast new areas for theatrical work but it also diffused the use of the word 'political' so widely that it began to lose its meaning.

In the narrow sense of the word 'political', relatively few plays would count, despite the impression left by the critical maelstrom of the 1970s. Where one draws the line is a matter of debate but plays with an explicit political purpose, rather than, for example, plays that simply refer to politics, are relatively rare. Plays that deal with revolutionary or working-class politics, not surprisingly, are even thinner on the ground. Apart from reasons external to the theatre, such as the absence of a mass revolutionary party, or lack of a widespread British political culture, one has to look to the broader definition of 'political' for an answer.

Any consideration of political theatre that goes further than the simple but true statement that all theatre is political has to move beyond the text to embrace the whole experience and practice of theatre: how it is made, for whom, by whom, representing whom, and so on. The 'everything-is-political' assertion is only useful when effects, whether conscious or not, are taken into account. That involves the relationships between the producers, the product and the consumers; these are difficult to analyse and, as yet, have received little systematic study. The standard thriller or farce can be seen as political but only in a wider context of what it does or does not say in its reproduction of and acquiescence in certain values, both social and dramatic. On the other hand, a twenty-minute agitprop show analysing and supporting a strike played to the strikers on a picket line is political in all its aspects and not just in the text alone; the existence of the text, aside from the curiosity of historical record, is meaningless without the context.

The issue of context — of intention, execution, reception and effect — raises a major problem of criticism. To what extent is there a set of judgements that can be applied regardless of context? In the past the problem has been largely evaded by critics adopting very narrow definitions of theatre and even within these erecting further sub-categories. Only work performed in particular, established venues was acceptable; other forms of performed art were pushed into non-theatre categories such as music hall or opera. Within theatre proper, anything with lots of music could be called a 'musical', anything with laughter a 'comedy', and for these, different and subtly inferior modes of criticism could be adopted. Within such rigid categories, what is deemed good can acquire a largely technical definition and the job of a critic is enormously simplified. But take away the categories — and this did happen, at least partially, because of the Theatre Workshop revolution — and the situation for the critic becomes difficult. Add to it a new generation of theatre workers who have insisted, quite rightly, that such categorization is a class-based and politically contentious issue and it becomes hazardous.

No-one would disagree that political theatre must be good theatre, in some general technical sense, to achieve its purpose, but that is a truism of all artistic endeavour. There are too many bad left-wing plays hiding behind their admirable purpose and too many bad right-wing plays hiding behind dominant but outmoded notions of artistic excellence for easy answers to be found, let alone accepted.

The established method of criticism remains literary and text-based, isolating the reproducible element from the where, how and why of its production and performance. In such a case it could be argued that a play cannot begin to be judged properly until a second generation has tested the text in production. The text is valued for qualities that stress its uniqueness, which, in terms of ideas, frequently means the skill with which complexity is achieved. But what if the uniqueness of the text is not paramount, if its ability to be reproduced is of secondary importance? What if the nature of the audience is quite different from the white, educated, middle-class adults normally taken as the model? What if the point of the play is not just entertainment however edifying, but something else — the dissemination of information or political influence, for example?

There is a further dilemma: if a play is not intentionally political then critics are often supposed to abandon their politics, the more so if they themselves declare a clear political affiliation. Equally, if a play is overtly political and clearly affiliated, then those who do not share its politics or who hold more ambiguous and contradictory political opinions are thought by its creators to be unfit to judge. It is, however, a political fact that the cultural clout is wielded in favour of the former category of plays rather than the latter; they are not equal victims nor two sides of the same coin. This is particularly true as education, training and the distribution and availability of resources generally favour the status quo, which has therefore an enormous power of incorporation simply because people need to survive.

We have chosen to approach these problems by examining the work of two prominent playwrights, John McGrath and Tom Stoppard, at the point where they occupy openly political ground.

In many respects these two playwrights are unlikely bedfellows for they inhabit distinct theatrical worlds. But they share a concern for form and, at the point of our contrast, for affecting consciousness directly, as well as for the relative merits of text and context in that process. Stoppard can assume his context — he does not have to worry about finding a new audience, only more of the same to keep his plays running. His primary concern is to perfect the text. For McGrath the context is everything, and that has to be continually fought for — a new audience and therefore a new type of theatre. The text is shaped by this overriding preoccupation.

Along with Pinter, Stoppard, the wordsmith, is in some ways the most successful postwar British playwright; few have combined such material success with intellectual and critical respect. Stoppard did not go to university but left school to work on a local newspaper and was attracted to the stage, he says, by — among other things — seeing *Look Back in Anger*. He wrote his first play in 1960. It was broadcast on television in 1963 and, having been rewritten, it was staged in 1968 as *Enter a Free Man*. Two radio plays, three short stories, five episodes of a radio soap-opera (*The Dales*), an unperformed television play and an unpublished stage play later, Stoppard's breakthrough came in 1966. This was the year of *If You're Glad I'll Be Frank* on radio, an adaptation of Mrozek's *Tango* for the RSC, *A Separate Peace* on television, a novel and, above all, the extremely popular *Rosencrantz and Guildenstern Are Dead* at the Edinburgh Festival fringe.

Rosencrantz and Guildenstern Are Dead was the turning point. Since then Stoppard has occupied an increasingly prestigious position in the national and international theatre, at home both in the two big subsidized companies and in the West End.

McGrath moved in the opposite direction, following at first a well-trodden establishment path — Oxford University, with work staged by the student company OUDS, adapting Chekhov, and success at Hampstead Theatre Club with *Events While Guarding the Bofors Gun* (1966). He also made a name for himself in television, as a writer and director, including work on the pioneering series *Z Cars*, and in the cinema, writing the screenplays for *The Billion Dollar Brain*, *The Reckoning* and *The Bofors Gun* (adapted from his own play). He was one of the most successful writers of the 1960s, in commercial as well as cultural terms. Having passed the establishment 'test', he turned his back on that prestige to pursue a single-minded course as an even more powerful figure in the alternative theatre movement. Between 1970 and 1972 he worked at the Liverpool Everyman. Out of that experience, and other attempts to work outside the system, he helped form in 1971 the touring group, 7:84, which divided a year later into a Scottish and English company. The name 7:84 stands for 7 per cent of the population owning 84 per cent of the capital wealth. To date McGrath has not written for any other theatre company than the two 7:84 groups, which he controls and for which he has succeeded in obtaining a remarkably high degree of central state funding. In 1984, however, 7:84 England lost its Arts Council grant despite having met the conditions required by the Council's new right-wing leadership.

Tom Stoppard

Stoppard has always enjoyed playing with ideas, including political ones, but it was not until *Every Good Boy Deserves Favour* (1977), *Professional Foul* (1977), and *Night and Day* (1978) that he openly embraced a political position in a political context.

Stoppard once described his aim as 'the perfect marriage between the play of ideas and farce or perhaps even high comedy'. (*Theatre Quarterly*, No. 14, 1974.) Like Peter Shaffer or Robert Bolt, he has created hugely successful commodities that deal with important ideas without letting the significance of those ideas take root. They give an audience a kind of intellectual titillation without requiring deep thought — merely an ability to keep up with the pace. Stoppard's early plays mainly explore philosophy and the morality that derives from it; the overriding theme is the clash between fixed and relative world views. The absurdities of *After Magritte* (1970) are given reasonable explanation; *Rosencrantz and Guildenstern Are Dead* and *Jumpers* (1972) challenge the materialist view: maybe everything is illusion, even death, even the search for meaning which infinitely regresses and can never be fixed. These plays, particularly *Rosencrantz and Guildenstern Are Dead*, established Stoppard as a comic master of great theatrical ingenuity, wit and verve. Only Pinter can match him as the most sustained exponent of an English-based theatre of the absurd, preoccupied with the pain of existence and with formal experiment to refine yet another version of the same vision. *Rosencrantz and Guildenstern Are Dead* works because it is light and fresh, in spite of its length. It gets nowhere, but that does not matter; it comes across as spontaneous, with the excitement of a journey that carries us along inexorably to an unknown destination. The early shorter pieces like *The Real Inspector Hound* (1968) work for similar reasons, even though their self-consciousness can be off-putting.

Jumpers marks a change because it takes the social aspects of the moral question to its centre; but in fact Stoppard is only interested in a remote debate within the conventions that he sets up for the play. A Radical-Liberal Party, which in *Theatre Quarterly* Stoppard called 'a joke Fascist outfit', has won the election and astronauts have landed on the moon. But the argument for a moral standard applicable at all times to all people becomes no more than a prop within the self-enclosed world of murdering professors and logical positivist acrobats; it is a technically well-executed conceit but in terms of social reality still doggedly abstract.

With *Artist Descending a Staircase* (1973) and more importantly *Travesties* (1974) Stoppard takes the moral issue to the heart of his work again, but still the world of the play precludes any direct relationship with the problems of the world that give rise to that issue. In *Travesties* he constructs a debate on art and commitment, exposing the three revolutionaries, Lenin, Joyce and Tzara, for their different dogmatisms. But it necessarily remains a *divertissement*; there are elegant, witty skirmishes around the issue in almost Shavian style, and arguments are tossed lightly before being lost in the needs of the entertainment. But there is no Shavian conclusion. The ending sums it up:

> CARR (*the Consular official and amateur actor at the centre of the play*): I learned three things in Zurich during the war. I wrote them down. Firstly, you're either a revolutionary or you're not, and if you're not you might as well be an artist as anything else.

Secondly, if you can't be an artist, you might as well be a revolutionary... I forget the third thing. [*Blackout.*]

Stoppard's investigation of social commitment takes a perhaps unexpected turn after *Jumpers* and *Travesties*. His three overtly political plays were designed to make an immediate statement about a contemporary political issue regardless of their longer life as 'works of art'. It is clear from the dates and the dedications that Stoppard was influenced by political events and wrote the plays with a definite political purpose: *Every Good Boy Deserves Favour (EGBDF)*, is dedicated to Victor Fainberg and Vladimir Bukovsky, and is a protest at the Soviet abuse of psychiatry to contain non-conformers; the television play *Professional Foul* is dedicated to the Czech playwright Vaclav Havel; a political counterpart to *Jumpers*, it marked Amnesty International's Prisoner of Conscience Year (1977) and in particular focused attention on the plight of arrested supporters of Charter 77, a petition signed by Czechs that year in protest against unconstitutional political repression. *Night and Day* is dedicated to Paul Johnson, well-known by 1978 as a born-again right-wing ideologue. The play, written at the time of a national debate on the closed shop in journalism in Britain, argues against such a practice. There is also *Cahoot's Macbeth* (1979), a short reworking of Shakespeare's play as performed in private and interrupted by the police, that is dedicated to another persecuted Czech playwright, Pavel Kohout.

EGBDF is the boldest play of the group, integrating into the action six actors and the musicians of a full orchestra (reduced to ten for its run at the Mermaid Theatre). The play revolves round the imprisonment of a dissenter in a hospital cell with a man certified as a lunatic who believes he commands an orchestra. The main problem is the failure to fuse the two sources of the play's inspiration — familiar Stoppard delight in having an orchestra at his imaginative disposal and the desire to write about a deeply serious and delicate human issue that is full in the world's gaze. The text without André Previn's music score runs to only two dozen pages. The action, cutting between cell, school and office, is necessarily sharp and quick, and the play is characteristically witty. There is no room for subtle argument or character — one is either with the author or not; its smartness either makes one nod affirmingly or recoil at the flippancy.

[ALEXANDER, *the dissenter and his son* SACHA, *go up a central aisle.*
SACHA *runs ahead; at the top he turns.*]
SACHA [*sings*]: Papa, don't be crazy! Everything can be all right!
ALEXANDER: Sacha —
SACHA [*sings*]: Everything can be all right! [*Music. Music ends.*]

It is a pure but tacky Hollywood finale — a gross, sentimental gesture of childish optimism in a situation which is painfully and all-too-obviously not going to be all right. Employing the arsenal of agitprop, he offers no persuasion or confrontation — nothing but an emotional consensus. The main subject is swamped by the overwhelming presence of the orchestra, the cleverness of the artefact and the absurdity of the ending.

Professional Foul works for all the opposite reasons: the medium of television seems to have imposed a discipline. Extraneous theatrical padding has gone and the cleverness has been assimilated into the plotting and characterization. It is a compact, precise piece of writing appropriate both to its medium and to its subject. It has the force, logic and pace of a thriller and is also funny without ever compromising its aim. It contrasts different attitudes and different cultures — English and Czech, philosophers and footballers, the student activist and the detached teacher; the central figure faces a real dilemma, undergoes a change and acts upon his new consciousness.

The air of moral superiority that makes *EGBDF* such a smug affair has here been replaced by dramatically sound persuasion, as if Stoppard has moved beyond a simple belief in the commonly shared attitude of his audience toward his subject; this is possibly due to television's heterogeneous audience compared to the narrow expectations of the average theatre audience. One does not need to agree with the most forceful philosophical position argued in *Professional Foul* — that the ethics of the state can only be the ethics of the individual writ large — to find convincing the general statement about contemporary Czechoslovakia and that type of oppressive state behaviour in any country.

As if taking his cue from the success of the conventional, naturalistic style of *Professional Foul,* Stoppard repeated this approach with *Night and Day* for the commercial stage. It was not a characteristic mode for him and he came unstuck. Both form and content have a curiously old-fashioned feel. As a case against the closed shop it is too obviously special pleading without sufficient theatrical or intellectual substance in support; the Wagner/Milne journalists' conflict is only thinly disguised as an argument clothed in dialogue. Stoppard's choice of characters and location — a fictitious African country in the grip of a rebellion against its black dictator — remain clichés. The play is peopled by whites, save for a black servant and the President. Having a jeep coming on stage or using the half-hearted device of inner thoughts being spoken aloud neither services nor breaks the grip of the traditional form and its attendant problems. Stoppard does not make the medium work. Instead, he apologizes for it. He seems frightened of having written a political play and is forever trying to hide the fact, but it will not go away. What he gains in distance by dealing with a hot British issue at one remove geographically and then at another remove by fictionalizing it, is lost precisely because of its distance from the hot British issue. A David Edgar would not have strayed so far.

The other major problem in *Night and Day* is the character of Ruth. Stoppard has rarely been concerned with character in the naturalistic sense and he has never been adept at women's parts, but in this play the weakness is crucial because Ruth is at the centre. She has the Stoppard wit ('I'm with you on the free press. It's the newspapers I can't stand.') but then offers little more than her highbrow sex interest. *Night and Day* never convinces and falls between all its stools: neither an emotional revelation nor a powerful political drama.

Nevertheless a major question remains: is artistic criticism undermined by accompanying political criticism? Should a critic be any less politically explicit than the artist? And should art be judged more successful the less explicitly political it is? Certainly these plays were successful in their effect. They were a significant contribution to shifting the cultural consensus on politics from the left-leaning position of the 1970s. Stoppard's adoption of an explicit political attitude formed a component of the general right-wing intellectual push which underpinned the election of a radical right-wing government in 1979. There is little doubt that *EGBDF* and *Night and Day* are dramatically inferior pieces to the earlier plays, but they suited Stoppard's political purpose and met the demands of that purpose: to reclaim political theatre from the Left.

John McGrath

John McGrath's political work raises similar problems. Just as an attack on *EGBDF* invites the reply that one is supporting Soviet repression, an attack on 7:84 puts one in the enemy camp of not supporting socialism or popular socialist theatre. Given that 7:84 is a touring company with the emphasis on the where and how of a performance, the critic has to take on board the totality before being able to comment. The familiar put-down response to the critic is that 'you missed the really wonderful performance in front of 800 miners in their club hall' and therefore cannot comment. Such all-too-rare experiences when ideals are realized in practice are to be cherished but they cannot be used to avoid necessary criticism; if such criticism had been more forthcoming it might have helped 7:84 to avoid stagnation.

In trying to formulate useful criticism it is necessary first to look at McGrath's stated aims which are clearly put forward in *A Good Night Out**, a collection of lectures he gave in 1979. With 7:84 he attempted

---

* *A Good Night Out: Popular Theatre — Audience, Class and Form* (Methuen, 1981).

to create 'a counter theatre, an emergent truly oppositional theatre, based on the working class' and, in the words of his manifesto, the way to do this was to give people 'a good night out'. He wanted to transform the theatre. Such an approach explicitly shifts the emphasis away from the text to the context, which may be one reason why McGrath has consistently and publicly voiced his views on theatre production and does not simply let the plays speak for themselves. This is in direct contrast to Stoppard who has written very little on the subject and who, for a playwright of his reputation, has given relatively few interviews.

Despite some curiously uninformed views on his predecessors, McGrath traces a heritage for 7:84 back through Joan Littlewood and Brecht to the Blue Blouse Theatre Group of post-revolutionary Russia. The link is their use of popular forms of entertainment. The chief stylistic influence lies in music and the central role of the performer, the flashpoint between text and context. McGrath's own 7:84 style lies somewhere between the epic and the naturalistic. The crucial factor is stage persona, mediating the performer's contact with the audience and with the other characters on stage. It becomes therefore the focus of different levels of reality, the total effect of which must create for the audience an experience over and above the individual interest in any one character or set of characters. In the book he launches a wholesale attack on the artistic and critical conventions of naturalism — the dominant theatrical method — arguing against the picture frame practice of separating audience from actor. Instead he looks to the conventions of working-class entertainment which for him have greater potential than those of the metropolitan elite. Here he is speaking for a number of other political touring groups who have placed strong emphasis on music, particularly in the cabaret style.

7:84 has toured Britain over a period of time and with a scope of enterprise that has not been matched by any other group. The Scottish company opened up a network of touring venues and made some important links with the Labour movement. As the number of overtly socialist groups dropped in the late 1970s, with those remaining often concentrated on a particular geographical area (like Red Ladder in the northeast of England), 7:84 maintained a national following because it stuck to its aims faithfully and loudly. Both 7:84 companies developed a brash, lively style that was as notable for its music and presentation as it was for its political analysis.

As a director and head of the company, McGrath has found the most complete answer to the problem of content, form and artistic control — more so than any of his contemporary playwrights for whom this was a major, recurring problem. It may not in the end have helped him. While avoiding the 'free-for-all, utopian fantasy', as he puts it, of group writing, his attempts to break down the 'insane hierarchies of the theatre' by respecting, and learning from, the skills of everyone on a collective and equal basis have been beset by persistent artistic and political dilemmas.

Whatever the pitfalls, McGrath's break with the world and drama of the 'middle class metropolitan elite' is important. After all, in *Events While Guarding the Bofors Gun* he had written one of the most powerful postwar indictments of alienation and the human waste and stupidity of our obsolete and hierarchical society. Yet McGrath felt keenly the limitations of both style and context: the Hampstead Theatre audience watching *Events While Guarding the Bofors Gun* could feel individually chastened and perhaps even a little superior at having witnessed a dehumanizing experience but they would hardly have been moved to any kind of action.

These kind of thoughts about the liberal wing of the establishment theatre led McGrath to his unequivocal break in form and content. The individual plight of apolitical characters was replaced by the revolutionary history of the struggle for socialism.

The shift away from the individual to the collective focus is most noticeable in those plays which reclaim the history of the working class, particularly the ones written for the Scottish company. This is no arcane exercise for McGrath but the effect of a Marxist tradition of analysis that says: to act on the future one must understand the present by looking at the past. Whereas Stoppard sets up a debate within the confines of the play and argues points back and forth like a game of tennis, McGrath traces a clear line through history that points the way forward. He takes on the mantle of playwright as historian, but as it is the history of the people that he is recreating he uses forms drawn from the people, notably music in what might be called a folk rock style.

In *The Game's a Bogey* (1974), McGrath presents the life of Glasgow socialist John McLean as a fast-moving variety act. Mining a similar area of history in *The Little Red Hen* (1975), he rekindles memories of a socialist future in direct challenge to the vision of the Scottish Nationalists as an old 'hen' tells her grand-daughter of the heroic figures of Red Clyde.

McGrath's most courageous attempt to find the link between the political and the personal is *Out of Our Heads* (1976), which tackles the controversial subject of alcoholism in Scotland. He pieces together the pressures of Scottish culture and political life to show how hard the fight is for a shop steward who tries to develop his socialist understanding in the face of overwhelming enticement to act the tough Scots male — reliant on and sentimental about drink at one and the same time.

The English plays are less localized than the Scottish ones, even if set in a particular area. They too support contemporary struggles in fictionalized but recognizable form while reflecting a less cohesive national identity south of the border. Here McGrath tends to tackle either more general problems, such as the power of the multinationals in *Lay-Off* (1975), or more personal ones. *Yobbo Nowt* (1975), inspired by Brecht's adaptation of Gorky's novel *The Mother*, tells of a working-class woman who breaks out of her domestic life to become a socialist inside and outside the home.

At the Liverpool Everyman McGrath wrote the first version of *Fish in the Sea* (1972), which 7:84 presented later (1975), updated and with new music by Mark Brown. The unsung daily round of working-class organization suddenly quickens into an occupation to counter the rationalization plans of the local factory's new owners, a multinational corporation. The play has a force and a unity that overrides the occasional stylistic mismatch between naturalism and popular entertainment. It represents McGrath's most successful attempt to combine the two — the credibility of individual character and the confidence of the musical, political idiom.

Characterization in this sense is absent from *The Cheviot, the Stag and the Black, Black Oil* (1973), the most ambitious of these popular history plays, which shows most clearly the influence on McGrath of the postwar expansion in people's culture: the work of Ewan MacColl, the folk revival, the oral history movement. In this play McGrath is at his surest as historian and entertainer, as educator and agitator. Sketches, jokes, songs in Gaelic and English, real and imagined people, famous and forgotten dates and little known statistics are pulled together within the overall form of a ceilidh in this panoramic history of the continuing exploitation of the Scottish Highlands.

In his foreword to the published text McGrath describes the ceilidh as the 'one truly popular form of entertainment in the Highlands... This is usually a gathering at which all, or most, of those present, with or without the aid of the whisky, sing a song, tell a story, play an instrument, have a good blether and occasionally end up dancing until the next morning.' Ceilidh parties had their political side, too, and in the west of Scotland had helped keep Gaelic culture intact.

In its use of the ceilidh and the obvious local appeal of the subject along with the wider significance of the history revealed, *The Cheviot* fulfils the requirements, and stands as the model, of McGrath's 'good night out'. It contains the necessary stylistic underpinnings: directness, comedy, music, emotion, variety, effect, immediacy, localism of place and localism of identity.

The model seems robust enough but, unfortunately, McGrath sustained the aims but not always the artistic product to go with them. Was the model he created one that inherently could not develop? It is interesting to compare it with the work done three decades earlier by the Theatre Workshop. McGrath is much less rooted in a formal structure derived from dramatic theory. He is also much more eclectic and less puritanical in the sources from which he derives his style. In *The Cheviot* he uses folk song and the traditional ceilidh. But he also uses rock music, stand-up comics and the whole vein of British music hall. Ewan MacColl in Theatre Workshop would have scorned much of this as cultural and imperialist pap, believing that this type of popular entertainment was reactionary.

McGrath identifies the typical 7:84 venue as a working men's club in Chorlton-cum-Hardy (a suburb of Manchester), where the standard fare is either romantic and sentimental music, or sexist, racist and anti-working-class comedy. Despite acknowledgement of this problem and an obvious desire to transform the material, McGrath seems very often to have poured his plays into a funnel occupied at the neck by a typical audience of white, male, manual workers. There is a change in his portrayal of women from the isolated middle-class women of *Trees in the Wind* (1971) through *Yobbo Nowt* to *Blood Red Roses*, and women are central to many of his plays, but it is very much a picture defined by the primacy of male-dominated, traditionally economic class struggle. McGrath would argue that he is reflecting reality but elsewhere he argues for changing it. Similarly, it was not until 1982 that he tackled racism as a central theme, in the rather ham-fisted *Rejoice*, and even then the black character was not a worker, as one might have expected from McGrath.

His enormous output on a limited number of themes — more than twenty plays in a decade — has inevitably meant repetition. The structure of the plays is often very weak, with over-long scenes punctuated by song in a pattern that is too familiar and lacking internal strength; characterization often becomes casual and superficial, too obviously shaped to the political needs of the plot where the job it is supposed to be doing requires more complexity. The songs cease to act as an important dramatic counterpoint and become aural wallpaper — more or less good pop songs. The difficulty with using forms wrenched from their original purpose lies not in the possibility of one-off achievement but in a gradual degeneration, as though some internal logic of the original begins to reassert itself.

McGrath was clearly aware of the possibility of such degeneration but he has also shown the other and opposite difficulty, namely that the attempt to preserve some pure cultural form leads to isolation. The problem is that a strong cultural hegemony *does* exist in the theatre and those who seek to break free are continually pulled back in ways that are much more complex than the simple material rewards emphasized in *A Good Night Out*.

As with Stoppard, the major critical problem goes beyond technical assessments. The conditions that produced *The Cheviot* as the strongest example of 7:84's work were as much political and social as they were artistic. But the model does have an intrinsic artistic merit that is susceptible to judgement regardless of context; the text is published, and not simply for the record. McGrath says: 'If other actors decide to perform a piece, they should try to create the same identification with what they say and do — something quite different from normal actors' learning of lines.' Yet with the performers who created the show no longer working together and, more importantly, the recent changes in the oil industry and the politics of Scotland, would any group want to revive *The Cheviot?* Was the valuable exposure as a BBC television broadcast an end rather than a new lease of life? Obviously, McGrath could always be approached to update where necessary but there comes a point at which the contemporary situation is so altered that a new play needs to be written.

Playwrights are usually judged on the texts they produce, but McGrath has dedicated himself to a type of theatre in which the text is not paramount and which ignores theatrical posterity. His success is the success of a formula which by definition must be familiar in order to work at all. The formula may be unique but it is still a formula in which traditional critical values, such as the importance of complexity, must take second place.

The shift of stress from creator of text to producer of text-in-context allowed McGrath to develop a vigorous model of popular political entertainment. But as guardian of the model he came to exclude those upon whom the model depends for its success — the collective of performers — and then to exclude critics altogether. At the moment when external conditions had changed to such an extent that the model needed appropriate alteration, McGrath was not able to make the adjustment. This process was deepened with the election of Thatcher. There was no equivalent artistic response to meet the radical break that her politics represent in postwar Britain — though 7:84 was not alone in failing to change. It was as if the company were waiting for the heyday of the early 1970s to reappear — a touch of the 'golden past' syndrome which can be a lurking danger in the type of historical analysis implicit in 7:84's plays.

The general external problem for groups like 7:84 is that the working class upon whom the emerging oppositional theatre is to be based is not their main source of support, although the militancy out of which 7:84 emerged was trade-union based. The group advocates a form of revolutionary socialism that requires the existence of a revolutionary party enjoying wide support; yet, like all the touring groups, 7:84 is non-aligned, and the Left is small and fractured, albeit influential. The plays rarely touch on, let alone reflect, such contradictions. They breathe an often necessary optimism, but sustaining that can lead to delusion.

As the model became tired, often through lack of preparation to meet the sausage-factory pressures imposed by the Arts Council, the politics of 7:84 became emotional and generalized to a point where they often lacked credibility: we need a revolutionary party but one does not exist — which leaves abstract appeals to solidarity; we need stronger trades unions but beware anyone who helps to build that movement by becoming an official; we need socialism, but that does not exist either — all is to come. While in no way dismissing the celebratory function of slogans or devaluing the inspiration to be derived from people seeing their stories and their values represented on stage, the continual appeal to an undifferentiated 'rank and file' of ordinary workers — which is composed mainly of white men or white women acting like men in a man's world — becomes an ever more tenuous gesture and the future becomes that much more abstract. McGrath, again, acknowledges this contradiction: 'Some will object that this kind of socialism has never been achieved: this is not true, but even if it were, it is no reason for not fighting for it.' He does not say where it has been achieved (and from the plays, he certainly does not consider the Warsaw Pact countries as socialist) nor does he say how to find a chosen dramatic form that can sustain the ideal.

McGrath's New Left rejection of Stalinism and its associations with high culture shares with Stalinism a similar 'them and us' stance. 'Their' theatre is two-fold — the commercial sector, which is historically outmoded and doomed to collapse, and the subsidized theatres that take their cue from the national centres of the National Theatre, the RSC and the Royal Court. Occasional pretensions to democracy or progressive thought, like staging safe and sanitized productions of political plays, are thought merely to seduce good people into their trap. 'Their' theatre is Stoppard, but it must also be, for example, Edgar, Brenton, Bond, whom McGrath dispatches with contempt. Yet these and many others have written plays about contemporary politics that are far from negligible.

For someone who has done so much to present history on the stage, McGrath has a curiously unhistorical view; present context overwhelms text, therefore one judges a play by where it is performed and not for what it says and how it says it. But where does that leave 'our' theatre and the 'good night out' recipe? It denies the possibility of learning from or using 'their' theatre even in the individual way that McGrath himself learnt. In a complex society there are many channels for presenting a vision of the future or an understanding of the present.

Given the importance of context for McGrath, the inevitable question arises: if what and how you write is shaped by your expectations of playing to a particular audience, then what is the effect on your work if your audience turns out to be different? This is not a variation of the hackneyed 'playing to the converted' argument but the larger question of the link between who is being represented on stage and for whom. McGrath's archetypal working men's club ideal assumes an old-fashioned notion of class that implies that workers will spontaneously respond to the socialist message if only you can get through to them, and to do that you use their culture. But what of those who either have no experience of the clubs or have a yearning for some other form of entertainment? McGrath under pressure always admits that his formula is not a complete prescription for political theatre but he never gives examples of other acceptable forms, let alone an idea of the range of theatre that might exist in a socialist society.

Surely a working-class audience, and particularly the socialists among them, can respond to complex ideas, to doubt and uncertainties as well as to optimism about the future? Nevertheless, there is an absence of self-doubt and genuine exploration in McGrath's work which, taken over the decade since 1971, has meant the relegation or even exclusion of those contradictions. Had they been faced by way of either internal or external criticism, the model might have developed and changed with new circumstances.

Certain assumptions have to be made to sustain a play in the first place, but the playwright's relationship to her or his chosen consensus inevitably intrudes on the play itself. With Stoppard in *Night and Day* it is the assumptions of the commercial theatre and the ambivalence toward this arena for his political platform that scuppers the play. It is even more of a problem in *The Real Thing* (1982), which picks up some of the threads of *Travesties* in its debate on politics and theatre but narrows the terms to the point of irrelevance. With *EGBDF*, the house of cards is a little firmer but the assumption of consensus limits the insight to the point of self-defeat. On the other hand, in *The Cheviot*, McGrath's assumptions bring a heightened awareness of audience that help to produce a successful integration of form and content.

The difference cannot be reduced simply to particulars, such as Stoppard's use of an orchestra or McGrath's use of the ceilidh. The real difference concerns a whole way of seeing and making theatre and its relation to the established and ascendant ideological system of the day. After helping to secure the release of Vladimir Bukovsky, Stoppard relates in the foreword to *EGBDF* how Bukovsky's presence at a rehearsal was '...disturbing. For people working on a piece of theatre, *terra firma is a self-contained world even while it mimics the real one.* That is *the necessary condition of making theatre,* and it is also our luxury.' [our stress] McGrath would have taken the opposite point of view.

Bukovsky's suffering inspired a piece that was premièred at the Royal Festival Hall, with the London Symphony Orchestra conducted by André Previn, an RSC star cast and director Trevor Nunn. The whole event was forbidding, prestigious and costly, with the snob value of a rare occasion. *The Cheviot* was inspired by centuries of struggle and played to local audiences scattered around Scotland who were often suspicious of the visitors invading their village halls.

The Cheviot embraces a history to speak directly to its audience about its own situation. It makes its wider references explicit and ends, like *EGBDF*, with a statement of hope for the future; but it is a statement rooted in the preceding events of the play. This stirring ending, though emotional as in the Stoppard play, is not a lament or a collapse into sentiment; it is shot through with the ideas raised in the play. It is sung and received in the wake of a story that has argued the need for struggle in the knowledge of many successive defeats. It has a beginning, a middle but, as yet, no end. *EGBDF* was written to enhance and flatter the expected ideological position of its audience which in general was one of being dominant in society. *The Cheviot* was written to move its audience out of its subordinate position — a task for political theatre of much greater complexity.

There lies the crucial distinction between these two types of political theatre. It is not to say that aesthetic values can be read off from political ones — a practice common on both the Left and the Right — nor that the aesthetic and the political have no connection. The point is that the struggle for one's beliefs, of which art is a component, requires different artistic and organizational efforts to meet different challenges depending on one's relationship to the existing systems of power and control.

CHAPTER FOUR

The Nation: This Sceptred Isle

Despite the evident class divisions in society, efforts to rebuild Britain in the three decades after the Second World War were promoted around the image of one nation and not two, but playwrights tested this image and found it wanting. This in itself was not new. Theatre has always had a critical social function and a tendency to generalize about political society; one could trace such a line back this century before the war from J.B. Priestley to Shaw and Granville-Barker via Auden and Isherwood. But during the postwar period the scope and intention were new because the situation was markedly different.

British society was, and still is, nurtured on the myths of an imperial power unable to sustain its historically brief but geographically extensive rule of the waves. Despite great social gains, the new postwar era promised by the Labour Party in 1945 did not come. Instead, in 1951, back came the old Tories who had been responsible for the Hungry Thirties and for taking the country into war by appeasing Fascism. Nevertheless, it was soon also clear that their moment was past; their appeal was distinctly to a romantic, Edwardian Toryism rather than to any modernizing force. The 'tonic for the nation' — the Festival of Britain — gave way to Suez in 1956 and a new appeal to an even more nostalgic aristocracy. A preoccupation among playwrights became 'who are we?' rather than 'who am I?' and the question brought an ever more pessimistic reply.

The 'England-in-decline' play became the hallmark of a new generation of playwrights in the 1970s as the moral and political crisis deepened with the failure of Labour's second chance to prove its worth. And the loss of empire, loss of world prestige and loss of moral certainty contributed to the emergence of the nation as a central theme for dramatic scrutiny. One theatrical indicator is how Shakespeare, the national playwright, can be seen to have written about the nation. His plays can be presented in a host of ways, but in the postwar period he has been increasingly interpreted as the dramatist *of* the nation. Within this process, however, the emphasis has shifted; compare the Laurence Olivier film of *Henry V* in 1945 with the RSC's production in 1975. The change from the heroic and patriotic in time of war and victory to the sceptical in time of peace is a measure of the shift in mood that can be seen in the drama of the postwar era.

Other concerns than the nation were certainly available to British dramatists after 1945 — the crisis of the individual psyche, of the artist, of religion, for example — but generally they were not taken up with the same enthusiasm or commitment. There was a brief flirtation with the Theatre of the Absurd and more widely with Continental European drama, including the plays of Max Frisch and Jean Genet, but in retrospect this seems as much a product of fashion as a predilection. Perhaps the likes of Samuel Beckett, Eugene Ionesco, Fernando Arrabal or Arthur Adamov were considered too 'foreign', abstract and avant garde — a reflection of an insular anti-intellectualism that is strong in many walks of British life. Early Harold Pinter and N.F. Simpson can be seen as part of this school but, whatever the similarities, they, like John Whiting before them, are resolutely English. Tom Stoppard is their real heir but he too has taken off in a very English way into his own self-enclosed world. Existentialism fared as badly; the plays of Jean Paul Sartre and Albert Camus found no true British equivalent despite the influence of the philosophy that can be seen in the works of a writer like John Osborne. The major external influence was Brecht, who seemed more in tune with the needs of the time.

After such an experience as the Second World War and Britain's first, fully committed Labour government with a sizeable majority, it was unlikely that drama would be completely asocial. Yet, although it was by no means all cabaret and American musicals, there was little immediate engagement with the new social reality of an emerging welfare state or with the War itself.

The verse dramatists were trying to define a new universal morality for the nation; they were inspired by religious sensibilities but had little concern for the reality of Britain's postwar situation. J.B. Priestley in *The Linden Tree* (1947) did confront the moral problems of building a socialist Britain, albeit rather remotely, but he was reflecting a mood that later became more strident and all-embracing. Linden, the red-brick university professor facing retirement, says: 'Sometimes our great common enterprise seems only a noble skeleton, as if the machines had already sucked the blood and marrow out of it'. He looks forward to a future generation of rebels when he acknowledges 'a kind of grey, chilly hollowness inside, where there ought to be gaiety, colour, warmth and vision'. John Whiting, in *Marching Song* (1954), tackled issues of national principle and conduct in war, but he was not writing overtly or only about Britain. Yet, even more than with Priestley, his *Saint's Day* (1947-49), the controversial winner of the Festival of Britain's play competition, prefigured a more disturbed mood. Had it been written twenty years later it too might have been hailed as a 'state of the nation' play because by this time it seemed almost impossible *not* to create such a beast, so vast was the range of metaphors and symbols mobilized to represent the national body politic.

The catalyst for change was the increasing disintegration of the British Empire that the Suez Crisis seemed to embody in 1956. Within a year of that fiasco, John Osborne in *The Entertainer* was dramatizing the nation as an out-of-date music-hall show. In a note to the play Osborne says: 'The music hall is dying and, with it, a significant part of England'.

In *The Entertainer*, Archie, son of an old music-hall comedian, is trying to keep his show going, but what Osborne calls 'truly a folk art' has been reduced to a 'Rock 'n' Roll New'd Look'. Osborne reflects on the state of the nation through a family story played as a revue; domestic scenes are intercut with excerpts from Archie's act. His attempt to rescue the business by putting his father Billy back on stage finally kills off the old England; on Billy's coffin lies a Union Jack with his hat, cane and gloves. The theatrical metaphor is complete. But if England cannot be revived by the old values what chance does it have with the new? Osborne offers an analysis through the passage of generations: Billy, who has preserved the old values but to no avail; Archie, who has cynically frittered them away; and the off-stage presence of Archie's son Mick, dying in a meaningless attempt to retain the remnants of an old empire.

At the close of the play it is not the flag we see but a nude tableau of Britannia. Yet the impression remains that Osborne has a warm affection for the tawdry show just as he has for Archie whose signature tune is 'Number One's the One for Me'. There is none of Charles Wood's anger, none of Peter Nichols' satire, none of Arnold Wesker's morality: the nation may not be what it used to be but it is still 'ours'.

Not everybody gives up like Archie: his daughter Jean makes a stand and refers to her brother Frank having been jailed as a 'conchie' [conscientious objector], unlike brother Mick who joined the army as soon as he was called up. There is really very little weight to these characters, however. Unlike Archie, they do not seem to have Osborne's favour. It is more as though Osborne felt that, like the working-class allusions in *Look Back in Anger*, such a point of reference was required. Frank is weak and appears to be 'made into a man' by Mick's death. Going against his earlier nature, he calls his killers 'wogs' and finally decides to look after number one. At last he has become Archie's true son, but there is no place for him in this England and he goes off to Canada. Jean is left as the defender of principle; she has been laughed at for demonstrating in Trafalgar Square but it is she who tries to stop Archie divorcing Phoebe and putting Billy back on the stage. She asks:

> Why do people like us sit here and just lap it all up, why do boys die, or stoke boilers... what are we hoping to get out of it, what's it all in

aid of — is it really just for the sake of a gloved hand waving at you
from a golden coach?

For Osborne the question is real but also rhetorical. Part of him longs
for a decent, earlier period, in which one laughed at the rules but never
seriously suggested that anyone broke them; it is as much a fiction as
his belief in individual solutions: both lead to a dead end.

Charles Wood

For many playwrights the specific and varied effects of imperialism in
decline that undermined any possibility of national cohesion has led to
different obsessions — a search for the nation's roots and a search for
the values that sprang from those roots. Two periods in particular have
been subjected to close scrutiny: the Second World War and the
Victorian period. War is always an important focus because it is
intrinsic to empire-building and, in wartime, key national characteristics are thrown into high relief.

Charles Wood is the playwright who has most consistently laid bare
the nature of the military and its values, from *Cockade* (1963) to the
lighter *Veterans* (1972), as well as in films such as *How I Won the War*
and *The Charge of the Light Brigade*. His play *H* (1969) is a vast
panoramic view of the inhumanity and idiocy of the relief of Lucknow,
celebrated by the Victorians and later conservative historians as an
example of English heroism. These ideals live on, and in *Dingo* (1967)
Wood savages their effect on the 'ordinary bloke' who always ends up
fighting — and too often dying — for his country. The central character, Dingo, feels that his compassion has been worn down and rubbed
away to nothing:

> Alamein, Alamein, Alamein… What was wailing, it was the wailing
> of my wife — it was the wailing of myself, it was the wailing of all I
> have seen die and it was nothing. It is such a pity this war was not
> fought for them… I might have kept my compassion, I might not
> have felt guilty, which I don't, because everybody will say it was
> fought for them. It was not. It was fought for all the usual reasons.

Wood was one of the first playwrights to tear the guts out of such
sacrosanct national myths and to blast through the genteel consensus
that shrouded the Second World War; his treatment can be linked to
that of the First World War in *Oh, What a Lovely War!* (1963) and it
continued the pattern of lambasting the traditional war hero; Haig in
Oh, What a Lovely War! is matched by Montgomery in *Dingo*.

The 1960s and early 1970s was a great period for destruction of
national myths. Even Queen Victoria and Florence Nightingale were
not safe when Edward Bond in *Early Morning* (1968) portrayed them in
a lesbian relationship. Sometimes this iconoclasm cut too close to the
bone, though ironically it was a German writer, Rolf Hochhuth, who

created the biggest scandal with *Soldiers* (1968), which alleged that Churchill had participated in the deliberate killing of a Polish war hero. But often there was a tinge of ingenuousness, of young men playing pranks that did not really threaten.

The approach during the earlier period, in *Marching Song* by John Whiting, for example, was that of a gentleman arguing his point; the emotions were guarded and held back. In the 1960s Charles Wood and others were releasing their feelings in a torrent. The opening image of the nation in Peter Barnes' baroque comedy *The Ruling Class* (1968), for instance, is of an earl accidentally hanging himself in his bedroom, dressed in a three-cornered hat, a tutu, long underwear and a sword, having just toasted 'England. This precious stone set in a silver sea'.

Peter Nichols

Such flinty, sardonic bitterness is peculiar to writers who lived through the Second World War, like the versatile Peter Nichols. Nichols, an idiosyncratic Utopian socialist of a very English, Orwell-like school, chooses to tuck his politics inside his effects. In *Poppy* (1982), he went further than Osborne in *The Entertainer* in taking his organizing metaphor from the theatre itself. In writing about the Opium Wars, and thereby tackling the economic basis for imperial and naval power, Nichols uses and subverts the theatrical form most closely associated with the period — the pantomime. In answer to the Emperor of China, known as Lasting Glory, Queen Victoria sings:

> Good honest folk subliminally know
> That romance helps maintain the status quo.
> If Lasting Glory wants to understand
> The real preoccupations of our land,
> He could do worse than spend a little time
> Deciphering the British pantomime.

The parody embraces Gilbert and Sullivan as well as Rodgers and Hammerstein, with all the panto paraphernalia: principal 'boy', dame, smutty and racist jokes. But the horror and hypocrisies of the opium trade get trapped in the debunking exercise and so the audience is let off the hook. A one-liner about the monetarist economist Milton Friedman and passing reference to the number of Hong Kong heroin addicts in 1970 are not strong enough bridges to the contemporary world of the audience; we can safely agree how terrible it all was in those bad old Victorian days.

In *The National Health* (1969), which is less complex, ambitious and harsh than *Poppy*, Nichols suffers from a similar 'bile-and-smile' split-personality but his metaphor for the nation in decline is spot-on — a drab National Health Service hospital ward 'down on its uppers'.

At first the play seems to offer no more than the trivial naturalism of a television serial like *Emergency Ward 10*. Gradually it takes on a new aspect, as serious issues, even life and death, come to the fore. As in *A Day in the Death of Joe Egg* (1967), Nichols uses humour to explore extremely painful subjects. Whether or not this allows the audience to escape the truth rather than face it is debatable. The strategy of being serious by stealth, catching the audience off-balance through jokes, is certainly open to that contradiction, as can be seen in all of Nichols' work.

In *The National Health* six male inmates chat to each other about their obsessions, illnesses, cures, hopes and fears. Through the dialogue one realizes that this is more than just the idle chatter of a random group. There is an obvious parallel in the awful regime to which each unique individual is subjected. Yet there is little direct reference to the nation as such amid the usual banter commonly found in hospitals. There are jokes about bed pans, mistaken identity of patients, 'Doctor in the House' students, games of 'Monopoly' and musing about the council pulling down your condemned terrace ('soaking wet but independent, you follow me'). Nichols builds impressionistically through highly realistic scenes full of recognizable situations and detail to the point where the audience is seeing a picture of 'our state' — archetypally for this period, the welfare state. The National Health Service, the greatest achievement of postwar welfare state Britain and Labour's monument, is seen in all its grimness though nevertheless preferable to the anarchy and pay beds of pre-war society.

Nichols' verbal currency is very English, from Churchill to the inefficiency of the Post Office, but the punch is supposed to come through the presence at the centre of the play of a black nurse who is in love with a white doctor. This part is played in front of the beds like a huge projected television soap opera, parodying in style the conventions of the romantic weekly women's magazine story and its TV equivalent. In fact the play is called in full, *The National Health or Nurse Norton's Affair*, reflecting exactly its dual persona. The father of the doctor is a famous surgeon at the hospital, who, while ostensibly in the business of saving lives and bringing happiness to his patients, is a sour old cynic forbidding the mixed marriage. Nichols crosses the racist line himself, not to mention the sexist, a move he no doubt would defend as being an honest reflection of his audience's attitudes and necessary to make contact with them; hence one of the contradictions of the strategy — the danger of reinforcing, or simply trivializing as mere fun, the very prejudices one is trying to expose. He debunks standard conservative opinions but is reluctant to offer any possible alternative. There is a fleeting reference to politics but it is never developed. Mackie (the old reactionary for whom Nichols appears to have some respect and attraction) talks to Foster, who admits to being a socialist.

> MACKIE: You religious?
> FOSTER: Personally no. I only ever go in church to see the stained glass — but I don't reckon you should do away with anything just because you don't believe in it. That's the meaning of freedom, live and let live.
> MACKIE: The early Socialists thought… if we achieved this, the rest would follow.
> FOSTER: Achieved what?
> MACKIE: This state we're in. This ward. Where men are prevented from death by poverty or curable sickness even the least intelligent… least healthy or useful…
> FOSTER: You've got to do what you can for people —
> MACKIE: Can't cure loneliness-boredom-ugliness… but at least you can see they're lonely on clean sheets… ugly on tapioca pudding…

Britain is a grumpy, chummy, muddling-along nation that does not like change but will accept it and learn to live with it.

Theatrically, there are some bold strokes in the play, such as the stylistic switch to and from realistic ward talk and the soap opera scenes, and, more strikingly, the use of a Max Miller-type male orderly who links the audience with the action, making us feel as though we are both the visitors to the hospital and the patients in it. This kind of audience engagement is important for Nichols, a basic concern of the piece being to achieve a sense of all being in the same boat. In *Privates on Parade* (1977), set in postwar Malaya, this is true only for the particular generation who went through military conscription, but nevertheless a crucial part of the dramatic appeal is to make the audience feel at home. The panto in *Poppy* and the soap opera in *The National Health* help to break down a class and social barrier in an implicit attempt to be accessible to as wide an audience as possible. Yet the search for such popularity seems to stop Nichols from going as far as he would like. He knows that theatre can hit very hard and he deploys all the techniques of imagery and language which would enable him to do this. But, at the edge, he draws back.

Nichols parodies this dilemma in *Born in the Gardens* (1979) while taking swipes at the English way of life and its resistance to change. A family has come together at the death of 'father'. The daughter Queenie, now a journalist in America, has been to the 'theeyater' the night before:

> QUEENIE: Sooner or later, no matter how the writer tries to slice it, the actors finish in a row delivering quote-unquote witty lines, and discussing the state of the nation… Everybody goes home depressed out of their skulls.
> HEDLEY: I'd have thought the West End theatre was the last place to look for an awareness of change.

Nichols' good-natured 'warts and all' view of the nation was not shared by the next generation of writers. The Brentons, Barkers and Edgars did not have direct experience of war or National Service. For them the key moments of national crisis were different, and far from wanting to make audiences feel at home, they set out to indict them for their part in those moments of crisis.

Class Conflict

The defining characteristic for many playwrights of the post-1968 generation has been the underlying importance of class. They comment on the state of the nation by emphasizing class conflict as the key to the past and by implication to the present and future too. This approach challenged directly the 'one nation' ideas that were crucial to pre-Thatcher welfare state politics. Influenced by Marxism, these playwrights trace an alternative historical thread of defining national moments back from the present through the General Strike in 1926, the English Civil War and even further to the Peasants' Revolt and the Norman Invasion. In these defining events, the clash of the particular interests involved is seen to epitomize the state of the nation as a whole, with the values of one side or section being embraced within a tradition of struggle that continues in the present.

The various plays produced in the mid-1970s for the fiftieth anniversary of the 1926 General Strike rejected class consensus and stressed class conflict as basic to society. *Nine Days and Saltley Gates* (1976) by Jonathan Chadwick and John Hoyland made the most explicit link between 1926 and the present. The play implies that the organized working class taking action to defend itself is acting not just for itself but on behalf of the whole nation — a reversal of the prevalent idea that the nation's interests are synonymous with those of its employers, or more extremely, with those of its bankers and merchants.

There is a correlation between the representation on stage of the working class as the leading force of the nation and the struggle of that class to take on this historical role. The militancy of the early 1970s led to the most positive expressions of this and to a revaluation of the opportunity presented at the end of the Second World War when, perhaps for the first time, the working class could really be seen to stand for the nation. Given what followed, it is not surprising that playwrights of a younger generation such as Steve Gooch in *How the Peace was Lost* (unperformed) should examine that defining moment critically. Sandra in Stephen Lowe's *Touched* (1977) can be seen as representing the hope and the frustration of that time, as too can the allotment in David Holman's *Dig for Victory* (1978), which becomes a symbol of the unfulfilled potential of the nation.

The development of the playwright as national recorder coincides with that of the playwright as historian, suggesting that a notion of history and change is integral to the ability to articulate a national dimension. The list of such historical plays is long, and comes mainly from the small theatre companies, although the big subsidized theatres were affected too. Bill Bryden at the National Theatre staged a series of plays (1977-79) — *The Passion, The World Turned Upside Down, Candleford* and *Lark Rise* — that used techniques pioneered on the fringe to build up a popular portrait of England in times past, as did the Royal Shakespeare Company's *Nicholas Nickleby* (1980), adapted by David Edgar. They emerged, however, as Sunday colour supplement pictures: warm, rosy and comfortable.

Alongside the appropriation of a historical moment or event, or of a section of society, to stand for the nation as a whole, there continued the metaphoric or symbolic use of a traditional focus: a room, a house, a locale. (In American drama, it is the bar; in English, it used to be the club, the country house or the drawing room.) The power of location as a generalizing agent can be clearly seen across a broad spectrum, from David Rudkin in *Afore Night Come* (1962), David Cregan in *Three Men of Colverton* (1966), and the work of Peter Cheeseman's company at Stoke, to the regional underpinning of plays by Peter Terson, C.P. Taylor, Michael Wilcox, Robert Holman and Nick Darke. Nigel Williams in *Class Enemy* (1978) uses an even more specific locale from which to generalize about the nation — a classroom in which issues of power and identity are worked out in both particular and metaphoric terms, prefiguring the roles that are played out in the adult world beyond the school. It is a classic example of conventional form and radical content.

Some playwrights have used the pre-war theatre's pre-eminent restricted symbol of nation — the country house — for their own ends; David Mercer in *Belcher's Luck* (1966) or David Halliwell in *The House* (1979) expose the class and psychological realities that the original symbol obscured. Joe Orton's version in *What the Butler Saw* (1969) uses the logic of farce to show the English as living in their own madhouse, an anarchic world of ever refracting images; here is an apt connection at the personal level with the state of the nation and national character which Orton has satirized in *Entertaining Mr. Sloane* (1964), *The Erpingham Camp* (1967) and *Loot* (1966).

There is a fine yet important difference between such work and similar plays that also take over a formula and extend or move the location and personnel along the social scale but without offering any measure for that scale. Alan Ayckbourn uses dazzling technique to expose an underlying disintegration of nation and class identity without making this explicit. His trilogy *The Norman Conquests* (1973) stands with certain plays by Noël Coward for pinning down a particular

English class, but it does not reach beyond the reproduction of a self-enclosed 'slice of life' observation. Such plays lack the broader-based social reality which by comparison or extension can assume a real sense of nation by embracing deeper conflicts and differences. This can be found most obviously in panoramic plays like Howard Brenton's *Epsom Downs* (1977), which takes on the national mantle by its choice of a special occasion — the Derby — that involves all classes. It is given a necessary historical perspective by the presence from the past of the suffragette Emily Davison, herself a striking national symbol.

A similar panorama can be found in picaresque plays that show a journey through the English social scene, like Barrie Keeffe's *Frozen Assets* (1978). Such sweeping dramas owe a lot to the Elizabethans and Jacobeans in both the boldness of their form and the ability to bring to life the whole of a society beyond the confines of a single setting. If *Epsom Downs* is comparable on a smaller scale to Ben Jonson's *Bartholomew Fair*, then Keeffe's *A Mad World, My Masters* (1977) makes such a debt explicit with his exuberant reworking of Middleton's play of the same name. Like many a Jacobean play, it was written and first performed during a Royal celebration (the Queen's Silver Jubilee). Keeffe's version was not of course commissioned by Buckingham Palace but by Joint Stock, the company also responsible for *Epsom Downs*. The world created by Keeffe is in deliberate contrast to that presented by the media at the time; Britain is not a harmonious nation cheering a popular monarch but a state built on corruption and breeding corruption. The Queen indeed meets her people — a London family from the East End — but far from the version that might be seen on television during Jubilee year, Keeffe shows the confrontation as the culmination of a twisting, double-dealing plot that, like life for this family, is propelled by lies, tricks, mistaken identity and mishap. Keeffe uses caricature to great effect and puts the blame for this state of affairs on those with the power and wealth who have achieved and sustained their positions through deceit. Royal pageantry is designed to divert the lower orders from this truth; the Jubilee is just another part of the paraphernalia that keeps the working class subordinate. Yet Keeffe is politically pessimistic behind the cheeriness. He takes swipes at trades union officials as much as at establishment figures, and the play ends with this epitaph to the working-class woman who 'had a go':

> Grandma Sprightly lies beneath this tree
> Died celebrating the Silver Jubilee
> She tried to take on the upper class
> Now the worms are gnawing at her arse.

The linchpin in Keeffe's national metaphor of madness and masters is crime, which figures largely in the work of many playwrights as a means of commenting on Britain. Crime is the focus in Snoo Wilson's *England, England* (1977), where he elevates gangsters (based upon the London twins, the Kray brothers) to samurai proportions; they rule a microcosm of the decaying nation with a rigid code of behaviour that provides constancy in a shifting world. Less grotesquely, Howard Brenton and David Hare in *Brassneck* (1973) show society to be oiled by graft which binds together cliques desperately holding on to their own bit of power. A similar picture is offered with great elan in John Arden's *The Workhouse Donkey* (1963) and also by Peter Flannery in *Our Friends in the North* (1982). Flannery is saying, like Keeffe, that ordinary people are corrupted by the machinations of the political and business system. A desperate family take the offer of a new house from the chairman of the housing committee rather than fight to expose him. Flannery links this to national and international corruption; ordinary people refuse to see the truth even when it is available (on rare occasions) and refuse to take political action to change the system.

As with much of the political writing since the 1970s, Flannery shows the point at which the world outside merges with the world of the theatre without the drama becoming documentary. He does not dramatize the nation itself but the sense of what the nation has become inhabits every scene.

Howard Barker

At another stylistic extreme the use of corruption to signify the state of the nation is most completely explored by Howard Barker. Barker is one of the most striking — and underrated — of theatrical innovators. He sees no point in being a playwright if the motivation is not political and his political concerns are almost exclusively national. Like Howard Brenton, he is known for his dramatic and linguistic boldness, as can be seen in the seance scene with the Prince of Wales on the field of Passchendaele in *The Love of a Good Man* (1979). Barker questions the motives of all who help to make war or profit by it, from monarch to politician, from bishop to building contractor, and he examines the attitudes of those who suffer the war, the soldiers and their relatives. As the contractor Hacker is about to lose his chance to make a mint out of building a cemetery for one million English dead, he says:

> England, what I would not have done for it on condition I wasn't out
> of pocket. [*to the Prince*] You people turn patriots into spivs.

This is a constant theme in Barker's work: the impossibility of moral responsibility in an immoral and disordered world.

In *Stripwell* (1975) he punctures the illusions of the English establishment through the figure of a judge, whose father-in-law is a venerable old socialist called Jarrow, whose son is the embodiment of laissez-faire capitalism, and whose lover is a young go-go dancer. The social contradiction at the root of *Stripwell*, which is amplified in *That Good Between Us* (1977), is that one cannot be good in a bad society; a liberal Home Secretary still has to defend the class power of the state. Like Keeffe, Barker links class power, madness and corruption and he returns frequently to the idea of law and prisons as the regulators of their relationship. In *Claw* (1975), society is a prison waiting to ensnare the working-class son who rejects his class because his father did not have the vocabulary to pass on the lesson of solidarity. Two waiters (one a former apprentice hangman, the other a bomber in Northern Ireland) turn out to be warders who kill Claw — the price of class collaboration. *Cheek* (1970) and *Alpha Alpha* (1972) both concern the English working class who turn to crime as an understandable though not politically effective response to the greater crime that is capitalism. In *Alpha Alpha* (loosely inspired by the Kray twins) the gangsters are seen as creating a mirror-image world to that of the capitalists.

In the worlds that Barker creates on stage his characters are likely to go mad if they understand that the world is bad; if they compromise with the bad, which means being corrupted, the world continues to get worse, and that too will make them mad. Taking the necessary action to make the world good, however, may also make them mad, because the world is so bad that no one can succeed. Even the artist Bela in *No End of Blame* (1981) goes mad trying to tell the truth. Barker's expressions of the nation as totally degenerate, bringing madness to those who try to change it, sometimes emerge as despairing shrieks.

The England of *That Good Between Us* is a spy-ridden conspiratorial world whose descent into authoritarian rule is the England of the near-future. The England of *The Hang of the Gaol* (1978) is the England of the present which takes as a central symbol for the nation a prison just burnt down. Both the prison — the subject of a Whitehall inquiry — and the failure of the inquiry itself stand accusingly for the state of the nation. Barker strips away the delusions of liberal reform: the nation is like the prison, a vestige of imperial power in which the inmates are ruled through a hierarchy that stretches from their own kind via intermediary ranks to the old-school-tie chap at the top. However much the inmates compensate for their subordinate position they remain at the bottom, to be improved by the decent governor, who sees his mission honourably enough as a civilizing one; yet by dint of his role in class society he cannot carry through his intentions and goes mad, the typical Barker fate. The Labour Party, as seen through its cynical Home Secretary, is in the whitewash business, placing more stress on staying in power than on principle. The Labour government's zealous servant, an ex-Communist investigator relentlessly unearthing the culprit, is trapped by the very system he hates but he continues to work for it. The gaol is called Middenhurst and this frame of reference is immediately established with the opening line, spoken by the governor Cooper to his wife Jane, who is looking at the burnt-out shell:

> COOPER: A bucket shitter did this...
> JANE: Taxpayers' ulcer bursts. John Betjeman prostrate with shock.
> COOPER: My lovely ringing corridors of English iron.

The typically English response to the arson is to hold an inquiry. 'No one ever died from injuries received from two hundred pages of HM stationery', says a screw who gives his colleagues a history lesson:

> In the beginning England was a bear garden. It was a paradise for yobbos... There was no neighbourliness... It came to pass... that a majority of English yobbos, weary of endless slash and chivvy, agreed to offer up their rights to one sole ruler, who would adjudicate and carry out the GBH on their behalf... and we got THE LAW... But it was not destined to last. Astonishing to contemplate, the yobbo who had been entrusted with the precious instrument showed inclinations to unscrupulosity... The law, this treasure of the human spirit, was seen to admit of much abuse... Jungle manners were on the cards again. Then someone thought of THE INQUIRY... All we know is that he bore the English way of life upon his shoulders and carried it safe through the sucking mud of discontent.

The civil servant carrying that burden of the inquiry is Jardine, who joined the Communists when they said they would 'shoot the barrators and nepotists' and handed his card in when they said they would now re-educate them instead. He is a Scot who reads the *Daily Express* to know what the enemy is thinking:

> When I did the Sinking Motorway Inquiry in the 60s I cross-examined underneath the flyovers. The knowledge they were standing under the products of their skimped workmanship did wonders for the contractors' evidence.

He comments on English taste:

> They have the *Guardian*, and they have Queen Elizabeth, and ye can no ask more of human wit and ingenuity than that.

And the niceties of the English language:

> ...we are in England, and in England you may think a man a liar but you are better not to call him one. That is called maturity. The more mature you are, the less you use the word you want. The purpose of wrapping meanings up in cotton wool is to stop them hurting. This is a very sick and bandaged race.

In the end he succumbs to the English system and in exchange for his knighthood agrees to cover-up. As his assistant says: 'England brings you down at last...'

Barker's anger is white-hot and his indignation fierce. In *The Hang of the Gaol* he fashions these emotions into a powerful indictment. He is saying also that the working class believes in the same notion of democracy as those who use that democracy to keep them subordinate. The representatives of the working class are presented as hopelessly compromised regardless of their private aspirations or worth, because of the role they have to play in propping up the state; similarly, individual goodness among the rulers is irrelevant to the power system. The title *The Hang of the Gaol* echoes the play's main proposition that the English ruling class has established over a long period an all-pervasive ideology of domination based on their real power that continually absorbs any opposition. It also carries the other meaning, that having got the hang of the system, the system hangs you. As such, *The Hang of the Gaol* is one of the strongest attacks on the reformism of Westminster's welfare state politics but it is also one of the bleakest visions of Britain as a nation in an irreversible decline. Barker sees no political action that is capable of saving it.

Although Barker is the great stylist of his generation his work is sometimes marred by weak construction and a repetition of imagery and vocabulary, particularly that drawn from an aggressive male sexual world. At worst this can produce an equation of social and sexual liberation carried over almost in its entirety from the liberation ideals of the late 1960s. In *Victory* (1983), for example, the Puritan woman wandering through Restoration England has to obtain some kind of pleasure and social release from being raped by a boozy Cavalier. In *That Good Between Us* the survivor of the political holocaust is the almost-animal Glaswegian rapist who possesses the vital spirit to keep going. At his best, Barker's unique imaginative creations are convincing on their own terms, though as representatives of a society that exists outside of the play they sometimes fall short at the point where the two are necessarily compared. The problem is that the style tends to keep the plays at a distance from Barker's intentions.

Despite his personal advocacy of socialism, there is often no perspective of such change in his work. The choices are stark — compromise or bust, but to compromise is also to bust. In *Fair Slaughter* (1977), which also includes the recurring idea of a prison and an asylum, Barker examines the impossibility of English revolution, at least in his time, and suggests rather eccentrically that one major reason is the lack of humour of the Left. The talisman of revolutionary socialism — the hand of Trotsky's train driver — is passed on after a series of failed attempts to fight for socialism. The gesture is symbolic, a spark of optimism, but in what? The audience is left to inhabit Barker's fictive world and, however pleasurable that experience may be, it remains at the symbolic level. As a statement about the English it may be true, but it reproduces what it criticizes the English for not having: a knowledge and sense of history that stretches from understanding the past to hope for the future.

In fact, despite the historical panorama of many of his plays, Barker
has very little concern for history as such. He searches back for
symbolic moments, usually those when something went disastrously
wrong, which he can use to illuminate present-day society. He never
says 'this caused this' but rather 'this is the same as this'.

At the heart of his work there lies an ambiguity about human
pleasure and passion. He clearly believes that one of the great problems of socialism is that it does not recognize pleasure. People smell
out the fact that socialism does not offer them a good time and, in the
end, they reject it because of this. *Fair Slaughter* and *Victory* probe this
idea most explicitly but it recurs elsewhere, in *The Loud Boy's Life*
(1980), for instance, in which it is the Enoch Powell look-alike politician who is rejected primarily because of his humourlessness. But at
the same time Barker himself does not wholly approve of pleasure. He
is attracted by it but seems unable to conceive of human passion except
in excess. The lack of a middle path produces exciting plays but they
tend to be on one note.

The initial image in Barker's plays counts for a great deal: the
burnt-out gaol; the Passchendaele cemetery in *The Love of a Good Man;*
the digging up of a dismembered body in *Victory*. Where these are
apposite, as in *The Hang of the Gaol*, they are magnificent. But sometimes their use is less clear. In *Victory* the journey to collect the body
becomes a rather vague central focus and so the play loses some of its
point. However, the scene set in the recently founded Bank of England
as nouveau riche conspirators squabble over running Britain behind
the facade of a weak king is one of the funniest and deadliest in
postwar British drama. It appears in one of the first plays of the
Thatcher period to analyse the recovery and advance of strident reaction while ending with a scene that at least keeps open the struggle
against such right-wing politics.

Barker is, surprisingly, one of the few playwrights to have surmounted the shock of a radical right-wing government. His most
resilient statement comes in *The Castle* (1985). This combines a
powerful central image — the huge castle built by a Crusader on his
return to England — and the process of human struggle and change,
which this time ends in hope rather than madness. In fact, Barker's
work has grown as some of his fears have come to the edge of
realization.

David Edgar

Barker's very English concern for the problems of commitment and
change is is shared by David Edgar, one of the major recorders of the
nation's political health. Edgar's huge output includes television plays,
short pieces, burlesques, epics and even a show that requires Mrs.

Beaton's recipe for plum pudding to be made on stage (using 36 eggs). In *Wreckers* (1977), written for 7:84, the focus is the law, examined in a London docklands setting as applied to crime (the ports and rag trade), to industrial relations (imprisoned dockers known as the 'Pentonville Five') and to the question of political legitimacy. The play looks at the arguments within the local constituency Labour party and the bid to oust the sitting MP. The nation's real criminals are seen to be the employers and the real wreckers are the politicians who help them. The law figures again in *The Jail Diary of Albie Sachs* (1978) in the shape of the eponymous lawyer imprisoned in South Africa under the notorious 90 Day Law. As passive resistance becomes a strategy of the past, the play not only records a remarkable personal tale of courage in the face of the interrogators but poses sharp questions for the privileged who still retain a conscience in the new, harsh political situation; it asks, can they stand the heat? It reminds them that if they turn their sympathy into action then there will come a point when they might have to face the full force of the new heat too. *Mary Barnes* (1978) looks at a different type of commitment and is a companion to *Teendreams* (1979), which was written with Susan Todd for Monstrous Regiment. The two plays move from the 1960s to the 1970s and, as in *Maydays* (1983), which covers the postwar years, they confront images of liberation and revolution with a dissenting reality. Nevertheless, in each case they suggest a positive growing process. For Mary Barnes it is her journey through madness amid the counter-cultural pretensions of a contemporary extended family. In *Teendreams* it is the journey to self-awareness for two women who were childhood friends, one now a teacher, the other a middle-class wife and mother. Both are challenged by feminism and harsh experiences. In *Maydays*, while two main characters shift from the Left to the Right in step with the national drift, two others learn to adapt to new times yet still stay true to their beliefs.

Edgar approaches the nation and Englishness via a different route from that of Howard Barker — or David Hare, whose play *Plenty* (1978), covers the same period as Edgar's *Destiny*. Against a backdrop of key events, Hare is impressionistic and personal, building a slowly emerging, composite picture that changes with the light. Barker is no less contemporary, no less real, but he creates a more fictional world. Suez becomes a gaol on fire, the limpid dialogue becomes blatant and blazing; his is a violent rather than an alienating nightmare. Edgar in *Destiny* is altogether more balanced, marshalling a dovetailed plot that aches with explanatory detail as much as it cries out for some of the personal detail which he deliberately rejected. As a former journalist, Edgar always researches his subjects thoroughly, and *Destiny* is the culmination of his documentary-based, agitrop apprenticeship during which he wrote some two dozen plays on national life, from the EEC and the Industrial Relations Act to the Rent Act, Concorde, the Plague and the health service.

Destiny, originally five hours long, remains a crucial statement about the state of the nation, both as a record of a history and as a political event itself within the theatre. The play's journey from The Other Place in Stratford-upon-Avon to the larger Aldwych stage and on to BBC TV was seen as a major breakthrough for a 'fringe' writer: an overtly political theme, set in contemporary Britain, achieving critical and audience success. *Destiny* became news in a way that *Look Back in Anger* had been twenty years earlier, and as *Maydays* was to become in 1983. Whereas Peter Nichols had dealt with racism and its economic environment by using the double-edged strategy of 'entertainment', Edgar showed another way. *Destiny* opens on Indian Independence Day in 1947. Sergeant Turner and a Sikh servant, Khera, are packing up the trappings of the empire. 'Is it true, sir, they'll all be able to come to England now, to live?' asks Turner. The Colonel says that it is Britain's obligation, but he represents an old-style Toryism that is on the way out. He goes home to 'another England/Rough and raw/Not gentle, sentimental as before'; being 'out of time' he dies.

With each scene at the start of the play Edgar establishes a different facet of 'another England'. He looks at the new-style Tories and the Labour alternative, but the main focus is the ultra-right in the form of the Nation Forward Party. The background to the rise of this party is carefully charted. Back home Major Rolfe identifies loyalty and the national interest not in terms of 'the miners, dockers, students, Irish or blacks' but in terms of the lower middle classes. They are the great betrayed.

> Their property no longer secure. Their status, in our age, increasingly irrelevant. And in place of national destiny, we've given them... it's not true we've lost an Empire, haven't found a role. We have a role. As Europe's whipping boy... And to play that role, we must become more shoddy, threadbare, second-rate.

To confirm that analysis, Turner's business is taken over by an investment trust in the shape of Razak Khan, a new-style Conservative. 'So where do I go now?', asks Turner. Edgar opens the next scene as if the answer is clear — to the left. A group in an upstairs pub room is discussing revolution, the vanguard, building the party, working in the unions. But this is Edgar's double-edged surprise; the comrades are in fact fascists celebrating Hitler's birthday.

Divisions within the ultra-right lead to an open platform of racism and neo-nazism with Turner as the party's general election candidate. The poll coincides with a strike at a local foundry over racism led by Khera, which is broken by the Nation Forward Party. The Labour candidate compromises, the Tories win the election and Turner gets

24% of the vote. However, Turner learns at the end that the firm which took him over is run by Rolfe who, as a representative now of monopoly capital, sets up a deal between his business interests and the fascists. Edgar clearly wishes *Destiny* to end with a challenge for he closes the play by quoting a 1933 speech of Hitler's:

> Only one thing could have stopped our movement. If our adversaries had understood its principle, and had smashed, with the utmost brutality, the nucleus of our movement.

Edgar intended this to jolt the audience who, it was assumed, had come to understand, though not to sympathize with, Turner. But as the play shows no effective alternative to the encroaching power of capital and fascism, this tactic remains a gesture. The right-wing arguments overshadow those from the Left. The strike is not prominent, for example, nor are speeches such as that of the strike leader, Khera, when he is discussing the role of the striker who has been arrested as an illegal immigrant:

> I come from Jullundur, the Punjab... Train the children to be quiet, subservient, respectful. So, to England, land of tolerance and decency, and found it hard to understand. But last year, I went home, on holiday, to India. Saw, with new eyes, just what the English did. And then I understood. There is more British capital in India, today, than thirty years ago... Even the poor, white British, think that they, not just their masters, were born to rule. And us, the blacks, the Irish, all of us — a lesser breed, without the Rule of Law.

While Edgar's focus is clearly on the Right, the imbalance is politically a problem. Edgar has dubbed it being 'irresponsibly responsible' but for the television production he did add a strengthening speech, just after the one quoted above. It is delivered by Paul who had worked for Turner:

> ...there's a funny moment, comes to you, you see your real friends. Came to me, a meeting of Barons strikers... Learning that it's possible too for them to make their future. Bit like the morning. Sun comes up, so slow, can't see it's changing. But it's growing lighter.

Paul has turned to the left while his friend Tony has moved to the right. This change boosts Paul who previously was dramatically much weaker than Tony. The audience knows that when Paul adds: 'No turning back. The need, to be our own. To change, the real world', Edgar has transformed the individual agony of 1950s drama into the collective problems of the 1970s.

Destiny does not lampoon 'our' rulers, or debunk 'our' leaders. It captures a crucial aspect of changing consciousness among ordinary people who identify with the nation in chaos by trying to reassert the cohesion of their race. As Rolfe says: 'We are under threat. The

British Nation and its enterprise. The two are indivisible... Unite the Durham miner with the Surrey stockbroker. An ideology...' The powerful scene played in front of a Union Jack, in which the Taddley Patriotic League joins forces with the Nation Forward Party, under-lines the erosion of values and status that is widely felt by white, working-class and middle-class English people, one result of which was Thatcher's decisive break in postwar politics. Nation Forward's general secretary addresses the meeting: '...what we have in common is greater, by far, than what divides us' — not anti-union but against their 'perversion for political ends', not anti-profit but against specula-tive profiteering. '...we all of us observe a gradual decay, a disintegra-tion, in our fortunes and the fortunes of our nation.' The scene is closed with a song:

> It was not part of their blood
> ... When the English began to hate ...
> It was not suddenly bred
> It will not swiftly abate
> Through the chill years ahead
> When time shall count from the date
> That the English began to hate.

Edgar is an honest playwright. He clearly reaches a conclusion in *Destiny* that he does not like — that the Right, not the Left, has an ideology that reaches down into the popular roots of Britain. Although he overestimates the potential of the neo-nazis, he is one of the few playwrights to see past the Left militancy of the early 1970s to a deeper vein of reaction which fascist parties helped articulate. In this he foresees the triumph of radical conservatism in 1979 as well as the riots and growing tension on the streets that Trevor Griffiths later was to reflect in *Oi for England* (1982).

To some extent Edgar redresses the balance of *Destiny* in *Our Own People* (1977), a committee of inquiry play about racial and sexual discrimination against Asian workers, which was toured by the Pirate Jenny Company. But his return to the theme of nation comes more explicitly with the two-part adaptation of *Nicholas Nickleby*, produced collaboratively within the RSC and using Edgar's experience of the collective process from his early days with the General Will group, 7:84, the *Mary Barnes* team and Monstrous Regiment. Its liberal conclusion, however, was different from the one that might have been expected had an alternative theatre group chosen to adapt the Dickens novel: that despite the poverty and exploitation shown in the plays, which results from capitalism, there is such a beast as a good capitalist who can retain a kind heart and care for stray orphans.

Edgar has continued his search for a microcosmic representation of the nation, and in 1985 he devised *Entertaining Strangers* for Ann

Jellicoe's large-scale community project in Dorset. (Jellicoe had already written and directed many similar plays herself, involving the local community and presenting a panoramic view of village life.) Edgar's epic tale, spanning the fifty years from 1824–74, tells the story of a Methodist preacher and his confrontation with the founder of a brewery. In its treatment of moral, military and mercantile themes, the play examines the foundations of a nation assuming its imperial role.

If Edgar is representative of playwrights who have taken on the nation as a distinctive feature of their work, there are notable exceptions to the trend. Edward Bond, for example, writes about the English as a means to a more universal statement. His reference point is not the nation, although in *Early Morning* (1968), *The Sea* (1973) or *Bingo* (1973), he goes more deeply into the English than, for example, Robert Bolt does in *A Man for All Seasons* (1960), which appears to be *the* play about Englishness. Bond, however, is characteristic in a different way of those who have explored the relationship between the nation and the state as a complex configuration in which race and power are intertwined with the development of capital.

With some exceptions, it is the English (white and male) who are taken to stand for the nation. This is a reflection of an historical ascendancy that is reinforced culturally by the theatrical dominance of London. Most of those writing the plays, putting them on and reviewing them, would be English or would accept English hegemony, with the West End and the national companies representing the highest rung on the ladder of achievement. This hegemony has been challenged in various ways, both in the regions and by other proponents of de-centralization or national independence, particularly among the Scots, who have their own distinct theatre tradition. The most serious challenge, however, has come with the struggle for Irish nationhood, which has produced contradictory effects in the British theatre.

The English theatre's debt to the Irish dramatic tradition is longstanding and immense, yet the work of a revered playwright like Sean O'Casey has been seriously neglected, although the two national companies did mark the centenary of his birth with major productions. Beckett also has an international reputation but his influence is shadowy, felt mainly through his challenge to conventional structure and narrative expectations. Irish playwrights based in Ireland have achieved only sporadic acceptance in London. It is as if critical acclaim is awarded in proportion to perceived distance from contemporary political realities. A good example is Brian Friel's *Translations* (1981), which transferred to the National Theatre. His reference to the current struggle was sufficiently oblique to the English mind for it to be ignored in the welcome accorded a 'well-made' play that celebrated language, or — if the reference was picked up at all — was seen as rather comforting, suggesting the need for greater understanding which could lead to reconciliation. The play, however, shows that knowledge and understanding have not yet led to political control of Irish life by the Irish but have aided the neo-colonial process.

In relation to its enormous political significance, Northern Ireland has received scant attention in the postwar theatre, although the British presence has affected the vision of many post-1968 playwrights such as Howard Brenton and Howard Barker. The irreducible core of the issue — self-determination — has been displaced in a variety of ways, mainly by ignoring it or by dissolving it into an isolated human dimension, which invokes sympathy or laughter but not much else. There has been little contemporary work in the two national theatres: Howard Brenton's *The Romans in Britain* (1980) does not move beyond the general point that the British presence constitutes imperialism that hurts the oppressed and distorts the oppressor. Ron Hutchinson's *The Irish Play* (1980) looks at the conflicting arguments through the eyes of the Irish in England, who act out the history and current reality of Ireland's struggles as a savage, comic inevitability. An index of the problem facing a playwright wishing to address an audience in England can be found in David Rudkin's *Cries from Casement as his Bones are Brought to Dublin* (1973) with its overwhelming need simply to relate the history of the Irish conflict and overcome a staggering and widespread ignorance.

Even among the smaller venues and the touring groups, it has often proved difficult to stage outspoken plays about Ireland. In 1972 Portable Theatre had great trouble finding a venue that would accept the collectively written kaleidoscopic show, *England's Ireland*, which attempted to shock its audience into an awareness of the horrors of the Irish troubles. In the same year, when John McGrath updated *Serjeant Musgrave's Dance* for 7:84 to deal with 'Bloody Sunday' and the Derry slaughter, the company's production of *The Ballygombeen Bequest* by John Arden and Margaretta D'Arcy had to be withdrawn on legal advice because of a libel action taken out by a landlord who was attacked through the play. To date, their epic serial on Irish revolutionary politics, *The Non-Stop Connolly Show* (1975), has only been given readings in England.

In the years since the introduction of troops into Northern Ireland the astute follower of alternative theatre guides might have been able to see plays dealing with interrogation and its techniques, Northern Ireland as a training ground for increased state authoritarianism in Britain, the psychology of terrorists, and the effect of sectarianism on both Catholic and Protestant communities. But even if one were to add Bill Morrison's farce *Flying Blind* (1977) and Stewart Parker's entertainment *Spokesong* (1975), both of which enjoyed wider audiences, it does not amount to a substantial body of work, whatever the individual merit. In each of the cases mentioned there is a good reason why a playwright has chosen a particular approach rather than another. What is striking is how, as a whole, this still leaves Ireland as a marginal subject, as if the violence inescapably associated with it has both kept it on the agenda yet forced it way down. Nevertheless, in the 1980s a group of writers like Seamus Finnegan and Daniel Mornin, who were mainly from Northern Ireland but working in England, did begin to challenge the situation. With Peter Cox's *Up to the Sun and Down to the Centre* (1984) and Ron Hutchinson's *Rat in the Skull* (1984) it seemed as though the challenge would hold firm this time.

The complex legacy of empire has been locked into other aspects of national prejudice and racism. Osborne's *The Entertainer*, which opens with Billy swearing, 'Bloody Poles and Irish!', stands in ironic counter-point to the multi-cultural potential of Britain that the collapse of empire made possible. Some playwrights have examined the legacy of empire in relation to the third world, using the English as a link: Christopher Hampton with *Savages* (1973), Ted Whitehead with *Mecca* (1977), *For the West* (1977) by Michael Hastings, or Nicholas Wright with *One Fine Day* (1980). Others have tackled the subject on home ground, although in the case of older racism — against the Irish or Jewish people, for example — the economic and political roots are often left untouched in favour of presenting alternative and positive 'human' images. With racism against black people, however, a number of plays have attempted to explore and challenge both personal and institutional aspects of this discrimination: *Nice* (1973) and *Welcome Home Jacko* (1979) by Mustapha Matura, for example, or *Borderline* (1981) by Hanif Kureishi. Plays on an anti-racist theme by black and white playwrights have not only presented a positive image of those discriminated against and often seen simply as victims, they have also shown them as active agents, coping with the wider causes of their situation as well as the individual effects.

While one could list many authors of plays dealing with this type of theme from the 1970s alone, the striking fact again is their absence from the major theatres; the exception is David Edgar, whose play *Destiny* (1976) was accepted by the RSC for its small Stratford-upon-Avon theatre before transferring to London. Of the black playwrights in such a list, only Trinidad-born Mustapha Matura enjoys a wider acceptance outside the small, community-orientated theatres, although a new generation — British-born — is beginning to emerge, for example Tunde Ikoli and Hanif Kureishi.

Until the late 1960s the Royal Court was the main focus for plays by black playwrights, such as Wole Soyinka or Derek Walcott, beginning in 1958 with *Flesh to a Tiger* by Barry Reckord, and Errol John's *Moon on a Rainbow Shawl*. Inter-Action's Ambiance lunchtime theatre presented a black power season in 1970 which included the fourth play by Ed Bullins that it had staged since 1968. But the first group to make any real headway was the Dark and Light Theatre founded in 1970 in Brixton in south London, which later became the Black Theatre of Brixton. From these modest beginnings has come an impressive range of groups and venues — Temba, Black Theatre Co-operative, Keskidee, for example — together with many experienced black actors and playwrights, such as Michael Abensetts, Edgar White, Trevor Rhone, Jimi Rand and T Bone Wilson.

Women playwrights on the whole have not addressed themselves to the concept of nation in any of its formations, which is surprising, given the opening up of new political perspectives. Yet several writers have shown that plays about the nation are not an inevitable consequence of historical themes. Caryl Churchill has demonstrated that imperialism — the immediate route of the contemporary nation — embraced a distinct sexual ideology but in *Cloud Nine* (1979) she makes no direct reference to any connections with national political make-up. Similarly, *Light Shining in Buckinghamshire* (1976) is clearly focused on a key, defining moment in English history but again the debate is centred on the construction of gender and identity. Perhaps a man would have turned that moment into a nation play, as Keith Dewhurst did in *The World Turned Upside Down* (1978). To take a different example, Louise Page in *Salonika* (1982) turns away from using war as the defining time for nations and instead uses it to define individuals in relation to society.

Maybe women playwrights have been more aware of the 'England in irreversible decline' cul-de-sac — that one can pronounce the nation dead only once. Perhaps this difference of perspective reflects the detachment of women from power and official history; it is not exclusively gender-related but male playwrights often seem to consider their obligation to be social and public in a way that is not shared by many women. A play like Stephen Lowe's *Touched* makes these wider links against the backdrop of Labour's postwar victory. Peter Whelan draws together another strand in *The Accrington Pals* (1981) as the nation goes to war against the Kaiser, leaving the women literally running the shop, and in *Clay* (1982) as the nation stiffens its sinews for possibly the final world war. But it is difficult to find a play that successfully juxtaposes the construction of the individual and the construction of the nation in their political and personal relationship to each other.

CHAPTER FIVE

Public and Private: The Gender Gap

It is a common practice to divide plays into public and private: those about events and ideas, and those concerned with personal relations between individuals. Yet in the past some of the most powerful drama, from Aristophanes to Büchner, has attempted to explore the connections between the two areas, and in the postwar period it has become clear that such a neat distinction can often be misplaced. Underlying the different ways that playwrights have tried to bring the public and the private into a single perspective — or to keep the two quite separate — is the gender gap, a basic feature of theatre that arouses great controversy. Most writers, directors and decision-makers in theatre management are men; they have been reared and educated in a mainly middle-class English cultural context, and it has to be recognized that this bias shapes the theatre's existence. In particular, it adjusts the focus of plays that deal with private life and its main component, sexuality.

Historically speaking, this bias is so ingrained and all-pervasive that to mention it, let alone to challenge it, brings forth the severest wrath and the greatest misunderstanding. It is easy to ignore other factors, especially class, and to become trapped into the idea that there is a form of writing or concern that is particularly 'feminine' with the converse judgement that there are some specifically 'masculine' areas which are inaccessible to women. Peter Whelan's *The Accrington Pals* (1981) or Steve Gooch's *Female Transport* (1973) are clear reminders that this is not necessarily the case. The familiar distinction between public and private plays needs to be refined in order to avoid such a gender assumption. The point is not that men are unable to write about private emotion nor that women are incapable of dealing with public issues. There is no inner force of gender that inescapably pushes men in one direction and women in another, but there is a clear if relatively unexplored relationship between gender and writing — in the use of language, choice of subject and general approach — that needs to be taken into consideration.

Any account of how the public and the private have been treated in postwar theatre has to begin by acknowledging the gender gap which exists within it. As an example, consider the way in which both a male and female playwright have treated the same subject of breast cancer and mastectomy: Trevor Griffiths in *Through the Night* (written for television in 1975) and Louise Page in *Tissue* (1978). Griffiths' play is charged with intense and personal feeling; there is no mistaking the deep anger felt by the author over the impersonal treatment of women having a mastectomy, an anger which is clearly rooted in some personal experience. It is a powerful and moving play, which invites a public response: that doctors and hospital administrators should be less callous and less clinical, and that patients need to be more demanding and less subservient. The individual characters serve to illustrate a set of general concepts: passive working-class woman, bewildered husband, authoritarian ward-sister, paternalistic male consultant, concerned male house doctor. The play isolates a set of progressive social forces, which are placed against a set of conservative forces. It is a sophisticated social statement which suggests 'How' and, up to a point, 'What', but ignores 'Why'. It takes for granted the choice of mastectomy as its specific subject, and moves beyond that to condemn the repression of institutions in general.

Page's play hardly deals with the fact of the operation at all and only marginally with the subsequent pain and embarrassment. Its issue is why it matters to have a breast removed and why the subject is taboo. It analyses how a woman is socialized as a child to think about her body and the expectations she builds up, and examines how removing a breast stirs up fears in which death, sex, and social and personal failure are all interlinked. It is a private play in the same way that the Griffiths' piece is a public play but it is a private play about social pressures rather than individual relationships; it is concerned with how an individual is formed within society. This is perhaps an easy case to argue; a man writes of mastectomy as an experience from which he is necessarily excluded whilst a woman can at least conceive of sharing that experience. Nevertheless the point has a wider relevance.

The hallmark of postwar British playwrights has been their concern to map out the main public themes of politics and the nation within a firm social framework. The starting point has been a public rather than a private perspective, with the fate of the individual carrying a political resonance. The audience is expected to possess some preconception about the role of different social groupings within this framework which the playwright can then either reinforce or, more effectively, twist and reshape; it is the deviation from the expected that gives the character a dramatic emphasis. Nearly all the great individual characters of the period (and there are relatively few of them) conform to this, for instance, Black Jack Musgrave in John Arden's *Serjeant Musgrave's Dance* (1959) or Maitland in John Osborne's *Inadmissible Evidence*

(1964). Nor is this confined to postwar British plays, for the common assumption of most European drama is that to assign someone a class and social position is to give that person an identity which the audience can recognize instantly.

In contrast to the British preoccupation, American playwrights have tended to the other extreme, with the focus being a private world and the fate of the individual being sufficient to itself without requiring wider validation in the public world — a curious reversal of the pre-war situation. Arthur Miller ventures onto the broader canvas, for example in *The American Clock* (1980), but even he is happiest when directing his concerns through domestic explorations, as in *Death of a Salesman* (1949). Tennessee Williams remains the key influence for the 'domestic' approach, followed by Edward Albee; the individual is very much up-front, with the social forces firmly in the background — something which is true even for the panoramas of social alienation presented by Sam Shepard.

One reason for the dominant presence of the individual in American drama is that assumptions about a person's social position are harder to make. The disintegrating cauldron of American society, with its mix of ethnic and social origins, makes it much more difficult to see automatically why people are as they appear to be.

In the past the premise of the British theatre rested upon the solidly bourgeois credentials of the theatre, the middle class watching middle-class life presented with a class focus so narrow that almost everything about the social formation of individual characters could be left un-stated. In a play like *For Services Rendered* (1932), Somerset Maugham could assume that his audience already knew everything that mattered about the past of his bourgeois family, including even the sexual repression which could scarcely be explicitly mentioned. He could then safely concentrate on his main theme: the disintegration of the social fabric following the First World War.

By the 1950s it was necessary for some writers to spell out the differences of class background and the effect that this had on indi-viduals, though it is difficult to find plays which treat this with any degree of complexity. The closest is David Mercer's vision of a work-ing-class childhood as one of immense warmth and security with material deprivation amounting almost to a moral bonus. But in most cases it remained sufficient to assume a pre-given understanding of how the people portrayed came to adulthood. The limitation of many plays about the working class is connected with this inability to bridge the gap between public and private, to explain what it is, at the level of the individual, that represents the class characteristics that are assumed to be so significant politically.

The bravura aspect of Bill Maitland in *Inadmissible Evidence* is that

Osborne dares us not to understand immediately why the man is as he is. 'You understand Maitland,' Osborne is saying, 'He is you and I challenge you to deny it.' The possibility of making such a challenge rests in part on Maitland's class but, perhaps more importantly, on Maitland's gender. Middle-class men are assumed to recognize what makes Maitland tick.

The adoption of social stereotypes as the basis of individual charac-ter is not necessarily a crude or ineffective device. It enables one to sit back and enjoy the mechanics of farce, for instance. In a more so-phisticated though less obviously enjoyable way, this is true of Harold Pinter. His revelations of character and negotiations of personal power do not alter or question social relations. In contrast, a playwright like John McGrath, who has written about women from a class point of view, has challenged prevailing stereotypes by offering opposing ones, in which individual character is less important than a common position in the social system.

For many postwar playwrights, and in particular the post-1968 generation, the stereotype marks a genuine failure. For them the slogan 'The personal is political' has a real meaning. Yet with few exceptions — mostly gay — the male playwrights who emerged in the 1970s had even less success than their predecessors in exploring the politics of personal identity. One of the preoccupations of the political movements around which many of these playwrights developed was the problem of Britain and the roots of national decay. Their work reflects this emphasis rather than, for example, any sustained examina-tion of gender or sexuality; nevertheless, this is often used as a metaphor for national decline and corruption — an expression of the very difficulty the playwrights have found in reaching beyond the acknowledgement of personal alienation.

The women playwrights who emerged in the 1970s tended to reflect the concerns of the women's movement, and the issues that came to the fore were sexuality, the 'construction' of female identity (particu-larly within the family) and the discovery of submerged and repressed aspects of female experience, all of which necessarily affected the way men were seen. It is important to note the considerable international culture that grew with the rise of the women's liberation movement, which encouraged a wide range of publications, including novels, poems and plays. Women playwrights began to re-define theatre, offering different views of contemporary experience, different inter-pretations of how such experience is categorized and different ways of expressing themselves. Just as the movement embraced radically dif-ferent views and changed its emphasis and momentum, the plays by women that put women at their centre differ enormously. The fact of such differences is a reminder that there is difficult ground to be covered in writing about women playwrights as a general category.

There is a rough parallel between this explosion in female playwriting and the great period of male private plays at the end of the last century when the new territory of the subconscious and repressed sexual urges was being explored. The comparison is only approximate but it does serve to indicate the gap which has existed in most postwar drama, a period in which at the very beginning Britain did possess two inheritors of the great tradition of plays about individual identity: John Whiting and Terence Rattigan.

John Whiting

Although Whiting's plays were performed only rarely in his own lifetime and have been neglected since his death in 1963, he remains a pioneer. *Saint's Day* (1951), *Marching Song* (1954) and *The Devils* (1961) all concern a central figure's relationship to an ideal and they all show how individuals are affected, privately and intensely, by the struggle against self-illusion and uncooperative reality in the pursuit of an absolute. The consequences of individual action never allow these concerns to remain private. In *Marching Song* the dilemma of the protagonist, a discredited general, relates to the fate of his nation. He massacred children in order to make a necessary military advance but, having been defeated, imprisoned and then released, he is politically, socially and emotionally destroyed. Through a scrutiny of the past that reassesses the present, Whiting links the different areas of failure in the most visible personal defeat, the general's inability to sustain his love or even to love anew.

Saint's Day by any yardstick is a complex piece that appears to have been written on the edge of despair brought on by the inhumanity of the Second World War and given the final bitter twist with the dropping of the atomic bombs. The play tells the story of a poet living among hostile villagers and ends in the death of his entire family; it offers only the merest spark of hope in human capacity for moral regeneration at the end of a very long, very dark tunnel.

The clearest link between social identity and sexuality comes in *The Devils* and is embodied in the figure of a parish priest, whose pursuit of intellectual, emotional and physical fulfilment leads to his destruction. Whiting paints a totally bleak picture of the individual's ability to realize in public a private passion.

Terence Rattigan

A similar stress on individual pain in the face of public pressure is to be found in the work of Terence Rattigan, who, like Whiting, was unable to find any strength in a collective situation. Rattigan is often seen as typical of the dramatists who were dislodged in 1956 by John Osborne and *Look Back in Anger*: cosy middle-class writers pursuing safe themes of middle-class life with drawing rooms, French windows and polite conversation.

It is certainly possible to put Rattigan in that context insofar as he wrote for a West End audience and did in many ways bow to the expected cultural norms. *The Winslow Boy* (1946) and *The Browning Version* (1948), to take obvious examples, are firmly within that most middle-class of areas, the English public-school, and in no way do they attack the values of such institutions. They accept their underlying virtues and offer criticism based only on things that are handled badly within that framework. Plays such as *French Without Tears* (1936), *While the Sun Shines* (1943) or *The Sleeping Prince* (1953) are indeed just middle-class confections. But considered as a writer about human emotions and the conflict between individual desire and social constraint, Rattigan is as interesting a dramatist as any of his post-1956 successors. One of his most revealing plays is *The Deep Blue Sea* (1952). It is simple in construction, worked out in one room with a time-span of a single day. It begins with a woman, Hester, being discovered after attempting a gas fire suicide. She is living with a lover, having separated from her very respectable husband ten months before. The husband is sent for and his pleas for her to come back are rejected. The lover returns, reads by accident the intended suicide note and walks out on her. Eventually he returns, expecting to be persuaded to stay. Instead Hester sends him on his way and, apparently, resigns herself to living on her own. The husband and the lover, as well as the secondary characters, are largely foils for the woman. The two men are stereotypes: a respectable judge, with a social life centred around polite and cultured dinner parties, and an ex-Battle of Britain pilot whose nerve has gone and who now does little more than drink, play golf and live off the memory of past exploits. The core of the play is the single and dominating sexual passion that Hester has for her lover.

It is interesting to compare just how explicit Rattigan is about this passion with the supposedly outspoken Osborne in *Look Back in Anger*. Jimmy Porter subdues two women by deploying what one must infer as sexual attraction. Yet sexual activity is hardly hinted at throughout the play. Osborne has remained a consistently prurient writer but never a sexually explicit one. On the other hand, Hester in *The Deep Blue Sea* is sexually avid for her lover, Freddie. When he first kisses her in greeting, she 'instantly responds, with an intensity of emotion that is almost ugly' (stage direction). The pressure on him is such, as he complains drunkenly to a friend, that early in their affair they had rows about his sexual response:

JACKIE: What were they about?

FREDDIE: [*uncomfortably*] Usual things.

[JACKIE *waits for him to continue.*]

[*explosively*] Damn it, Jackie, you know me. I can't be a ruddy Romeo all the time.

JACKIE: Who can?

FREDDIE: According to her the whole damn human race — male part of it anyway.

Passionate emotion, whether repressed and concealed or allowed to blow up with disastrous consequences, runs as a thread through Rattigan: the desperate grasping of a strange woman's knee in *Separate Tables* (1954); Alma Rattenbury in *Cause Célèbre* (1977), besotted with a 17-year-old; T.E. Lawrence in *Ross* (1960); even, in a different non-sexual way, the lonely classics teacher in *The Browning Version*. To be fully human for Rattigan is to be passionate, but one does not always freely choose the object of one's passion. In a society based on the suppression of passion, one must either endure life without social acceptability or suffer the effects of painful self-control.

In *The Deep Blue Sea* Rattigan uses the device of the struck-off doctor, Miller, who lives in the same house as Hester, to confront a way of living with this dilemma. His past offence is referred to obliquely and obscurely. An obvious answer is that he was involved in an abortion but another 'crime' that fits is that he went to prison for some homosexual offence. (*The Deep Blue Sea* was originally conceived as a play about homosexual love.)

MRS. ELTON [*the landlady*]: ...You know what people are and what he did wasn't — well — the sort of thing people forgive very easily. Ordinary normal people, I mean.

Now Miller works as a bookie's runner and helps out at a children's hospital. He responds to Hester's plight instinctively but bleakly.

MILLER: To live without hope can mean to live without despair. That word "never". Face that and you can face life. Get beyond hope. It's your only chance.

Hack through life simply because it is there. 'For me the only purpose in life is to live it,' says Miller, and Hester follows his advice. When Freddie comes back she refuses to respond to his advances, denies even the possibility of missing him. The last word in the play is 'Goodbye' and the last actions are of Hester burying her face in his clothes before folding them away, having turned on the gas again, but this time only to light the fire. It is not the victory of reason but a pained assertion of individual control.

Rattigan was homosexual and saw himself as a humanist. Yet living in the immediate postwar decade when social change was, at least in principle, on the agenda, he failed to respond dramatically to the needs of the time. He acknowledges passion and then recommends retreat from it as the only possible way to survive. Rattigan was not really kicked off the stage by Osborne; he remained a successful if less constant presence in the West End theatre. But artistically he seems to have followed Hester's path: a discreet and measured retreat from a world of danger.

There is, in fact, considerable overlap between the concerns of Rattigan and those of Osborne. But whereas Osborne, at least verbally, allowed his characters full rein in the expression of their passion, Rattigan asked them to subdue it. Osborne's existential philosophy required, if not urged, that an individual should push himself (the gender is deliberate) right upstage. Rattigan proposed retreat in the face of a dire alternative.

Harold Pinter

The same concerns, approached from a different angle, can be seen in the plays of Harold Pinter, who proposes neither retreat nor front-line battle. His tactic is altogether more oblique. He stands as a central but aloof figure in postwar British drama. He is one of Britain's best-known writers yet he has stood apart from the general trend towards broadening the social base of theatre and has pursued with great success his own version of intellectual solipsism. (This, however, should be distinguished from the vision of Samuel Beckett to whom he has been compared frequently but mistakenly.)

Stylistically Pinter has been enormously influential, probably more than any other contemporary British playwright. There is a pattern to a Pinter play — passages of apparently random and condensed conversation, ordered, heightened and interspersed with long and oblique stories suddenly produced by one of the characters. It occurs again and again in the work of later playwrights, elevating the private world of the half-remembered anecdote or personal obsession to an unspecified but apparent general significance. It is always the 'feel' of a Pinter play that matters; the slightly eerie sense of things stirring under the skin and expressed in silence and reservation rather than direct comment. It is very English.

To a considerable extent it is this discretion which accounts for Pinter's popularity. He was found difficult at first but once the new rules had been learnt his work allowed audiences to project the ordinariness and confusion of their own lives into something invested with a greater drama. Every halting and nervous conversation around a dinner table can be accorded the quality of a Pinter play even when very little or nothing at all is stirring under the skin. Many actors love doing his work for the enormous flexibility and degree of intonation which he offers them. A former actor himself, few other contemporary playwrights provide such space for interpretation and nuance in performance. It is possible to perform a Pinter play with almost any sub-text — a pointer to both the strength and weakness of his work.

A large part of this achievement is his distinctive verbal technique, which has been copied (usually to worse effect) in many television and stage plays to the point where 'Pinteresque' has become its own self-evident description. His susceptibility to imitation points to his importance in loosening theatrical form and shifting expectations of character and narrative. Yet finally one has to confront the central question of whether anything exists in his work beyond technique, and if not, does this matter?

The position of a writer such as Pinter, distanced resolutely from any kind of direct social comment, is, in its own terms, secure and consistent. It is the response of Osborne, in that he writes for himself and not for an audience or, in the classic expression of modern apostasy, that of the elder Auden*:

> No more movements. No more manifestoes. Every poet stands above... The ideal audience the poet imagines consists of the beautiful who go to bed with him, the powerful who invite him to dinner and tell him secrets of State, and his fellow poets.

Pinter, of course, is no apostate, and remains as the one major British dramatist to have turned his back on social comment while Tom Stoppard and even Alan Ayckbourn have succumbed to such temptation. Yet the structuring of technique, most notably, for example, in *No Man's Land* (1975), *Old Times* (1971) or *Betrayal* (1978), is itself a comment. Pinter writes about real society and he exists in a real world. He does have a philosophical view, which is that while truth may be absolute it is only ever subjective and relative. His work explores the problems of time, of perception, of memory, rooted in the insecurity of personal identity. The violence, both explicit and implicit, is a measure of that insecurity, and the concentration on power games, the ritual of personal and geographical territorial struggles, is a measure of the drive to come to terms with that insecurity. Whatever the location of those struggles, which is usually the primary social unit of family or marriage, the core for Pinter is sexuality.

Sexuality is, after all, the commonest worm beneath the skin. But Pinter is not neutral in what he says about sex, perception, power or personal relationships. This can be seen in the most successful of his plays about sexuality, *The Homecoming* (1965). It is the work which secured his reputation, being played by the Royal Shakespeare Company for eighteen months before going in triumph to Broadway. The plot is simple to the point of absurdity. A son, Teddy, returns with his

---

* W.H. Auden: *Poets at Work* (1948).

wife, Ruth, to his family home in North London. He is a successful academic in the States. His mother is dead. His father, a butcher, Teddy's uncle and his two younger brothers remain in the all-male household — the lumpen working class existing, in Pinter's half-spoken way, on the verges of criminality. For David Mercer or David Storey this would be the beginning of another excursion through class betrayal, but Pinter's interest is different. At their first meeting Teddy's brother Lenny makes a sexual proposal to Ruth; the relatives all turn on her sexually, graduating from a fondle to a dance, with the youngest brother going with her to his bedroom.

Teddy accepts all this with a puzzled aloofness even when the family decides that the best thing to do is to set Ruth up as a working whore, a job which it is implied she has done before. She accepts this and Teddy leaves alone. In the final moments the remaining men group round her, predatory and frightened, competing for her and fearful of failing with her. The family is seen as both a tightly bonded group, as in *The Caretaker* (1960), and as an arena for sexual competition. The patriarch father, Max, unable to cope with the implied sexual demands of Ruth's continual presence, collapses on his knees, whimpering and begging for a kiss. The outsider has been brought in — on her terms but within their context. She becomes the new mother and offers the possibility of sexual gratification as well.

The Homecoming is an unpleasant play not just because of its overt content but because of the use Pinter makes of his muscular technique to build up an erotic charge. It is a masculine play written like a thriller but given a skilful gloss of intellectual content sufficient to allow audiences to feel good about seeing it. It was called shocking in the mid-1960s and is still seen as such.

In the wake of *Lady Chatterley's Lover* and its like it was usual in the 'swinging sixties' to believe that working-class men had a direct approach to sex which gave them a virility denied to the middle classes. It was the era of rough trade with a new brand of working-class sex-symbols: actors such as Michael Caine, rock stars like Mick Jagger, even photographers like David Bailey. It is this belief in the class-bias of sexuality that Pinter uses so effectively.

The upwardly mobile men portrayed by Mercer and Storey feel that they are culturally and politically enfeebled by losing contact with manual work and its environment. Their class virility is drained through education. Pinter, however, goes to the jugular. The sensitive philosopher Teddy is 'emasculated' in a more direct manner; he cannot satisfy his wife sexually whereas his brother can. Lust rather than love wins the day; marriage is an empty bourgeois convention. But while other playwrights at least try to come to terms with their perceived problem, Pinter simply shows it off for effect. Look at the lower orders, he is saying. The men are in touch with their bodies and with their instincts. They know how to operate; size up a woman at a glance and, if she wants sex, and mostly they do, have her there and then on the sofa. It is both a prudish and a lascivious attitude.

The character of Ruth is one of many women presented by Pinter as powerful, potentially devouring and yet elusive; she stands in line with Stella (*The Collection*, 1961), who tells her husband she slept with a complete stranger in a hotel, Kate (*Old Times*), whom husband and old woman friend fight over, or Emma (*Betrayal*), the centre of the sex triangle between husband and lover who is her husband's best friend.

For Pinter the world of sex is alluring; it is forbidden and forbidding. You enter it illicitly — hence the prominence of women as whores and the constant references to underwear and fantasy. (There is also an uneasy and submerged suggestion of gay sexuality in many plays like *The Homecoming*, *Old Times* and *The Caretaker* that is left unexplored.) Pinter's plays express a view of sexuality that is hostile to women, conceding to them a pseudo-matriarchal dominance that exists to satisfy heterosexual male appetites. The subjectivity of the form is not the same as openness or, even less, a position of neutrality.

Joe Orton

An *enfant terrible* in the classic Romantic mould, Joe Orton revelled in the role of social outcast and was defeated, fatally, by the success with which he played this role out. In the three years between the production of his first play *The Ruffian on the Stair* (1964) and his violent death in 1967, Orton acquired a reputation for taking to a logical and comic extreme the so-called 'permissiveness' of the decade in a theatrical world still constrained by the Lord Chamberlain's censorship. His achievement was to embrace openly and passionately the contradictions that he saw inside everyone, and to fashion his frenzied vision of the chaos and cruelty inside English respectability into a bold but elegant stage architecture.

In *The Ruffian on the Stair* and the first stage success, *Entertaining Mr. Sloane* (1964), Orton's concerns are in stark contrast to those of the early Harold Pinter to which his work has been understandably but unhelpfully compared. Orton attacks head on: *Entertaining Mr. Sloane* has the panache of *Loot* (1966) but not the control. The grotesque characters of *Loot* offer a vivid picture of English life through stylized distortion, but this accomplished comedy of human avarice and corruption relies on offence and shock to a degree that dates it quickly. Orton's obliteration of all moral standards allows no element of judgement and therefore robs the play of the more serious purpose of theatre that he intended. This is most nearly overcome in his great farce *What the Butler Saw* (1969), produced posthumously, in which the principle of role reversal and mistaken identity speeds the action to its sobering climax.

Orton's sexual jokes sum up not just his view of the repressed

English but also his only view of any kind of liberation — male-centred, sexual, flamboyant, unresponsive to social reality. Counter-pointing the elegant and the gross, Orton catches the duality between the drive of passion and the impossibility of its true fulfilment. He indicts society for producing such terror and pain where there should be joy, but nowhere does he relate this to an ability to struggle for love or caring. In the end his single tone lets society off the hook; he becomes the safety valve and no longer the accuser. He creates a world that the audience can enter and leave with safety precisely because such excess can be cathartic in a reassuring and conservative way. *What the Butler Saw* is now firmly established in the repertoire of English theatre, which is an index of how limited and containable an apparently radical impulse can be.

Orton, like Pinter, was able to exploit the fashion of his time for the supposed magnetism and virility of the working-class male, which was usually allied to a male view that women really wanted the niceties of bourgeois life to be swept away and to be sexually possessed by this new force. The lower-middle-class 'outsider' of the 1950s who had become a classless radical was now transformed into a deliciously threatening yobbo.

Attempts to puncture the new macho myth have frequently led to fantasy or madness in drama as an indication of the impossibility of truly breaking free from the designated social and sexual roles. Some-times this is purely personal, as in David Storey's *The Restoration of Arnold Middleton* (1966) in which the conflict between the private and the public, the emotional and the rational, leads to neurosis of psycho-tic proportions when the character's normal state becomes his abnor-mality; his sanity is his madness. Sometimes it is linked to political dilemmas as well, as in the plays of David Mercer, who dramatized the instability caused by an inability to live out one's beliefs. In David Halliwell's *Little Malcolm and his Struggle against the Eunuchs* (1966), Malcolm, expelled from technical college for leading other students astray, forms his own political party to oust the college principal using a bizarre blackmail scheme. Malcolm has the eloquence of an Osborne 'anti-hero' though his journey is one of self-discovery rather than self-justification.

This kind of territory was most disturbingly explored in the 1960s by followers of Antonin Artaud and Jean Genet and was taken up by the RSC in its 1962 season of new plays at the Arts Theatre, notably with David Rudkin's *Afore Night Come* and Fred Watson's *Infanticide in the House of Fred Ginger.* Two years later the RSC launched its Theatre of Cruelty season and produced, among other things, Peter Weiss's *Marat/Sade* (1964). Common to all these attempts to examine the various overlappings on the private-public axis is the linking of sex and violence. Rudkin, a rare and idiosyncratic poet, continued to explore this territory more consistently than any other writer; his two most politically explicit plays are *Cries from Casement as his Bones are Brought to Dublin* (1973), in which homosexuality is the trigger for new political awareness and action, and *Ashes* (1974), which focuses on infertility as a personal parallel to political impotence in Northern Ireland. The same concerns can be seen in *The Sons of Light* (1976) and *The Triumph of Death* (1981).

The use of sexuality as a metaphor for the wider political system embraces many different views of both sexuality and politics. Yet throughout the postwar period one of the most persistent ideas of sexuality presented by those who made such links could be found in a host of plays attacking middle-class mores, savaging the conventions of the family or lamenting the onset of the middle-aged 'male menopause'. It was an approach that contained an overriding image of the sex impulse as an innate and individual force which had to be contained, expressed or repressed. This supremely male view was given expression in female form when the Lulu figure was brought to an English theatre in 1970 by Peter Barnes in his adaptation of Frank Wedekind's turn of the century plays *Earth Spirit* and *Pandora's Box*. Barnes had previously linked sex and anarchy in *The Ruling Class* (1968); and in *The Bewitched* (1974) he carried even further his extraordinarily powerful exploration of the malaise of society as the malaise of the individual psyche writ large. Barnes connects the egalitarian and the erotic, the health of democracy with the ability to love, and suggests that the individual needs to be set free from the traps of a socially determined role. David Edgar, adapting a contemporary case history, makes a similar point in *Mary Barnes* (1978); here the political context forms a backdrop to the creation of a social environment in which the 'patient' can come through, influenced by the psychoanalytical thinking of R.D. Laing. Other playwrights applying sexual-political correlatives have drawn on different psychological theories, for example, Caryl Churchill's use of Reich in *Objections to Sex and Violence* (1975).

Freud and Jung are clearly as important as Marx, especially for those who have benefited from the abolition of the Lord Chamberlain's censorship powers in 1968. This has meant a loosening of restrictions, although not their abolition. A private prosecution was brought against Howard Brenton's *The Romans in Britain* (1981), for example, not for its political views on imperialism but for a scene of forced buggery.

The removal of censorship and the eruption of sexual liberation at the end of the 1960s certainly made British theatre more sensational for a time, at least at its edges. The fare provided for West End audiences changed little; we were presented with a tastefully lit nude in

Ronald Millar's *Abelard and Heloise* (1970), and *Oh! Calcutta!* (1970), devised by Kenneth Tynan, ran for a decade, but this over-self-conscious set of explicit sketches about sex that gave erotica a bad name did not turn Shaftesbury Avenue into a new Jerusalem. There was a shift in what was considered acceptable in terms of language and subject matter that reflected changing social attitudes but most of the explosion occurred well away from the traditional theatre and was generally imported from the USA.

The best work was strikingly innovatory, like that of the Living Theatre from America and in its wake Les Trétaux Libres from France, both of which visited London in 1971, offering a vision of individual freedom and the breaking down of bourgeois boundaries between art, life and politics. Other exponents of total and physical theatre condemning entirely their social and cultural system made a similar impact, in particular Café La Mama and the Open Theatre from America which both came to London in 1967 and strongly influenced the course of British theatre. Happenings became multi-media events; the Traverse in Edinburgh and the Arts Laboratory in London spawned other experimental centres and touring groups, some of whom developed a form of theatre known as performance art. The work of such companies — for example, Freehold, The People Show, the Pip Simmons Theatre Group, Welfare State — is almost by definition freed from most of the assumptions of a writer-based theatre and much of it has vanished, unrecorded. This strand certainly represents a major impulse of the alternative theatre, the reverberations of which can be seen in the women's theatre, in the work of playwrights like Howard Brenton and Snoo Wilson, and in the enormously influential 1970 Peter Brook production of *A Midsummer Night's Dream*. For some it really was the Age of Aquarius even if it was difficult to pin down exactly what that meant. But underlying the exuberance there lay a hollowness and sense of alienation. There was not, after all, a new dawn, only more dancing to wilder music.

The plays that drew on or assessed sexual liberation are, by and large, bleak. The characteristic reaction of the young playwrights in the immediate post-1968 years is a shriek of moral outrage and disgust rather than any celebration of a new era. The general feeling could be summed up by Chris Wilkinson's touring shows, *I Was Hitler's Maid* (1971) and *Plays for Rubber Go-Go Girls* (1972), which present contemporary society as a form of violence fuelled by pornographic male fantasies. Two other plays from the beginning of this period serve as further illustrations to confirm the trend: Heathcote Williams' *AC/DC* (1970) and Trevor Griffiths' *Apricots* (1971).

AC/DC is not a play in the traditional sense, though it acquired a sensational reputation at the Royal Court's Theatre Upstairs. In the first half five characters in an amusement arcade blast away in a whirlwind of heightened language about sex, psychic energy and madness. It is the language that matters. Nothing actually happens, not even any sex, despite the mysterious sexual combinations said to have occurred in a photo-booth seconds before the talking started. In the second half a woman penetrates herself with a roll of celebrity photos; a man masturbates watching her. Finally she drills a hole in his skull to release the pressure. He screams, then smiles. The intent is exultation, a celebration of the rejection of all values in favour of psychic anarchy. Anything is allowed as the only hope of combatting the psychic capital-ism of the media that is gradually stealing the brains and soul of humanity. The language stutters at times and falls back on repetitive jargon but it also achieves part of its point; the flow of association and jokes demonstrates that conceptual freedom does exist somewhere out there beyond the airwaves. However, the cumulative effect is depress-ing. It is in the end a masturbatory male fantasy which culminates in paranoia. It is not a celebration after all; gender and the social assump-tions attached to it are seen as irrelevant and the collective instinct is shown to be empty of promise. Underlying the general apprehension is fear of women. Sadie, the masturbating and head-drilling woman, is the one person with any real sense of self and that self is man-hating. She does not trepan the man to exorcize him but to kill him.

The thread of women-fearing (which can easily become women-hating) runs through John Osborne, Harold Pinter, David Mercer and the post-1968 generation to a writer like David Hare without a break. It is almost the defining mark of male dramatists who have written since the War about personal-public relations and sexuality. It exists too, though in a mediated and muffled way, within the plays of Trevor Griffiths.

Griffiths is, by self-definition, a writer about politics, but in most of his work there is an oppressive sense of sexuality that carries a political correlation. He is concerned to expose the betrayal of true socialism but he makes nevertheless a continual connection, explicit or implicit, between political power and sexual potency which would not be out of place in the political practice of those he is criticizing. In *Occupations* (1970), it is Kabak, the Comintern emissary and a cynical betrayer of revolution when expedient, who possesses the sexual virility. His poli-tics are mirrored in the way he treats his dying wife and exerts sexual control over her maid. Gramsci, the sympathetic revolutionary, is portrayed as sexually neutered. In *The Party* (1973) the first scene takes place in a bedroom after unsatisfactory sexual intercourse; the TV producer, Joe Shawcross, who is politically lost, ends the scene by masturbating. (He is seen against projected images of May 1968 in Paris — a sign of his political ineffectiveness.) In *Comedians* it is Gethin, the born-again Stalinist, who retains his implied vigour, and Eddie, the failed liberal comic, who tells of the guilty and surreptitious sexual arousal he felt when visiting a concentration camp. (It is interesting to note that in the rewritten versions of both *Occupations* and *The Party* Griffiths toned down the sexual references.)

The only play that Griffiths has written directly about sexuality is *Apricots*, a brief two-hander. Its theme is desolate and lonely sex. A married couple talk about the sex they have shared the previous night with another couple. They make love slowly and without achieving orgasm. Eventually both masturbate. Each talks about the past: moments when sexual discovery was exciting and the possibilities of further exploration seemed endless. Now, it appears, everything has been explored but found to be empty.

In an interview (condensed in the introduction to the published text of *Apricots*), Griffiths says that he clearly wants this wasteland not just to represent a failure of sexual desire but to have a wider, social significance. He seems to believe that implicit in the play is the impossibility of considering personal relationships as autonomous — they take their meaning from the conditions of society and the world. But in no sense can this be taken as obvious within the play. The woman or the man could as easily be activists with a revolutionary socialist party as middle-class executives. They have a baby but this is excluded from the consideration of their relationship. It is not even made clear whether they have a particularly affluent life. In the absence of such information, *Apricots* becomes just what Griffiths wants to prevent — a morality play about the dangers of too much sex. Hovering around is the distinct suspicion that in such a life it is the woman who gradually becomes dominant as her sexual needs emerge.

> ANNA: Yes. You can. You will. I want you to fuck me hard and strong and long. I want you to make my cunt sing with it. Scream with it. I want you to get in there... prick and balls and body and mind and senses and conscience and remorse and hope. Everything. I want it *all in there.*
> SAM: No. I can't.
> ANNA: Yes. You can.
> SAM: I can't. I can't.
> ANNA: You won't. You mean.

There is something a little frightening about Griffiths' writing on sexuality and personal relationships though it is veiled behind a strong intellectual vigour. There is a suppressed sexual element in the ritual that ends *Oi for England* (1982) when Finn and Gloria transform themselves into gladiators ready for street warfare. Although Gloria is shown to be a fully-fledged fighter, her gender has been obliterated by the uniform she has donned, and it is Finn who closes the play in speechless fury. What Griffiths implies is that only an enormous assertion of masculine force can prevent female sexuality from taking over, and he equates political force with just such a masculine urge. In

Comedians Gethin's assault on the female dummy in his comedy act is as much sexual as political and leaves a final impression that the equation is a necessary one. What this image suggests is an accurate representation of some aspects of contemporary politics, socialist or not. What is disturbing is that Griffiths never openly questions the assumptions which lie behind such politics. In this sense he observes rather than comments.

Gay Theatre

It was in response to 'male' politics that the women's and gay liberation movements developed. The plays which followed in their wake have made the major contribution to the exploration of the public-private axis. Much of the work, particularly in the gay category, is little more than a preliminary exploration. It was, after all, still a sensation for two men to kiss on stage in 1970, and the simple fact of presenting homosexual life has been the major component of much gay theatre.

Gay playwrights such as Somerset Maugham, Noël Coward, Terence Rattigan and Tennessee Williams often channelled their vision through heterosexual situations. Club performances allowed more explicit presentations, notably when the Comedy Theatre was taken over in 1956 as the New Watergate. There followed an immensely successful two-year season with plays by Arthur Miller, Tennessee Williams and Robert Anderson. This experiment persuaded the Lord Chamberlain to drop opposition to the staging of plays about homosexuality and gradually they became commercially viable. In 1960 Rattigan's *Ross* openly dealt with an English hero's discovery of homosexual feelings, and in 1965 *The Killing of Sister George* by Frank Marcus centred on a lesbian relationship, though it implicitly confirmed the dominant view of gender by making fun of the two women. (The play ran successfully in the West End while in the same year John Osborne's *A Patriot for Me* was forced to perform under club conditions at the Royal Court.) Ironically, the Lord Chamberlain's censorship role was removed during the run at the Royal Court of Christopher Hampton's *Total Eclipse* (1968), which deals with the relationship between Verlaine and Rimbaud.

The most clearly political gay plays were those produced by Gay Sweatshop, a group formed in 1975 during the gay season at the Almost Free Theatre in London. At first predominantly male, the group later involved more women, splitting into two separate groups in 1977. It is illuminating to quote Michelene Wandor*, the author of

---

* Michelene Wandor: *Understudies: Theatre and Sexual Politics* (Methuen, 1981).

one of the group's plays, *Care and Control* (1977), about the clash of theatrical style in Gay Sweatshop:

> The men drew on an already familiar camp and drag tradition, which they both celebrated and tried to stand on its head, whereas the women leaned more towards the newer agitprop documentary-based styles, as a means of showing hitherto suppressed experience as it really is.

Care and Control itself provides a good illustration of the point, being based on the experiences of two lesbian mothers facing attack through the courts on their right to child custody. Other interviews and source material were gathered before Michelene Wandor was asked to script the play, which expanded its focus to deal with notions of family life and sexuality. It remains one of the few plays to explore directly the role of the state in the area of sexual politics.

The two main plays produced by the male section of Gay Sweatshop, *As Time Goes By* (1977) and *The Dear Love of Comrades* (1979), are celebrations and discoveries of a male homosexual history. In this they parallel many feminist plays written in the 1970s that set out to discover women in history. Where they differ is that the dramatic emphasis is not so much on the strength of that historic presence — though *As Time Goes By* emphasizes the existence of men like Magnus Hirschfield, who founded an international homosexual organization in the 19th century — but on the moment of the individual decision to face the consequences of a particular sexuality.

As Time Goes By by Noel Greig culminates in one of the key moments of sexual politics: the Stonewall riots in New York in 1969 when gay men fought back against police harassment. The in-built knowledge of that moment provides the point towards which all the preceding, relatively unconnected and schematic scenes move. There is little need for more dramatic construction.

The Dear Love of Comrades by Noel Greig and Drew Griffiths picks up on one episode in *As Time Goes By* — the life in the 1890s of the British socialist Edward Carpenter. It is a much more complex piece, which looks at Carpenter's efforts to combine both his public life as a campaigning socialist and his private life as a sexually active homosexual. Finally he commits himself to living openly with one man and effectively turns his back on organized socialism.

Both plays offer a lot more than pleas to 'come out of the closet'. They present the legitimate hopes and fears of gay men about society and, more boldly, they are careful to consider the complexities of gay sexuality. Although the final scene of *As Time Goes By* in the Stonewall bar ends on the almost mythic moment when gay men did fight back, it is largely composed of rather lonely monologues.

The dramatic worth of such work is not reduced by recognizing its context nor acknowledging that much of its purpose lies in the very fact of its presentation. Gay women and men on the stage playing gay women and men, not as caricatures but as real historical figures, remain a rare occurrence. One exception is Michael Wilcox's play *Accounts* (1981), in which two brothers struggle to survive on a hill farm in the Scottish borders with their widowed mother. Wilcox's work is representative of a small body of plays that feature homosexuals — usually male — without being directly concerned with gay politics. While Noel Greig continued to place his work in the political arena, in such plays as *Poppies* (1983), produced by Gay Sweatshop, which deals with gayness and the fight for peace, other writers chose to make their statements more obliquely through plays that contained gay characters. This could be fashionable, as in the resurgence of interest in ex-public school spies, or it could be challenging, as in a humorous and tough play like Tom McClenaghan's *Submariners* (1980). Gay Sweatshop had cleared away many obstacles, a fact acknowledged by the American writer Martin Sherman in his play *Bent* (1979) about two gays in a concentration camp. But during the 1980s the impetus has come once again from the USA. This has been most sharply concentrated on the AIDS epidemic, which has forced the 'personal-is-politics' slogan to be scrutinized in completely unexpected ways.

Yet despite the breakthrough achieved by such work in allowing a different dimension of the public-private axis to be presented, it remains locked largely into its own circumscribed area. Plays about homosexuals tend to be just that; there is an absence of work which has both homo- and heterosexuality within the same frame.

Feminist Theatre

The most sustained challenge to the dominant notions of public and private began in the early 1970s when there began to develop a theatre for women by women as distinct from a theatre in which women had a peripheral presence. It followed earlier, isolated, examples of breaks in traditional playmaking by women playwrights such as Shelagh Delaney and Ann Jellicoe, whose shifts in form are related both to their subject matter and to their particular perceptions of that content. Jellicoe's *The Sport of My Mad Mother* (1958) and *The Knack* (1962) prefigure later stylized exposures of male sexual power yet, as with Delaney's work, they had little immediate effect beyond the production of the plays themselves. The wider and specifically female-oriented challenge was still to come. Its contemporary origins were twofold: the striking agitprop of street theatre, and the imaginative multi-media work of the London-based Arts Laboratory. The first used hard and direct physical images to create immediate impact, for example the

flashing lights at nipple and crotch in the counter demonstration
against the Miss World Competition in 1971. The context can be
judged from the arrests of those involved in street theatre at the
Festival of Light demonstrations in the same year. The other source
used music, movement and lighting as much as words to create its
overall effect, as was seen in Jane Arden's extraordinary *Vagina Rex and
the Gas Oven* (1969) and *A New Communion for Freaks, Prophets and
Witches* (1971).

Such work cannot be displaced from its time; to recall the Women's
Street Theatre Group performing to celebrate the International
Women's Day march in 1971 is not to recreate just a moment of
theatre but a point when women, a few of whom were in the theatre,
came together on the streets and celebrated their collective courage.
But it had important consequences for British theatre.

Firstly, it brought together women who were determined to set up
channels through which writers could work outside the heavily restricted patterns of conventional theatre. By creating performing
groups, workshops and performance venues and by steadily influenc-
ing the artistic policy of a number of established theatres such as the
Royal Court, they provided a much-needed point of purchase for
women playwrights. Some of these began their work in this environment; others, such as Pam Gems and Caryl Churchill, had their
artistic horizons radically shifted by the startling impact of the women's
movement. The general atmosphere was of collective work, so that
categories of actor, director, playwright, designer and musician were
blurred and often interchangeable. Such a breaking down of artistic
barriers has had a profound impact on the women involved, precisely
because it emerged out of a wider experience within a movement
centrally concerned to contest pre-given social and professional categories.

Secondly, the content of the work was developed as much around
image as around words. This is not to say that women playwrights in
the following years have not deployed a very wide range of language.
The intricate verbal patterns of Caryl Churchill's *Top Girls* (1982) or
Michelene Wandor's skilful adaptation of Elizabeth Barrett Browning's *Aurora Leigh* (1979) are obvious examples. But there has been a
consistent concern with images which has been specific to women's
writing and set it apart from most contemporary male playwriting. The
general approach has derived mainly from a historical point of departure: that of exploring the social construction of women within a
male-dominated society, and of either presenting alternatives to the
stereotypes or using those stereotypes in a subversive way.

In Bryony Lavery's *For Maggie, Betty and Ida* (1982), for example, the
main technique is to bring together stories and songs about women,
both past and present, that build up cumulatively. Similarly, Claire

Luckham's *Trafford Tanzi* (1980), charts the development of a woman through childhood, school, marriage and eventual liberation depicted as a series of wrestling bouts.

Throughout the broad range of images and techniques used by women playwrights, personal experience dominates; its roots lie in isolation, but what is of interest is that which is held in common, hence the importance of a gender identity and of group situations, of linking women's experiences and emphasizing sisterhood. There is the need to recount again and again the everyday experiences of women that are often dismissed as insignificant, and to reinforce the reality of women's lives through resort to history. The attempt to embrace both feminism and Socialism has been the most direct confrontation of the private and the political, and has emanated mainly from touring groups such as Red Ladder or The Women's Theatre Group. Not surprisingly it has been no easy task. The two slogans presented on separate banners at the end of Red Ladder's *Strike While the Iron is Hot* (1974) represent a political and a theatrical problem. One read: 'Women will never be free while workers are in chains' and the other: 'Workers will never be free while women are in chains.'

Another difficulty stems from an even more basic element: women's interaction with men. Increasingly this has come to be referred to rather than portrayed; it is as hard to find plays by women that can deal adequately with male characters as it is to find adequate female characters in plays by male dramatists. One of the few plays which attempts this from the female viewpoint is *Kiss and Kill* (1977), scripted out of collective work by Susan Todd and Ann Mitchell for the feminist group Monstrous Regiment. The core of the interaction that they define is violence. Two men are portrayed on stage; one more is heard on the telephone; another exists by reference. In relation to these four men there are four women who, by and large, protect or console each other against the almost uniformly antagonistic nature of the male/female relationship. The impact of these antagonisms is undermined by the unevenness of composition and the fact that the only man portrayed with any great sympathy, an American Vietnam veteran, is much the weakest character.

Kiss and Kill is a disturbing play in that it seems to suggest, unwillingly but clearly, that there is no way that men and women can co-exist without some form of male domination. At the end the women get together for their own purposes and the two men go on holiday together. In between the scenes with adults there are inserted scenes with a gang of girls whose leisure life consists of running wild around the streets and gardens, pouring contempt on their parents. The implication of this is never resolved. Does the breakdown of the relationships amongst the adults imply the breakdown of child-rearing? Or are these wild children the ones who will find the solution?

Pam Gems

The two main playwrights to have emerged from women's theatre, Caryl Churchill and Pam Gems, both put children and child-bearing at the centre of their work. (In private plays by male dramatists the focus is usually sex.) Although in a properly developed society women would rear children equally with men as well as retaining independent, working lives outside the home, Churchill suggests that women as yet have little real choice except to opt for children, with all the associated problems, or to deny totally a vital part of their femaleness and humanity. Pam Gems comes to much the same conclusion. Unlike other women playwrights who emerged with the rise of the women's movement and the mushrooming of small venues, Gems was a young adult during the War and had brought up four children in the postwar years. She turned from radio and television writing in the 1950s and 1960s to her first stage production in 1972, since when she has had her work presented across the theatrical map, from the smallest touring venue to the main stages of the big two national theatres, with one show, *Piaf* (1978), going into the West End and on to Broadway.

Although she was involved in the development of feminist theatre, particularly the 1973 Women's Season at the Almost-Free and the two subsequent productions by the Women's Theatre Company, Gems has distanced herself from feminism, which she sees as polemic, preferring instead drama's role of subversion. Nevertheless, her preoccupation with the autonomy of women is one shared by the women's movement, the main difference of emphasis being the importance of motherhood. Her basic concern is the way women survive and assert their own identity in the face of male and class pressures, but it is in no sense a Utopian vision. She deals explicitly with two political revolutionaries in her adaptation of Marianne Auricoste's *My Name is Rosa Luxemburg* (1976) and in *Pasionaria* (1985), and travels the social scale in her four most important plays, *Piaf, Dusa, Stas, Fish and Vi* (1976, formerly *Dead Fish*), *Queen Christina* (1977) and *Camille* (1984).

Dusa, Stas, Fish and Vi picks up from *My Name is Rosa Luxemburg* and *The Project* (1976), later reworked as *Living Women* (1984), the problem of a middle-class woman who embraces socialism with a passion that excludes all else. Fish, who owns the flat that she shares with the other three women, has been left by her lover. Dusa's husband has run off with the children, and Vi, who changes fashion like everyone else changes clothes, suggests she should steal the money for lawyers from Stas, a psychotherapist earning money by prostitution to enable her to study marine biology. Following a debate about Dusa's children and the scruples of survival, Fish, the socialist, speaks directly to the audience:

So why is Rosa Luxemburg relevant? ...she believed that the mistakes made by people doing things for themselves were more valuable than any theory coming from an elitist committee... Rosa constantly demonstrates that the emergence of women thinkers in politics modifies Marxist theory as we know it... To be outside may be oppression. To be inside may be total irrelevancy. It's not just a matter of equal pay...equal opportunity. For the first time in history we have the opportunity to investigate ourselves... Rosa never married Leo. She never had the child she longed for... She writes to him from Zurich about seeing a fine child in a park, and wanting to scoop him up in her arms and run off with him, back to her room. Usually when people write about her nowadays they leave all that out. They are wrong.

But it is Fish, the only political person in the play, who is the one character who cannot survive. She chooses death because she is faced (like Rosa) with the impossibility of love. Rosa, however, died for the cause whereas Fish's death achieves nothing. It is a harsh condemnation of politics. The implication is that a struggle for self releases the self but a struggle for others leaves the self dried up.

In *Piaf* this tension is removed as the play demonstrates the indestructibility of a gut class reaction. Expressly undercutting the mythology of working-class waif turned glamorous international showbiz star (even to the point of having Piaf urinate on stage) Gems relishes the connection between sexual freedom, fame and autonomy based on streetwise resilience. When Piaf moves into the Ritz despite not getting any bookings, she taunts her manager:

> You think we all want to get ahead. Like you. Pile it up for tomorrow. When's tomorrow? Nah, I was born lucky. Never had it. Don't want it, never had the bother. OK, a bit draughty, but I know all I need to know... You think being born working class is like having a disease.

But the anti-romantic picture is in its own way a form of romance. Piaf suffers terribly, and the price she pays is drug addiction and the lonely pursuit of sexual passion through performance.

Queen Christina spans the 17th-century life of a real historical figure who was brought up as a man to succeed to the Swedish throne but then was expected to act as a woman and give birth in order to preserve the succession. She abdicates and searches for another way of life, only to find that her male lover with whom she has settled is also using her. At the point of wanting to kill him, she realizes that she cannot because she has discovered herself at last. By choosing this frame Gems is able to ask basic questions about the construction and make-up of sex roles and their position in the class and sex hierarchies of power. There is a clear statement that while gender may be the guide, the rest is learned; by implication this means that it can be learned differently. At the opening, the King blames the loss of another son on the Queen. 'What is it with women? Weak!' But then he points to the only surviving child, Christina.

KING: She's fit enough. Intelligent.
AXEL: But the wrong sex. With a weak succession it'll be anybody's game, we can't have a woman.
KING: Make a man of her then.
AXEL: How?
KING: Training.

Christina's Renaissance journey through fighting, hunting, politics and bi-sexual encounter to abdication and heterosexual living gives her a unique access to the choices available. In answer, Gems moves towards defining a femaleness that is strong and open but pacifist and home-centred — a controversial vision that provides little leverage on contemporary opportunities available to women. Christina pieces together a new identity:

I have *been* as a man. I have commanded. I have signed death warrants, consigned regiments to the sword... Must it always be the sword? By God, half the world are women... they've learned subversion, to keep their teeth in their mouths and the rope off their backs, why not try that? ...who are the poorest of all? Women, children...the old. Are they fighters, the creators of war? You say you want me for the fight, and it's true I was bred as a man, despising the weakness of women. I begin to question the favour. To be invited to join the killing, why, where's the advantage? Half the world rapes and destroys — must the women, the other half, join in?

In contrast, she discovers the pleasure of ordinary women:

...the smell of ironed clothes. ...lace — Food ...baking... And babies. The smell of babies. I like the smell of babies — can that be wrong?

Gems defiantly thrusts to the fore the central, complex problem of women's automony, their relation to children. Christina, now unable to give birth, continues:

Women submit, not from weakness, but for love. I have been betrayed. This... (*slaps her abdomen*)... I have been denied my birthright. I have been denied the very centre of myself.

Gems' conclusion on the advances made by women is hard-headed and designed to puncture any illusions. Despite the potential for controlling biology, the power to do so is still very much in male hands. Her strategy is oblique. She admires those like Fish who do make a fight but cannot see that as any way forward. Fish, for example, is robbed of any sexual politics. In the end, instead of trying to find a way in which socialist politics can meet the feminist, Gems prefers the battle for the individual through the woman taking control of what defines her.

Another generation of women playwrights has begun to emerge who, unlike Gems and Churchill, have not had their lives shifted by the sudden jumps of the late 1960s and early 1970s. The women's movement was part of their adult horizon and they have reacted to it quite differently. Louise Page, for example, combines quite effortlessly both social history and personal experience in one complex thread in *Salonika* (1982), a mesmeric and disturbing piece in which a woman travels with her daughter to the beach of Salonika where her husband died in the First World War. There they confront two young men — the ghost of the dead soldier and a living beach-bum — as well as a male admirer of the mother who has travelled from England to find her.

Page does not write about the obvious theme — the horror of war and the loss felt by those left alive. She takes this for granted and instead pushes much further into the unravelling of age and youth and the offering up of human lives not to war but to the construction of social roles. Young men die, pointlessly, and in their absence women live patched and makeshift lives.

Page does not draw back from the needs of women for physical sex, and by transferring attention away from the young to the old, she manages to move beyond the bleakness of vision which has visited some of her immediate precursors. The same is true of Andrea Dunbar's *Rita, Sue and Bob Too* (1982), which achieves, in its opening scene, that rare moment, a really funny and physically explicit sexual encounter. Dunbar and her contemporaries, such as Sarah Daniels, look at a generation living in an economic wasteland, accustomed to harshness and the breakdown of relationships, accepting that men are normally unreliable and yet still managing to find enough energy and humour to get on with the business of living.

It is too early to assess the new mood but one of the most hopeful features of the work of many women playwrights is its boldness. In the wake of the women's movement, which has rewritten the political agenda, the theatrical agenda has been altered too, for both men and women, with the effect that the conventional notions of public and private have been seriously challenged and redefined.

CHAPTER SIX

John Osborne: The Curate's Ego

John Osborne occupies an ambiguous place in postwar British theatre. Unwittingly he has passed into its mythology as a founding father, thanks to an unprepossessing play that is, nevertheless, an irremovable reference point in the renewal of British drama. In the twenty years following *Look Back in Anger* (1956), he wrote twenty stage plays (fifteen original and five adaptations), seven television plays and one film, yet critically he has fallen further and further out of favour. Without ever making a clear break, Osborne has gradually drifted out of the theatre, growling at the critics and attacking what he sees as a takeover by pinkos and trendies. One of the reasons for his irritation is that it was Jimmy Porter who kept the English Stage Company alive financially and thereby allowed it to play its crucial role in stimulating new writing and laying important ground for the emergence of the very alternative theatre that challenged what Osborne stood for and which became one of his pet hates.

Before this alternative arrived one did not talk about contemporary theatre without mentioning Osborne. But, just as he was said in 1956 to have kicked Rattigan off the stage, he too was superseded by the arrival of the new generation. Even the revival in 1978 at the Royal Court of one of his strongest and most representative plays, *Inadmissible Evidence* (1964), with Nicol Williamson re-creating the lead role, did not generate any new interest in Osborne or stimulate a re-assessment. A similar fate befell the revival of *A Patriot for Me* (1965), in 1983.

Any assessment of Osborne's work is difficult because, to his credit, it does seem to defy labels; the range of subjects and variety of treatments look like products of inexhaustible creativity and unceasing experiment. The most often quoted reason for the difficulty lies in his own manifesto: 'I want to make people feel, to give them lessons in feeling. They can think afterwards.' (in *Declaration*, MacGibbon & Kee, 1957). Osborne has always rejected the idea that he was any kind of intellectual or that he had a position to argue. Yet, despite his protestations, a clear philosophy does emerge, which can be summed up by a quote from Jean in *The Entertainer* (1957): 'We've only got ourselves.'

In 1957 Osborne was talking of the theatre as a 'weapon'. Its use? 'There is room for many kinds of theatre, but the one that matters the most is the one that offers a vital, emotional dynamic to ordinary people, that breaks down class barriers, and all the many obstacles set in the way of feeling.' By 1961 the transcendence of feeling over social factors had taken root in absolute individualism: 'It's possible to write for yourself and to write for a few people at the same time. It's also possible to write for yourself and write for everybody. But it's not my job *as a dramatist* to worry about reaching a mass audience if there is one... Ultimately, after all, the only satisfaction you can get out of doing all this is the satisfaction you give yourself.' (*The Twentieth Century*, Vol. 169, 1961.) Osborne, like Harold Pinter, set his face explicitly against the current of popular theatre and tied himself to the safest of artistic positions — absolute self-expression.

Even allowing for *Epitaph for George Dillon* (1958, with Anthony Creighton) and *The Entertainer*, Osborne's early declared intention to ask about the lives of ordinary people was never achieved. His basic concern as a dramatist — to please himself — was identical to the basic concern of his drama: the investigation of self. (By his own acknowledgement there is a lot of autobiographical material in his plays.)

Osborne's approach is romantic and subjective, and his work is marked by the existential philosophy current in the 1950s. It is also atheistic and materialist, especially when linked to contemporary reference or resonance: for example, his treatment of history in *Luther* (1961) or *A Patriot for Me*. This explains why many commentators have talked of Osborne's commitment. However, his committed political work is represented not by his major work but by a satirical, journalistic group of plays — *The World of Paul Slickey* (1959), *Plays for England* (1962) and even *A Sense of Detachment* (1972) — which, by their artistic failure, underscore the lack of wider commitment and the individualistic stress of the main plays. The revue style of this work falls down because it is too personal and not objective or analytical enough. In general, the social and political underpinnings of his plays are external and incidental, although often precise and functional (as in *The Entertainer* when, for example, the son is killed in Cyprus). Even in *Luther*, described by some critics as his most Brechtian play, Osborne constructs the action around psychology and not around the clash of class or power interests and their relationship to ideas, however much these may impinge. *A Patriot for Me* offers the most fruitful attempt to explore self and society, but, ironically, because the central figure, Redl, is underwritten compared to other Osborne heroes, it loses in vigour what it gains in breadth.

Osborne's plays from 1956 to 1976 fall into two periods. The first, during which theatre censorship was still in force, is dominated by rhetoric — wild, bold and energetic, running up and down the emotional scale. These are the plays of the 'actor-heroes': Porter, Dillon,

Rice, Luther, Maitland. The second period (in which *A Sense of Detachment* is the exception in style) is one of reflection, with more obviously conventional settings within the 'well-made play' tradition and attempts at more equal characterization, though with the dramatic stress falling still on one individual: Pamela in *Time Present* (1968), Laurie in *The Hotel in Amsterdam* (1968), Gillman in *West of Suez* (1971). By this time Osborne has become more concerned with the role of the artist; and with his last stage play to date, *Watch it Come Down* (1976), the cultured few, who are as much yahoos as those destroying their country retreat, are presented as the carriers of a civilization worth saving: chilling even if ironic.

The distinguishing feature of the first group of plays is the energy of the language, and of the second, its enervation. It is not so much a shift from rebel to reactionary as a change in the tone of voice, for there was never any great depth to his early rebelliousness. Osborne's *bêtes noires* are present throughout: the young (there is nothing likeable about the young in *Look Back in Anger*), egalitarian democracy, journalists (especially critics), royalty-watchers, God-worshippers, upper classes, middle classes, working classes (only the 'gifted' get off lightly), foreigners (i.e. non-English), demonstrators and, particularly, women (with the necessary corollary of gays). They are all parasites, that is, not true to themselves, or if they are, then with rotten selves to be true to. Their pursuit of self is not allowed, and is usually seen as an obstacle to the full realization of the Osborne hero. The rest of the world forms a conspiracy against this hero, whether it be in the shape of party ideology, sexual involvement or the welfare state. They are different traps designed for the same end: it is always someone else's fault — Alison's not Jimmy's in *Look Back in Anger;* a betrayed Britain not Archie's in *The Entertainer.*

Osborne's pursuit of self, which is expressed mainly in the themes of sex and art (for him the key arenas of emotional and verbal self-realization) is primarily linguistic, and it is this that makes him an important figure. It is the language of his towering characters that earns him a place in theatre history and establishes him as part of a continuity in that history. It is an odd irony that it is Osborne, with his particular use of language, who is the bridge between the two postwar continents of the pre-1956 and post-1968 theatres.

For Osborne the writer, language is paramount. This is shown overtly in the plays that deal with artists: 'Words are important... when millions of people seem unable to communicate with one another it is vitally important that words are made to work. It may be old-fashioned, but *they're the only thing.*' (our stress). So says the writer, Gillman, in *West of Suez*. It is language that defines Osborne's central preoccupation with and exploration of sex, which, as a constant topic, is referred to verbally but not expressed physically. Language for Osborne defines class and, more importantly for him, a sense of nation. In *The Enter-tainer*, a play that openly uses the music hall as a metaphor for the nation, Billy, the admired relic of a past age, looks back: 'We all had our own style — and we were all English. What's more we spoke English... We all knew what the rules were, and even if we spent half our time making people laugh at 'em we never seriously suggested that anyone should break them.' It is a pity that Osborne does not bring to bear in any of his plays such an acute awareness of the political role of language.

His main creations — the 'actor-heroes' — are shaped by their language, even at the basic level of holding the stage verbally and saying more than anyone else. Osborne himself was an actor and joined the English Stage Company in 1956 as such. It is not difficult to fit Porter, Maitland, Luther and Rice into this tradition, especially when these and other roles have been created by leading actors such as Olivier, Richardson, Scofield, Finney, Williamson and Bennett. It was not in the *New Statesman* or the *Times Literary Supplement* that George Devine and Tony Richardson put their famous 'new plays wanted' ad, but in *The Stage*, the actors' trade-journal. Not surprising, therefore, that they came up with an actor as their first new writer, and one whose characters themselves are actors — individuals on display. Osborne inflates and gives his main roles an emotionally overcharged, spon-taneous high profile, played up-front through maximum use of lan-guage and minimum of sub-text; they are stars, playing the star's part, which is their lives. Osborne's bargain-basement reading of existen-tialism is that one must come to centre-front stage and stay there, fighting off all competition for the limelight.

Despite the fractured, anguished and contradictory self that is al-ways revealed, the heroes are the plays' driving force, with language as their unifying factor. This produces, at best, a fierce intensity and a direct, untrammelled relationship between audience and main actor. Osborne writes in an anti-theoretical English tradition based on a 'university-of-life' pragmatism. In his autobiography* he never touches on why he wanted to write except that childhood unhappiness seems to have led to an exploitation of his one talent — verbosity. Out of the conflicts of his neurosis — wanting to be a playwright but frightened of not being good — came a non-naturalistic style of bold and liberating gesture. This verbal torrent, overtaking the dynamics of plot or character, makes him a true precursor of the 'literary' alterna-tive playwrights, the Barkers and the Brentons, whose sheer intensity of language may also on occasion carry more weight than their analyses.

---

* John Osborne: *A Better Class of Person — An Autobiography, 1929-1956* (Faber & Faber, 1981).

Osborne admits to being more interested in excitement than in construction and it shows in most of his work. Yet he seems oddly irked by the problems of craft, particularly in *A Sense of Detachment*. At various points he seems to want to demonstrate that he too can write a 'proper' play with all the conventional requirements of character development and plot. But, appropriately for a writer who obsessively explores self, the form of his plays is almost invariably cyclical; life goes on, reality goes round. Osborne strips away or evades until an external event breaks through to end the pattern or to start it up again at a different level. The interruptions are arbitrary, as if he felt he ought to end an act on an up-note or finish a play with a bang. *The Hotel in Amsterdam* ends with a classic *deus ex machina* which could have appeared almost anywhere in the closing stages. *West of Suez* and *Watch it Come Down* end with quite unbelievable interventions of the hostile outside world. It is as though Osborne, aware that plays have to end, can only break into the relentless cycle with an external event, the realism of which is neither interesting nor relevant. *A Patriot for Me*, like *Luther*, tells a story but without real development; the treadmill of external reality trundles on, reinforcing the retreat into the refuge of the self.

This ambiguous relationship to self is most clearly seen in Osborne's treatment of sex, even though he is one of the few male writers to put it at the centre of his work. Whereas Terence Rattigan (with whom he shares a common concern for passionate emotion) writes about the problems of the lid coming off, Osborne unscrews the hatches and blasts forth with undertones of a real personal fear. Sex is presented as what you are: an imperative, an urge, which you try to control but cannot. You have to go on doing it to confirm your existence (as a man) and that means a battle to preserve your self. As with the Osborne 'actor-heroes', it is a performance; underneath is the fear of failing to perform adequately. In *Inadmissible Evidence*, for example, Maitland, returning home after sleeping with his lover, agonizes in case his wife will also ask him to perform. Women are traps, ready to ensnare and then devour you. When Osborne writes about a woman, as in *Time Present*, he presents her as if she felt exactly the same as a man.

Alongside the constant anti-women references and hatred of children, Osborne also pours out vitriol toward gays. Yet this relationship is more complex than it seems. Jimmy Porter says:

> Sometimes I almost envy old Gide and the Greek chorus boys. Oh, I'm not saying that it mustn't be hell for them a lot of the time. But, at least, they do seem to have a cause — not a particularly good one it's true. But plenty of them do seem to have a revolutionary fire about them, which is more than you can say for the rest of us.

Gay men are not lumbered with women so they have the possibility of control. Redl, the gay hero of *A Patriot for Me*, explores this and emerges as the only Osborne character to express his sex freely; he understands his relationship to external reality and learns the limits of his control. But it necessarily ends in death, because he has broken the rules. This play, despite the furore which greeted its first performance, is not about homosexuality: it is about the limits of self-expression. Osborne's exploration of sex is aggressive and painful, desperate and fearful, trying to get to the heart of the matter but increasingly convinced that the centre will not hold. This never-to-be-fulfilled search is accompanied by a longing, and later a nostalgia, for a time when the self could be in harmony. The past is conjured up in a childlike manner, unreal except to the individual; it is experienced as a loss and ultimately as a betrayal.

Fear pervades all the plays. The anguished outbursts of the early works become the bitter or melancholic pain of the later ones, but at the centre of all of them is fear. The early dynamism of Osborne was fed largely by frustration — eight years as a repertory actor (after a brief spell as a trade journalist) with no recognition for his talent. There was little in his early experience to give any assured guarantee of success. The fear in his early plays is essentially concerned with a belief that one will ultimately be found out and exposed as some kind of fraud.

Despite the self-centred feel of his plays, the nature and dominance of the fears, the male-orientation, the refuge in subjectivity, they are also statements about Osborne's own time; these are his chosen subjects and his chosen treatments. The success of his strategy can be measured by the fact that many critics call him compassionate and mistake his directness for truth, and see his outspokenness and willingness to parade prejudice as honesty. This is comfortable for those in the audience who can find cathartic release in the experience of having someone else to take the sting out of attitudes they wish they did not hold. There are no countervailing forces in Osborne's plays to suggest a different way of thinking or acting; they tend to operate on one plane within a narrow set of social relationships and concern an equally narrow range of attitudes (even if supposedly widely held). Within their frame, the plays are truthful and honest. But in the partial and selective choice of that frame, virtues are not attributed to those whom Osborne does not favour, and positive change is never countenanced.

The most successful example of this strategy is in *Inadmissible Evidence*, which raises to new artistic heights the projection of an unpleasant and uncomfortable individual as a modern hero. The play opens with a characteristic Osborne stage direction that is addressed as much to a reader as to a director or actor. It reads: 'The location where a dream takes place.' Yet the whole point of the play is how *real* Maitland is, although he cannot always recognize the reality. (A further stage direction talks of slipping in and out of unreality.) Osborne says, 'The structure of this particular dream is the bones and dead objects of a solicitor's office', and he pays close attention in the most realistic fashion to the paraphernalia of office life and to its daily routine. The bedrock of the play's dramatic tension is Maitland's psyche as it erupts, clashes and fractures against his office, the other people working there, and the predatory outside visitors (whom Osborne specifies are to be played as ciphers). Office objects become important, especially the telephone, which is Maitland's lifeline but also the line that cuts him off from the world.

The opening of *Inadmissible Evidence* is archetypal: the office that imprisons Maitland is also a courtroom. There is a bench with a judge, a Royal Coat of Arms which gives an initial generalized application to the play as if to say, this is typical of today's England, and a dock with Maitland in it, on trial for unspecified lewdness and debauchery. It is a familiar Kafkaesque image. This dream setting is made convincing by the detail and specificity of language in contrast to the ambiguous crime. Picking up from Osborne's television play *A Subject for Scandal and Concern* (1960), which deals with the last man to be convicted for allegedly taking the name of God in vain and who conducts his own defence, Maitland decides to defend himself and is immediately confronted by the judge changing the rules.

Maitland is not presented as special or abnormal, and neither is he an artist or privileged communicator like Rice, Luther or Gillman. He is middle-class but not seen as enjoying anything more than the just fruits of life in the prosperous England of the 1960s. The opening moments in the court define Maitland the man and also his habitual nightmare — that of being caught out for minor professional malpractice. From there it changes to the theatrical representation of the nightmare coming true; alone in the office, Maitland becomes an object like the other office objects, deserted by colleagues, friends and family alike, living through the recognition and reality of total isolation. He tells the court in a jumbled, self-ironic manner that he is a drinker with hypochondriac tendencies who nevertheless has become boss of his own firm:

> No, but I never seriously thought of myself being brilliant enough to sit in that company, with those men, among any of them with their fresh complexions from their playing fields and all that, with their ringing effortless voice production and their quiet chambers, and tailors and mess bills and Oxford Colleges and going to the opera God knows where and the 400, whatever I used to think that was... I have always been tolerably bright... But, to start with, and potentially and finally, that is to say, irredeemably mediocre.

The attempt to use formal legal language is subtly parodied throughout to show how one gets trapped in the business of conforming to the rules and habits of others at the expense of one's own self-expression. Osborne picks this up more ferociously in Act Two when Maitland confronts the series of clients whose real life stories are submerged beneath their legalese. Maitland even swears an oath (affirmed, of course, being a modern man) which is a public gesture toward a ruling notion in which privately he has little faith; in his case it is to a technological society of:

> ...automation and the ever increasing need, need, oh need for, the
> stable ties of modern family life, rethinking, reliving, making way for
> the motor car, forty million by nineteen...

The stuff of conventional life is antipathetic to Maitland, who gathers steam in the office as the sexually offensive boss with a mouth instead of a brain. He calls the new clerk, Jones, who is the prosecuting counsel in the trial scene, a 'Tent peg. Made in England. To be knocked into the ground... He's got all the makings of a good, happy democratic underdog.' He rants against 'vote wheedling catchfart' politicians, 'colour supplement culture', 'slabs of concrete technological nougat', and the 'people who go up every year like it was holy communion to have a look at the Christmas decorations in Regent Street.' He harasses his secretaries and when possible screws them, preferably on the office floor. Osborne makes him unpleasant on purpose, both because he does not want to have easy sympathy — there would be no point — and because he feels that in our society the spirited ones are often those who, like himself, do not share conforming attitudes.

Osborne undercuts any hints at special pleading through irony or contradiction, yet he builds the whole play as a case for it. Maitland's sense of self is highly conscious, paradoxically for one who loses self. The severity of the structure and the uncompromising single focus can only work if the audience is still interested in Maitland at the end. This is a big gamble and an enormous achievement: to sustain, with no other plot, a single, distasteful personality in decline. One by one the other characters abandon Maitland — the chief clerk Hudson, his secretaries, his daughter (who never speaks) and his lover — and with each departure he becomes less himself, until he is the one finally to say goodbye to his wife and remain alone, the alienation complete. Maitland attacks as he is deserted and destroyed and, because we see the play entirely through his eyes, the reduction of the others to ciphers (and in his daughter's case, to silence) makes dramatic sense. As ciphers they tell us more about Maitland than about themselves; the most emphatic dramatic expression of this is when the actor who plays the new clerk, Jones, reappears as the client Maples, whose trouble with the law concerns his homosexuality. Central to Maitland's loss of reality is his loss of sexuality. His isolation is seen as a female conspiracy; Hudson's departure, a blow to his business pride, is less hurtful than that of the secretaries, his daughter and his lover. The distance between himself and the world has narrowed to vanishing point. It is this single-mindedness, carried through by the language which takes over plot, that allows for the success of the play. It is the language that carries the nuances, the ducking in and out of different realities, the complexities on the road to the final silence. The language is always explicit, communicating directly to the audience across the proscenium arch.

But why is it that such articulacy, such a self-aware pattern of perceptions, cannot prevent that final isolation? In the trial Maitland says: 'I have always expected this, and consequently, I have done my best to prepare myself as well as I can.' Yet, despite this level of self-consciousness, his preparations are inadequate. He cannot hold on to his friends or family and he can no longer overcome alienation through sex, let alone through words. In fact, the more he speaks, the more inevitable seems his doom. At one point he says, [it was] 'as if I only existed because of her [his wife], because she allowed me to, but if she turned off the switch... turned off the switch... who knows? But if she turned it off I'd have been dead'. Whether or not he is actually speaking to her on the phone at the end of the play, he does turn off the switch, as if in final recognition that the preparations are complete. Just before that, when only Liz, his lover, remains, he says that she 'may be the last to pack it in, but pack it in she will'. He complains of being ignored yet says to Liz: 'I'm tired of being watched by you, and observed and scrutinized and assessed and guessed about' — which is precisely how he himself treats other people. He even reminisces: 'There was a time...' This is a common feature in Osborne — nostalgia for a time *when*: when life was ordered properly, when national values were intact, when people were whole. In front of his cool, distressed daughter, Maitland's nostalgia becomes: 'I always used to think that when you're the age you are now I'd...' — the change of tense seemingly requiring just an effort of will but clearly now impossible. He can no longer choose the next step.

By now Maitland has moved from consciousness of the problem without analysis ('I don't have any idea where I am... I ought to be able to give a better account of myself. But I don't seem to be functioning properly.') to statements of belief in the face of the final collapse that are articulate and lucid (to Liz: 'There *are* other qualities besides courage... Cowardice, for instance.') But then, in the moment of realization, he actually does choose, but negatively, accepting the departure of Liz. He has the chance to rescue the relationship but does not.

LIZ: I was thinking... perhaps you'd rather I didn't come away for the weekend. [*Silence. He faces her.*] I just thought you seemed... as if... you might... want to be alone.
    [*Pause.*]
BILL: I was only waiting, from the moment you came in, for you to say that.

The male ego wants the independence to choose to be alone on its own terms but not actually to be lonely.

Two days in the life of Bill Maitland come to stand for a whole lifetime of accumulating awareness of disintegration and of that disintegration itself. The inadmissible evidence — the complexity of Maitland in all his relationships, thoughts and emotions, from the trivial to the profound — has been displayed, but it is no defence. Or is it? Osborne obviously implies that it should be, and that the power of the figure he has presented is such that an audience will have sympathy for him, will perhaps even identify with the trapped animal. But unlike the characters of a play by Tennessee Williams (a writer towards whom Osborne feels an affinity) Maitland is a victim with clear choices. Osborne pulls off a dramatic sleight of hand by investing Maitland with modern tragic status when he does not warrant it (a temptation that Terence Rattigan resists in *Separate Tables*). Sheer verbal power, the associative and dissociated speeches, the stabbing bursts, the flowing passages, the half-assimilated jargon, the dramatic sustaining of a stream of consciousness, all this projected in the directness and the nakedness of the first person, convinces us that in seeing all the evidence one cannot condemn. Osborne's romantic liberal belief is robustly argued through, but it cannot hide the hollowness inside. It is, in a grand historical sense, the crisis of male supremacy. The irony is that the very power of the description of the alienation suggests the possibility still of overcoming it.

Inadmissible Evidence is an extraordinary exercise in defending that which it appears to destroy; the male ego, in laying waste to all around it, can still survive dependent on nothing but its own resources. Maitland is its ideal hero — the man above, the man rejected, the man surviving without social props, the man resurgent even in defeat. Despite the apparent collapse of his own life, Maitland comes across as the supreme life-force that is inevitably destructive precisely because that is what complete maleness is all about. Osborne goes way beyond any simple male chauvinism. What he defends is both the necessity and the dominance of the male because in his view men alone have the true sense of the individual. The winning of this trick, at least within the theatre, is Osborne's supreme dramatic achievement. There is a part of the social construction of all men which corresponds to Maitland, and Osborne draws on it relentlessly.

In 1967 Osborne said: 'A theatre audience is no longer linked by anything but the climate of disassociation in which it tries to live out its baffled lives. A dramatist can no longer expect to draw many common references, be they social, sexual or emotional. He can't generalize in the old way. He must be specific to himself and his own particular, concrete experience.' (*The Times Saturday Review;* October 14, 1967.) In fact, he does generalize from his experience, as a man, and asserts that experience to be superior. Maitland has loved, even to his limits, though describing his own 'little worm of energy' as 'fibbing, mumping, pinched'. But it is superior, we are told, to what his daughter's generation stands for — 'all that youth everyone's so mad about and admires'. (Osborne must be aware of the irony, given his own initial enrolment as an Angry Young Man.) 'But there isn't much loving in any of your kindnesses... not much kindness, not even cruelty, really in any of you, not much craving for the harm of others.'

Whatever the causes for Osborne's settling down to a comfortable life of fame and alimony, the plays after the mid-1960s contain nothing to compare with Maitland's compelling and uncompromising self-enquiry. Osborne remains a major dramatist and yet he is another playwright who seems to have abandoned (or to have been abandoned by) the stage. Noël Coward, maintains Osborne, evolved a smooth style for evasion. He himself evolved a rough style for it. But it is difficult to avoid the conclusion that, despite the ferocious stance, Osborne's departure from the theatre is derived from an inability to cope with its acutely personal demands. Unlike other playwrights who have rebelled against the system — John Arden, Arnold Wesker, John McGrath, for instance — Osborne has made few practical efforts towards change. He clearly wanted to be a star, revelled in the attention given to him when, surprisingly, he became one, and tried to live up to all that is demanded of stars. Yet there is a feeling that he was never convinced that he had *really* succeeded, unlike, say, Arden, who passed the exam and then proceeded to pull down the whole school. Osborne seems continually impelled to resit his own internal tests.

The most haunting moment of *The Entertainer* is Archie Rice's repeated refrain, 'Why should I care? Why should I let it touch me?' In Osborne's bleak existential philosophy this is the riddle that is central to much of his work but remains unresolved. Perhaps, in the end, he has simply grown tired of asking.

CHAPTER SEVEN

Arnold Wesker: The Trilogy and the Spirit of Socialism

Arnold Wesker can be placed alongside John Osborne, John Arden and Harold Pinter as one of the major influences in postwar British theatre in changing the standing of the playwright. He has also helped to change the meaning of theatre, both in his writing and, as with Arden, in his work as an activist. Not only did he bring on to the stage characters from a different class with a different set of concerns from the traditional theatrical preoccupations of his time, he also attempted to broaden the popular appeal of theatre through the organized Labour movement.

In recent years, however, Wesker has fallen from fashion in Britain. Ever since his protracted and public dispute over the RSC's rejection of *The Journalists* in 1972 he has lost the place in the British theatre that he had more than earned with *The Kitchen* (1959), *The Trilogy** (1958-60) and *Chips with Everything* (1962). He remains a prolific playwright and he has also written critical essays, poems, short stories and a book for children. In countries as diverse as Sweden, Cuba and Israel he is one of the best-known British dramatists. The reasons for this divergence between Wesker's domestic and international reputation cannot be fully explained here but it is perhaps linked to a certain kind of solidity and moral worth in his plays that fits in much better with the status and values of theatre abroad, particularly in northern Europe and socialist countries, with their more formal moral systems.

Paradoxically, the failure of the Labour movement project, Centre 42, in the mid-1960s coincided with the flowering of many aspects of the Wesker vision, though outside what he considered the main channel for reaching the new, working-class audience — the trades unions. The growth of a network of arts centres and locally-based companies

---

* We use this common term for the three plays, originally presented at the Belgrade Theatre, Coventry: *Chicken Soup with Barley* (1958), *Roots* (1959) and *I'm Talking about Jerusalem* (1960); all three plays are separate pieces but they share characters and themes.

was soon in full flood, though Wesker's views on art and irreducible
cultural standards put him in opposition to many of the new practitioners, thus intensifying his isolation.

While it is impossible to consider Wesker's plays entirely divorced
from such concerns, it is also dangerous to relate any of them too
directly. Wesker's interests as an activist and playwright are clearly
linked though distinct: the influence of his experiences in socialist and
trades union politics on *Their Very Own and Golden City* (1964) or *Love
Letters on Blue Paper* (1977), for example, is obvious. But more curious
is the continuity of feeling that two such plays express, given the years
that lie between them. Wesker has chiselled away at his central preoccupations but the trajectory has taken him deeper into his own world
without this necessarily illuminating anyone else's quite as much. Both
plays seem much more distant than, for example, Osborne's *Inadmissible Evidence*, which was written the same year as *Their Very Own and
Golden City*, or Bond's *Saved*, which came the following year; and,
while thematically close, *Their Very Own and Golden City* inhabits a
different moral planet from a play like Brenton and Hare's *Brassneck*
(1973). It seems as if an iron curtain of critical astringency dropped in
the early 1970s and Wesker chose not to cross to the other side,
perhaps because his own pursuit of ideals against the constant batter-
ing of unyielding reality led him to fight the good fight increasingly
alone. Fittingly, his own history as an activist and playwright is fore-
shadowed in the movement of his *Trilogy*, which also reflects the wider
problems of the British Left in coming to terms not only with a project
like Centre 42 but also with finding a model of socialism appropriate to
Britain.

In the *Trilogy* Wesker charts the fate of the socialist ideal from the
anti-fascist fervour of 1936 to the Tory Britain of 1959. He shows
individuals trying to combine their desire for change with the reality of
living in a hostile and harsh society. What interests Wesker is families,
in both the social and the political sense, and the loyalties which bind
them — the experience of belonging to a small group that is simultaneously under pressure from the external world and, in the political
sense, is concerned to change that world. The plays explore the
experience of being political and of belonging to an extended family of
comrades with whom one wrangled and fell out but to whom one was
ultimately bound in a common fight against the outside world. The
plays of the *Trilogy* also show the mingling of that wider family with the
much more closely defined family of mothers, fathers, sisters and
brothers uniting to survive against the pressures of society.

The heart of the *Trilogy* is morality, and socialism for Wesker is
morally defined. Socialists are those possessed of moral certainty who
try to express this in their social lives. Socialism is not presented as
being primarily developed through patient, unrewarding political work,

through learning or through collective discussion, although all of this is recorded. Its roots lie in moral emulation, in particular the passing of the spirit from generation to generation. The focus of the plays is how that morality passes along a chain, from one person to another, and how some take up the burden while others falter and refuse or cannot accept it.

Four central characters demonstrate the process; Sarah and her son Ronnie Kahn, Dave Simmonds and Beatie Bryant. Sarah carries within her the same fire that was kindled in her youth in Hungary; it needs no sustenance other than faith and, apparently, it can carry on through any setback. She is the most fully formed character, possibly because, of all the many autobiographical influences in the *Trilogy*, she represents the most dominant factor in shaping Wesker's own life. There were many Sarah Kahns in the organizations of the postwar Left, and in various ways these women gave those organizations their rank-and-file backbone. They were the people who in youth acquired a sense of purpose about politics that nothing could dislodge. They might have acknowledged but would seldom have articulated to anyone outside the 'family', the reasons why they kept going. Sarah Kahn ends *Chicken Soup with Barley* with a passionate explanation:

> You think it doesn't hurt me — the news about Hungary? You think I know what happened and what didn't happen? Do any of us know? Who do I know who to trust now — God, who are our friends now? But all my life I've fought. With your father and the rotten system that couldn't help him. All my life I've worked with a Party that meant glory and freedom and brotherhood. You want me to give it up now? You want me to move to Hendon and forget who I am? If the electrician who comes to mend my fuse blows it instead, so should I stop having electricity? I should cut off my light? Socialism is my light, can you understand that? A way of life. A man *can* be beautiful. I hate ugly people — I can't bear meanness and fighting and jealousy — I've got to have light. I'm a simple person, Ronnie, and I've got to have light and love.
>
> ...Please, Ronnie, don't let me finish this life thinking I lived for nothing. We got through, didn't we? We got scars but we got through. You hear me, Ronnie? You've got to care, you've got to care or you'll die.

Politics has come to mean perpetual struggle and the survival of a personal moral commitment; the salvaging of a life that can only be saved by passing on that moral commitment to the one individual left whom she can influence — her son. He all but collapses under the weight.

Sarah is a displaced Hungarian Jew, shaped by the rag-trade sweat-shops of London's East End. The three other central characters are quite different. They come from backgrounds that are both less grinding and more socially ambiguous. There is little, for example, in Beatie

Bryant's depressed rural working-class family to inspire much moral fervour. Behind the *Trilogy* lies this unexpressed dilemma; Wesker's concern is that the moral fire of Sarah Kahn cannot be reproduced in such new contexts but that, in some way, it has to be.

The first play, *Chicken Soup with Barley*, centres on Sarah, and Wesker's impassioned treatment of her emphasizes one of the continuing problems of his later work. He wants to find the individual roots of a person's politics. Yet what he finds with Sarah is an endless regression of experience in which the same face is presented. Wesker never analyses why Sarah is a Communist nor why she should remain committed when everyone about her falls away. In Act I, with the local Party branch preparing for the Battle of Cable Street (in 1936, when Fascists attempted to march through the East End of London), Sarah springs to life fully-formed with her twin inspirations and obsessions: the family and Communism. She is presented as an innocent who has picked up a particular vision of the world to which she clings because it makes sense to her:

> MONTY: ...It was all so simple. The only thing that mattered was to be happy and to eat. Anything that made you unhappy or stopped you from eating was the fault of capitalism. Do you think she ever read a book on political economy in her life? Bless her! Someone told her socialism was happiness so she joined the Party.

But Sarah is not very happy personally; her happiness never enters anyone's mind, least of all her own, despite the fact that she insists, in the face of her sister-in-law's coldness as a trade union organizer, that, 'Love comes now. You have to start with love. How can you talk about socialism otherwise?' Yet there is a strong though implicit undercurrent that Sarah is a monster feeding off the emotions, and particularly the pleasures, of those who surround her, demanding that she be seen as the selfless provider. Wesker never, even by the most indirect allusion, enters the most sensitive and revealing area, that of the sexual relationship between Sarah and her husband Harry. It is not a question of a lack of explicitness in the theatre of that time; more that Wesker seems unwilling to raise the spectre. There is throughout the *Trilogy* a very reserved, even puritanical, view of sex, which may come from the two social backgrounds represented — the Jewish working-class milieu and the rural working class. It is very difficult to envisage Beatie Bryant in *Roots* actually making love in the afternoon as she asserts; it comes across as the kind of activity Wesker sees as symbolizing the outer fringes of bohemian life. Sex occupies a peculiar place in Wesker's plays because an abiding theme is love — the difficulty of achieving it, how we are diminished by not so doing, and the joy if it is achieved. Yet Wesker's impassioned challenge to puritanism is generally romantic and confined to the image not the act, as if the deluge on stage and television of everyday sexual naturalism has convinced him to embrace more abstract forms.

The Four Seasons (1965) is an extension of Sarah's plea for love but in a highly stylized, almost balletic, form. The love in *The Old Ones* (1972) or in *The Merchant* (1976) is fractured, dyspeptic and displaced but ultimately strong, again through family and friendship rather than sexual encounter. In *Love Letters on Blue Paper* the nub of the relationship is explored in the most distanced of effects — correspondence posted by Sonia to her dying husband and broadcast through speakers around the auditorium.

Such barriers occur throughout the *Trilogy*. Sarah has married her opposite; Harry is a man whose life is presented as one long illicit search for the most accessible pieces of immediate and simple happiness: knowing the time that the pictures begin though not that of the march; going off to eat salt-beef sandwiches when his daughter is near death from diphtheria; the man remembered by a former comrade as 'having a fine tenor voice'; a man finally reduced to stealing jelly-babies and retreating to infancy by shitting his pants — the final act of a weak man who has given up caring. Harry Kahn's pleasure carries the tang of sin instead of being the spiritual state which comes from great ideals, as it *ought* to be. Yet one of the things that makes *Chicken Soup with Barley* such a good play is the constant undercutting of this by sympathy for the feckless Harry.

This tension between the spiritual and sensual side of happiness is another main concern of Wesker's. Several of his plays are built around an epicurean celebration which stands both beyond individual dilemmas and yet also reveals them more sharply, as when the workers turn on their boss during a party game that forms the climax of *The Wedding Feast* (1974). In *The Old Ones* the central event heals rather than wounds; one comes to respect the battling, defiant old people who are brought together to celebrate the feast of the Sukkoth, a thanksgiving festival for the harvest of the fields. The pleasure of the shouting, singing and dancing is far removed from the original religious significance, which is ironically counterpointed as the family has to follow the instructions in a book to get the ceremony right. A more chilling use of a religious setting is the warning shot sounded by *Caritas* (1981) in which the denial of material reality in pursuit of an ideal leads to the logical conclusion of social isolation and madness. It is a chilling echo of *Roots* which moves on from *Chicken Soup with Barley* and the possession of the spirit to its acquisition and, in a semi-religious way, to salvation and redemption.

The dramatic problem with *Roots* is similar though much more accentuated than that of *Chicken Soup with Barley*. Like the two framing plays in the *Trilogy*, it is centred on the same milieu of London socialism, but this time in terms of the effects it has on someone who is a stranger to it. It is full of people who co-exist, however fitfully; they are crude, they fight, they appear unaware of many aspects of human experience but nevertheless they do acknowledge each other. One of the strengths of *Roots* is the precision and care with which such acknowledgements are described. The neutral word 'acknowledgement' is appropriate because much of the statement of *Roots* is its assertion of just how impoverished and lacking in humanity most of these relationships are. The cruel insensitivity is maintained to the very end as Beatie receives her letter of rejection from Ronnie Kahn against a background of contemptuous dismissal. Wesker, however, does consider why they have arrived at this state — the oppressions and fears of rural agricultural labour, the constant uncertainties of death and enforced absence — and he is not unsympathetic.

Beatie is the central character, and although her motivations are crucial they remain almost wholly unexplored. She has gone away to work at a hotel as a waitress, has met Ronnie Kahn, pursued him, gone to bed with him, followed him to London where she works, paints, makes love in the afternoon and is harangued, almost continuously it seems, by his pompous and self-opinionated remarks. All this is such a sharp break with her dull youth and unadventurous family that it needs some explanation to make sense. Why did she go? In an obvious way this is easy to answer: because life at home was so horrible that even the odious Ronnie was preferable. But that does not get us very far, for how do the chosen few break through the constraints of even the most blinkered society to see some greater purpose beyond it? Why Beatie? Did she know of the road she was travelling? When she met the redeemer did she understand what he was? Wesker chooses not to answer these questions because his investment lies in her conversion. Beatie does not come across as a particularly sympathetic character, perhaps less than Wesker had intended. She is afraid of the old and the sick, she is over-assertive and inquisitorial and she displays no affection or particular interest in her family whom she nevertheless uses as a refuge. We are asked to accept her as another innocent, someone who has somehow passed through the tawdry existence of her immediate society while retaining her childlike quality. Obliquely she is Wesker's way of searching out the origin of Sarah Kahn, as though, blocked in the direct historical search, he had shifted his reference-frame.

All the parts of the *Trilogy* end with self-revelation in the form of assertions. Beatie's is the least convincing though the best known, perhaps because it is the most appealing. It springs from the same contemporary soil of Richard Hoggart's and Raymond Williams' cultural commentaries. There is a lament for a lost working-class culture, and anger at the sapping qualities of material prosperity. There is the definite stand against repressive influences and corrupt-

ing commercial culture in all its social forms. Beatie's pain and conflicts are spontaneous; her final speech is not presented as a battle past
the pain to attain a genuine kind of self and social knowledge, but
comes across rather as the spirit being passed on, of faith suddenly
being acquired, the gift of tongues:

> Did you listen to me? ...Jenny, Frankie, Mother — I'm not quoting
> no more... Listen to me someone. [*As though a vision were being
> revealed to her.*] God in Heaven, Ronnie! It does work, it's happening
> to me, I can feel it's happened, I'm beginning, on my own two feet —
> I'm beginning...
>
> [*The murmur of the family sitting down to eat grows as Beatie's last cry is
> heard. Whatever she will do they will continue to live as before. As Beatie
> stands alone, articulate at last.*] CURTAIN.

There is in this the same kind of elitism that Sarah Kahn possesses:
that of being the special figure who by virtue of acquiring the gift of
caring and feeling also becomes marked out as someone who has to be
accorded a special tolerance. Wesker's feelings seem mixed. Clearly
this spirit fascinates him and attracts him as a form of power (especially
given his own commitment to the transcendental value of acquiring
education and culture) but it also repels and frightens him.

Much of the balance of feeling, however, is restored in the final
piece, *I'm Talking About Jerusalem*. This is the tightest play in the
Trilogy and yet it is probably the least known. There is a good deal of
padding in the previous two, particularly in *Roots*, whereas *I'm Talking
About Jerusalem* is much denser and filled with a group of characters
who all take on a life rather than being subordinate to one dominant
figure. Furthermore, the play has, in the character of Dave Simmonds,
a person who genuinely learns from experience. He is the only one in
the *Trilogy* to undergo a genuine transformation. Sarah Kahn remains
defiant but essentially static while Beatie Bryant is static until the one
moment of acute revelation. Ronnie Kahn, the most unsatisfactory of
the major characters, appears only to suffer and never to develop,
though he ends the *Trilogy* with his own form of self-awareness:
'We-must-be-bloody-mad-to-cry!'

The common feature of all these characters, despite their political
positions, is the distance that separates them from the mass of the
population. Only in the opening scenes of *Chicken Soup with Barley* is
there any sense of the Kahns being involved in a mass movement, a
moment of struggle seen on the Left as a symbol for one of the points
in British history where socialist and popular aspirations coalesced. It
is inevitable that by using this starting point, Wesker is unable to break
out of a view of the Left that is one of decline. Dave alone seems to be
conscious of this separation. Work, he suggests, is the crucially alienating process of modern capitalism. It is modern production that reduces

people to slaves, bored and drained of any ability to assess or change their circumstances. Distancing oneself from the mass of the working people then becomes an inevitable stage along the road to freeing oneself. Wesker seems uncertain how far he wants to approach this issue. In *Chicken Soup with Barley* he suggests that Dave has actually been so repelled by his experiences of the working class in the army that he wishes to cut himself off from all further contact. But this direct experience is not developed in *I'm Talking About Jerusalem*; it becomes absorbed in a general thesis about the alienation of work. (This is a far cry from the very detailed and loving exploration of the pressure of work in *The Kitchen*.)

Dave's ambitions are defeated; he is forced to return to London, to a personal and domestic survival and, probably, to begin to lower his standards of craftsmanship in order to do even that. But it is a different kind of defeat from the unconscious, or at least unacknowledged, sapping of Sarah Kahn or the bewildered twistings of Ronnie. It is a slow and calculated retreat, grudgingly and sadly made but not a capitulation. After the fierce conflict between Dave and his brother-in-law Ronnie at the end of the play, Ronnie sinks to his knees in despair while Dave busies himself with the everyday details of the future. However, we are left with a strong sense that something will survive in Dave and even be reborn. Yet it is Ronnie who has the last words in the *Trilogy*; Dave goes back to the corrupting metropolis: 'They say you can sell them anything in London.' The cot, with Dave and Ada's baby in it, is carried off to a potentially hopeful future, despite its limitations and problems.

The success of *I'm Talking About Jerusalem* lies in the measured way in which Dave's position is put under systematic attack from various quarters: the cynicism of Dave's wartime friend Libby Dobson; the practicalities of the Kahn sisters; Ronnie's visions; and the materialism of Dave's apprentice. Dave has even turned his back on his time fighting in Spain. The attacks are never unfair nor are they wholly conclusive. There is a careful and scrupulous balance which makes Dave's retreat very real, as he finds that his answers cannot be wholly conclusive either. *I'm Talking About Jerusalem* is centrally concerned with the necessities of compromise and the possibility of preserving some integrity through such compromise.

The most intriguing and most important incident in the play, from the point of view of understanding the core of Wesker's position, is the strange episode of the stolen lino. The Simmonds have moved from London to live and work in the country. Dave is working as a farm handyman to earn money to put together a craft-furniture workshop. Whilst working there he takes a roll of abandoned lino from the farm. For this piece of minor larceny he is sacked by the farmer, a country gentleman figure. The episode has no apparent effect on the lives of the Simmonds. The job is of no importance, the farmer is never seen again and the furniture workshop is merely set up a few months ahead of schedule. Yet in terms of the moral perspective of the play the incident is crucial, for what it suggests is a moral failing in Dave, a weakness which will prevent him from ever overcoming the barriers to his ambition. It inserts a seed into the play which must be accepted as fully considered by Wesker, given that it is hardly necessary for plot development. This has two important implications which decisively colour the play thereafter.

Firstly, Dave's defeat is given an air of tragic inevitability. It seems that Wesker is asserting the impossibility of escape from contamination by society except in some sense by the pure in heart, which Dave is not. The incident brings together a strong theme of the *Trilogy* — the town/country opposition — in a way that seems to sum up the defeat facing those who seek rural escape from the corrosive conurbations, however understandable and worthy that route might be. (Wesker's own brother and sister did leave the capital for Norfolk.) It also ties in with *Roots*, which shows that rural life, for those born to it, can be just as stultifying and hard. The grass may look greener on the other side, but it is not. There is no escape wherever you are except in personal, moral terms, by struggling to achieve grace. It is impossible to find such grace by merely shifting one's physical residence. There is a contrast implicitly struck between the innocents like Sarah and Beatie, who pass through society with their ideals intact, and those like Dave, who have a more ambiguous position but who do try to change their lives. The ultimate failure of individual sanctity or retreat as a solution to moral dilemmas is pushed to the limit in *Caritas* in which a woman is literally immured to escape from the world, while the Peasants' Revolt offstage expresses simultaneously the necessity of a collective struggle and its inevitable defeat.

Secondly, within Wesker's moral framework, there has to be a complete acceptance of the morality of the lino issue; Dave was wrong to have taken it and the farmer was right, though harsh, to sack him.

This has a central implication for the *Trilogy* (though nowhere expressed as sharply as in the lino episode) that capitalism, although severe, is not, at its centre, irredeemably immoral. The major implication for Wesker's socialism, as for that of many others, is the refusal of the masses to be enlightened, as though the root of this failure lies in separate and individual refusals to accept something that is available to all. The only suggestion that there could be any external block to such discovery lies in Dave's attacks on the nature of industrialization, attacks which are constantly weakened by, for example, the free choice made by his apprentice to work in a factory rather than a craft workshop.

But can the class system be overcome by enlightenment? Can ex-

ploitation be ended by education? The problem is that Wesker tends to
see the working class along an idealist axis of heroes or victims that
ultimately offers an inadequate model for understanding the real
situation. This position is intensified in *The Wedding Feast* when the
workers, repressed by social custom but released by the freedom of a
wedding celebration, are condemned for their inhumanity to the boss;
the divisiveness of class is lamented with an accepting melancholy.
Wesker's morality is rooted in this concentration on the need for the
individual to choose, rather than on any condemnation (except at the
most superficial or generalized level) of the society which constrains
and oppresses the individual; we all have to face a tough life, whether
in town or country — it is up to us to do something about it.

> DAVE: You child you — visions don't work.
> RONNIE: [*desperately*] They *do* work! And even if they don't work
> then for God's sake let's try and behave as though they do — or
> else nothing will work.
> DAVE: Then nothing will work.

It is a bleak view and yet Wesker never wants to leave us defeated;
despite the constant disillusion, he still seems to prefer the dreamers.
Wesker does not come to terms with political practice, except as
offstage events, because he does not analyse the roots of the vision.
Sarah just has it; Beatie picks it up but we do not know what she will do
with it; Ronnie is bitter that he has not got it: 'I say all the right things, I
think all the right things, but somewhere, some bloody where I fail as a
human being.'

It is the 'some bloody where' that Wesker tries to dramatize because
that is what most people find most difficult to discover. For Wesker the
activists are those with a conferred spirit rather than those with a
coherent response to external pressures. Dave is the only character
who attempts such a response and he is driven back and back by
reality. Activists could be both idealists and effective at Cable Street, a
fusion of the public and the personal when innocence and politics
coincided. The nearer Wesker takes us to the present, the further away
he gets from such a communion of interests; the activists, to remain
pure, become ever less socially effective. Challenging the contamination of society becomes more personal and passive.

Wesker says in a note to the *Trilogy*: 'I am at one with these people; it
is only that I am annoyed, with them and myself.' A classic Angry
Young Man statement? Wesker certainly wanted to write about ideas
as emotional, human entities — not a very English thing to do, as the
folk in *Roots* are meant to show. In this respect, Wesker is a man of his
time along with Osborne and the others, kicking against what they saw
as a deadening affluence, both intellectually and emotionally. But only
Wesker has held on to this moral vision with an exclusive passion.

In *The Journalists* he rails against the misuse of ideas and words to cut 'better' people down to the size of the 'inferior' perpetrators. The opposite impulse informs *The Merchant*. It opens with Shylock, in the Venice ghetto with his Christian merchant friend, Antonio, making a catalogue of his superb private collection of books which should have been burnt ten years before by order of the Pope. The play is predicated on the joy of words and dispute, of their lasting value beyond the graves of their creators. In the last scene Antonio, at a picnic in Belmont, speaks to Portia in what it is tempting to take as an index of Wesker's own feelings:

> What mixed blessings in these last years of my life, to meet an acerbic old Jew who disturbed my dull complacency; and you, blossoming with purpose, reminding me of a barren life.

In the *Trilogy* Wesker's upbringing provides the spread and the force of the plays, placing his own dilemma in a powerful, convincing context. In the later plays, however, the private paradox often becomes more consuming than the situation that gives rise to it, as the moral ground of the debate becomes less and less identified with socialism in any of its interpretations save the most individual. It is not that private matters are of no concern to socialism, nor that there is only one way to explore the links between the two. Far from it. The problem lies in how successfully such connections are charted. In many cases Wesker's preoccupations undermine rather than sustain the cohesion of the plays. *Their Very Own and Golden City*, which appeared after the first difficult experiences of Centre 42, has an epic framework and socialist values at its core but it is clear that by now these values have become so abstracted from reality that the touching poetic vision of the play seems no more than romanticism, a shout in the wilderness. The road to *Caritas* and immuring is not such a long one.

There is a danger in comparing later works to the earlier standards by which a playwright makes a name, particularly when the marker is as good as the *Trilogy*. One can miss what is new and developing, and one can succumb to a self-fulfilling commentary: Wesker will never be as good as he was. Yet Wesker as a playwright is the counterpart to those on the political Left who in the mid-1960s, having defended a beleaguered position for two decades, suddenly found the ground moving under their feet. Despite a continuing, courageous concern for the primacy of humane values and their exploration in drama, Wesker has never again been able to express this preoccupation with the force of the *Trilogy*; the same questions recur but the dramatic answers become more elusive.

CHAPTER EIGHT

John Arden and Margaretta D'Arcy:
Uneasy Lies the Head...

John Arden is often seen as the most problematic of the postwar British dramatists. There are those on the Left who see him as the exemplar of the bourgeois writer who, having passed through the classic channels of London avant-garde and establishment theatre, turned his back on it and wrote instead plays for and with the revolutionary socialist movement. As a consequence, it is felt, he has been spurned by the traditional theatre, has been denied control of his work and has had his artistic reputation denigrated. For others, who may be roughly defined as the conventional critics, Arden's reputation stands precisely on the group of early plays written before the turn, namely those that were presented at the Royal Court — *Waters of Babylon* (1957), *Live Like Pigs* (1958), *The Happy Haven* (1960) and, in particular, *Serjeant Musgrave's Dance* (1959) — and the two plays performed by National Theatre companies: *The Workhouse Donkey* (1963) and *Armstrong's Last Goodnight* (1964). This camp maintains that Arden on his own is a master of his humanist craft; the later work is dismissed or seen as inferior, and Arden's collaboration with Margaretta D'Arcy is regarded as the key to this break.

In support of this view, the radio play *Pearl* (1978) can be held up because it falls into the second period but is a solely John Arden creation (though D'Arcy's influence, at least in terms of theme, is clear); it is a conventional piece of great power in a solid classic mould, in form though not in content. It should be remembered, however, that the early plays were not all written alone and did not have an easy ride at the time. The English Stage Company turned down the first play that Arden submitted but George Devine later stood by him while the critics in general were bewildered by his work and the box office was bad. Although *Serjeant Musgrave's Dance* has emerged as a 20th-century classic, it was more or less condemned at birth in 1959 and given only qualified approval in the 1965 Royal Court revival. It was not until 1981, with a new production at the National Theatre, that the play's stature could be taken for granted.

By then Arden had moved to Ireland, his new solo plays were being performed only on radio and the collaborative work had all but disappeared from British theatre. In 1982 Arden's first novel was published. The rupture had proceeded so far that the inclusion of Arden and D'Arcy (who is Irish) in a book on British playwriting would seem to some to be inappropriate. Nevertheless, the impact of Arden's plays and of the collaborative work produced in Britain as well as the importance of the experiences of the two playwrights in British theatre more than justify their inclusion. It is also crucial to challenge without going to the opposite extreme the artistic judgement that divides the canon into two, with a supposed break in form, content and the deployment of traditional skills whenever D'Arcy appears to pull Arden into the yawning pit of propagandist agitrop. In fact, the bulk of Arden's work has been written collaboratively, beginning as early as 1960 with *The Happy Haven* and there is a clear continuity through to the later Irish plays.

There have been many conflicts along the route of this work. D'Arcy and Arden have been thorny individuals for many theatre managements. But difficult writers are legion; the theatre thrives on the alleged creativity of the tension they cause. Although the abrasive nature of some of the skirmishes with Arden and D'Arcy has derived from political differences, there is a deeper cause, of which the politics is an expression. This is the attempt by D'Arcy and Arden to make theatre a live event which draws on and communicates directly with its audience outside of traditional constraints.

Like many other playwrights, D'Arcy and Arden increasingly felt the need to control the conditions of work on their plays. What hastened their departure from British theatre was as much the nature of the control they demanded (and the way they demanded it) as the actual content of the plays. The turning point was their dispute in 1972 with the Royal Shakespeare Company over the first production of *The Island of the Mighty*, which ended in D'Arcy and Arden picketing the Aldwych Theatre and dissociating themselves from what they claimed to be a travesty of their original play. The details of this dispute are complex and contentious, but it is worth noting that their demands included the right to involve in discussion not only the actors but also the entire theatre staff — technicians, ushers, front-of-house.

Their argument questioned the supremacy of the system in which both executive and legislative power — and thereby artistic control — is vested in one and the same person or function, namely a director. The triumvirate of nationally subsidized companies that then offered the main chance for new writing were (and still are) run as more or less benevolent dictatorships by directors. Arden and D'Arcy were challenging a system that in practice denied the primacy of the playwright in artistic input. To them the director of a new play is properly concerned with how the playwright's meaning is best presented on stage but not primarily with the meaning itself. Meaning precedes and outlives directional interpretation and comes from the playwright through the text.

The dispute also highlighted the problem of artistic contribution from other sources — actors, music, design — and how to make theatre genuinely collaborative. Experience in the alternative theatre, where interlocking artistic and political differences have jeopardized projects just as much as elsewhere, is a reminder that the British system of subsidy offers little chance to test other approaches properly. D'Arcy's and Arden's position in this area is paradoxical. On the one hand they have championed the cause of non-professional theatre and of drama that is not structured through traditional hierarchies and functions. On the other, the personal position of artistic autonomy and control they have taken up frequently has much more in common with, say, the theatre of Ibsen and Chekhov, than with that of many recent writers who have grown up within a framework of more democratic theatre groups.

Arden and D'Arcy have often worked outside the conventional professional theatre, for example, with left-wing groups such as CAST at Unity Theatre on *Muggins is a Martyr* (1968), or 7:84 on *The Ballygombeen Bequest* (1972), *Serjeant Musgrave Dances On* (1972), and *Vandaleur's Folly* (1978). A nativity play, *The Business of Good Government* (1960), was produced with villagers in Somerset; *Ars Longa, Vita Brevis* (1964), which formed part of the Theatre of Cruelty season, was developed from children's games and later performed with children at Kirbymoorside Festival; *The Royal Pardon* (1966) was a community play developed at Beaford in Devon. Most remarkable was the Easter weekend at Liberty Hall, Dublin, the headquarters of the Irish Transport and General Workers' Union, when a mix of professionals and amateurs presented the six-part *Non-Stop Connolly Show* (1975).

One consistent aspect of this work is fun — a word not immediately associated with Arden and D'Arcy but inescapable when one looks at the way in which passion and argument are presented forthrightly with humour, exuberance and vitality throughout their work. Any attempt to approach the plays naturalistically or without an ever-present image of performance will miss the point, as often has happened. The plays represent the dramatist as painter, with words as some of the brush-strokes and action as the canvas. Detail and realism are not foreign to such emblematic art; on the contrary, they give it the power of direct statement, the cutting edge of satire, the force of cartoon, that subverts the habits and traditions of empathetic theatre on which the dominant dramatic mode of European humanism is based. Despite the differences between, for example, *The Workhouse Donkey* and *Serjeant Musgrave's Dance*, this elan is common to both; they share, as the other plays do, a multiple inspiration in ballad, in that productive moment of poetry and drama where the Tudors met feudalism head on, and in contemporary political events.

When Arden and D'Arcy presented *The Hero Rises Up* (1968) at the Roundhouse, they defined their practice as asymmetrical, 'curvilinear', improper — features of the supposedly conservative Celts who were to be improved by Roman 'rectilinear' propriety. This spirit of libertarian rebellion speaks throughout the plays. Authority is to be defied, especially if it is trying to order your life, as happens to the old people in *The Happy Haven*. In the right circumstances this passion will erupt in even the most respectable folk — hence the double life of architect/ pimp Krank in *The Waters of Babylon*, the riot by the decent people in *Live Like Pigs* or the private desires of the reforming Chief Constable Feng in *The Workhouse Donkey*, a play truly in the robust tradition of popular English drama.

There is also a concern for the nature of government and the paradox of individuals caught up in a system of authority. It is most comically explored in the figure of the policeman, for example Feng, or the constable in *The Royal Pardon*, and it is seen at its most concentrated and powerful in the figure of the soldier, particularly Black Jack Musgrave, unable in the end to identify with any form of authority — the supreme characterization of anarchy in British theatre.

The other strong presence is that of the artist — tellingly, the soldier in *The Royal Pardon* becomes an actor. At a more complex political level, the theme of the artist is explored in *Armstrong's Last Goodnight* through Lindsay, the urbane poet who plays a directly political role, and through the public poets who form the strongest links between the three parts of *The Island of the Mighty*. This trilogy, begun in 1953, and nineteen years in the making, offers the most imaginative and far-reaching attempt in postwar drama to dig up the ancient roots of Britain; it tackles the Arthurian legend as a political reality, and demystifies the romantic Victorian vision.

All this is brought out in the presentation and style of performance: actors and musicians come on to a platform, which is erected on whatever stage or space already exists; they play out their scenes against one of a series of backcloths — Camp, Raid, Fort, Woodland, Ruins, Seascape, Mill, Snowscape. The actor is important as presenter rather than as an interpreter of character, and is required to use a near-pantomimic anti-heroic style which allows the humour, and particularly the irony of the situations, to be fully displayed. Music is used throughout, not just to punctuate and accompany but also to provide a strong rhythm for certain pieces of action. Costume, colour and props are all simple and striking.

The trilogy charts the movement of history through stories. Part One tells the story of twins, Balin and Balan, who kill each other unknowingly in a tribal ritual. Part Two deals with Arthur's defeat and Part Three tells the story of Merlin's end. Characteristically, the three parts stress the clash of different worlds and of their values, customs, ways of life. As in all Arden's plays up to this point, the interest lies in how and why the conflict has developed and how the contact is negotiated. The arena is always historical rather than private. Arthur is trying to impose Roman rule after the Romans have left and has to be superseded; he is a lame king, which foreshadows his defeat, but it is only when we learn how he was made lame that the significance of the defeat becomes clear. The great Christian leader has to confess that he was made lame in a strange and ancient ceremony. Further, he reveals that not only is the leader of the opposing army his son but that he, Arthur, killed the mother, his wife, because she was also his sister. Ideology and customs may be suppressed by conquering invaders or internal oppressors but they do not disappear; they live on to inspire future generations. *The Island of the Mighty* shows that military victory is but a first step in winning a war and that war itself cannot wholly destroy a society.

The underlying theme of the three parts is the survival of an underground and subversive culture, which is carried, though not always understood, by the poets. This survival of a sustaining custom in the collective memory, ready to erupt later at some chosen moment, is a prominent but unexplained feature at odds with the precision of the rest of the trilogy. Although the theme is dramatically very powerful, it does undercut the politics of the rest of the play. The events of the trilogy are set against the tough life of the people, though this, like their resistance, is less clearly dramatized than the actions of their rulers. The people's resistance, while being celebrated, is at the same time being denied by being romanticized; the notion of a secret elite, with the poet figure unknowingly holding the key to the rituals, represents an emotional retreat from the actual struggle of resistance which is fought out in flesh and blood.

The Island of the Mighty is not an antiquarian exercise although, like *Armstrong's Last Goodnight*, with its 'sort of Babylonish dialect' (Arden's description), it could not be described as immediately accessible. Equally, it was not part of the project to draw the explicit parallels that, for example, Howard Brenton later made in *The Romans in Britain* (1980) between Britain's past and its present role as an imperial power. *The Island of the Mighty* is a rich and swirling drama, telling an exciting story but it is also a puzzle. In *Serjeant Musgrave's Dance*, written at the time of British colonial activity in Cyprus and Aden, Black Jack brings home the bones of his comrade killer in an imperialist war as an act of individual revolt — he wants to cure the illness by further, fatal, doses of the same disease. But he is also commenting on the political reality of the 1950s as the bones of

Empire came back home to Britain. In *Armstrong's Last Goodnight* the great warrior chief Gilnockie and the clan system he represents have to be tamed because historically the development of English-Scottish relations required border 'peace'. In some ways a sequel to *Musgrave*, *Armstrong's Last Goodnight* was written against the background of the post-independence struggles in the Congo. Political ends are again achieved through a necessary savagery but this time behind the mask of civilized behaviour. With these plays, political connections and other contemporary implications have to be sought by the audience, whereas in later Arden/D'Arcy plays the political links are made explicit.

The contrast between implicit and explicit links can be seen in *The Ballygombeen Bequest*, which is the first play by D'Arcy and Arden to express, in any full sense, Marxist inspiration. The contrast is made starker by the coincidence that it too opened in 1972 but in the Falls Road, Belfast, far from London's West End and the Aldwych Theatre. *The Ballygombeen Bequest* marks a vigorous renewal within the Arden/D'Arcy popular tradition and ranks as a landmark in the history of a particular form of alternative theatre alongside the later *Non-Stop Connolly Show* and 7:84's *The Cheviot, the Stag and the Black, Black Oil* (1973).

If *Serjeant Musgrave's Dance* is a ballad, then *The Ballygombeen Bequest* is a revolutionary song. *Serjeant Musgrave's Dance* is far from simplistic; it has the construction, directness and power of a ballad; it is a story told within a tightly controlled poetic form that uses precise, primary contrasts — Black death, Black coal, Black Jack, Red uniform, Red blood, Green apple. It shows the political limitations — and dangers — when ideas which fuel people, like liberalism or pacifism, remain abstract. Musgrave's problem is his inability to connect his anger and protest with that of the striking miners, whose cause, to him, was 'not material'.

In *The Ballygombeen Bequest* the action is approached in several but connected ways. An English absentee landlord, Hollidey-Cheype, inherits land which includes a bungalow and a cottage that has been lived in rent free for over a century by the O'Leary family. He swindles O'Leary of his historic rights but the eviction is resisted by the son Padraic who returns home after working in England. With the cynical help of local small businessman Hagan, Padraic gets Republicans to blow up the holiday bungalow. Padraic is then fooled by two agents, one British, who is posing as a BBC film-maker and who was tipped off by Hollidey-Cheype, the other from Dublin, tipped off by Hagan. Padraic is wrongly arrested by the British Army and dies under interrogation. His body is left in the South as if killed in an internal IRA dispute. Hagan gets the bungalow cheap and Hollidey-Cheype seeks his fortune in Europe.

The story offers an example of colonial and neo-colonial exploitation in social, economic and political terms. This is achieved through different theatrical styles: the landlord is in the Arden emblematic tradition of the constable or the doctor, while the interrogation is chillingly realistic; the ending is pure music hall, as Hagan and Hollidey-Cheype scrabble for bank notes in a custard-pie fight using the funeral meats and spurred on unseen by the risen dead body of Padraic. The authors explicitly link this story from a small part of Ireland to world events. A narrator sings:

> The fat men of the fat half-world
> Had food on every plate.
> The lean men of the naked world
> Grew leaner every day
> And if they put their faces up
> Their teeth were kicked away.

The accumulated detail of the play's bold statement is very persuasive though its life was cut short by a libel action. (The same story appears again in *The Little Gray Home in the West: an Anglo-Irish Melodrama* (1978).)

Arden has dismissed unsympathetic critics of his Marxist development and of D'Arcy's influence, saying that he was 'affirming from his own hard experience the need for revolution and a socialistic society,' and stating that he was 'convinced that his artistic independence and integrity will be strengthened rather than weakened by so doctrinaire a stance'.*

For those who persist in dividing the canon into 'Arden' and 'non-Arden' as synonymous with good and bad, politically uncommitted and committed, the achievement of *The Ballygombeen Bequest* must be hard to comprehend. Harder still to appreciate would be the staggering qualities of *The Non-Stop Connolly Show*, which has been dismissed by most of the few traditional critics who have seen or read it as banal propaganda.

In theatrical terms there is a direct line from *The Workhouse Donkey* through *Serjeant Musgrave's Dance*, *Armstrong's Last Goodnight*, *The Island of the Mighty* to *The Non-Stop Connolly Show*. Written in six parts, *The Non-Stop Connolly Show* describes the life of the Irish revolutionary James Connolly from boyhood to his execution by the British after the Easter Uprising of 1916. The cycle includes an entire play set in the USA during Connolly's time there, which is almost exclusively concerned with American Labour politics, as well as plays that are concerned with major events in Irish labour history preceding the Uprising.

Like Arden's most praised earlier work, the cycle contains the very

---

*John Arden: *To Present the Pretence: Essays on the Theatre and its Public* (Methuen, 1977).

stuff of drama: paradox, dilemma, action, intrigue, conflict, doubt, development, fun, song, verse, colour. The actors are required to be agile, to be in command of speed and rhythm, to sing, dance and play many characters. At its heart are people fired with ideas, testing them in practice as they make history: King Arthur down the telescope of history has become Connolly in front of our very eyes.

Who else in the contemporary theatre but Arden and D'Arcy could have held together such diverse strands under the spinning weight of their centrifugal tendencies? *The Non-Stop Connolly Show* has fair claim to being one of the finest pieces of postwar drama in the English language. It is a disgrace that none of the big English companies has even tried to present it. And yet the gigantic effort shows its cracks; politically, Arden and D'Arcy pull the carpet from under Connolly's feet and cast an ambiguity over their own intentions. These they outlined in the introduction to the published plays as being two-fold: in Ireland, among other things, they wanted to show that the 1916 Uprising was necessary and that the contemporary anti-imperialist struggle has an historical validity; in England, they wanted to emphasize how the unwillingness of the British Labour movement to support Irish self-determination has been a major reason for the continuing bloodshed. The balance of their argument comes near the end of the final play in a crucial political and emotional scene when Connolly decides whether or not he should join the uprising planned by the secret Republican Brotherhood. One by one the classic arguments against insurrectionary politics are put and one by one Connolly fashions an answer to them. Finally, one last objection is put by the symbolic bird who has appeared to him:

BIRD: Prohibition number seven:
      Do not deceive yourself that you are given
      By Jesuitical justification all the cause
      You need to make upon your own your private wars!
      Private perhaps, so slyly personal the real deep guilt and grudge
      That drives James Connolly to this sharp knife-edge...

CONNOLLY: See the slave of a slave taking orders from her boss
      So that *his* boss may be toppled with the minimum of loss...
      Very well: I am a man who will hazard his whole life
      And those of his friends because he knows his wife
      Has got from him alive such little good.
      Very well, perhaps I do shed blood
      Perhaps I do make war
      For no-one else but her —
      What's wrong with that: she is legion, I can't count
      How many of her there are, and what they want
      I do not know how to explain —
      But I do know that to do nothing
      Will do nothing to relieve their pain.

With an uncharacteristic blood-lust statement — 'We're going out to be slaughtered' — the decision is taken to put the Citizen Army into the Easter Uprising, deserted and to be defeated. Its justification? That a way was shown; that Dublin in 1916 opened up a path for all the popular uprisings of the 20th century.

CONNOLLY: For nearly thirty years I tried
To clear the world of those who now have had me tied
Into my chair and shot at till I died.
They always claimed that they were here to stay.
They did not ask us if they may.
And altogether they asked so very few
That when the fire and sword flew
At them in Russia, China, Cuba, Africa, Vietnam
And indeed once more in Ireland, my own home,
They could not credit what it was they'd done,
Or what it was in Dublin we'd begun
At Easter nineteen hundred and sixteen —
We were the first to roll away the stone
From the leprous wall of the whitened tomb
We were the first to show the dark deep hole within
Could be thrown open to the living sun.
We were the first to feel their loaded gun
That would prevent us doing it any more —
Or so they hoped. We were the first. We shall not be the last.
This was not history. It has not passed.

Again and again one is pulled back by the magnificent range and quality of the writing which runs through a spectrum of prose and poetic styles. Arden and D'Arcy are in every way writers as well as polemicists. Yet it is doubtful that one would leave a production of *The Non-Stop Connolly Show* convinced by the final argument. One might be sadder, wiser, possibly more committed; but it is a fundamental weakness that, finally, all the solid, patient and detailed work that Connolly and others undertook (in particular the building of an endur-ing Irish trade-unionism, which is scrupulously portrayed and argued for in the earlier parts of the cycle) is abandoned in favour of empha-sizing a noble and tragic end. Connolly is given the classic role of the isolated and abandoned hero coming to terms with his existence and the inevitability of his death. The questioning bird is stylistically a break within the cycle, appearing as Connolly enters a dreamlike confrontation with himself and figures from his past.

The final resort to psychological conjecture is both unconvincing as a link between the personal and the political and out of keeping with the general style of debate in the play. Furthermore, it returns Connol-ly to the classic mould of European humanist drama: the individual hero flawed by his own internal self-doubt.

This ambiguity in dramatic structure has links with the romantic notion of secret resistance found in *The Island of the Mighty* and to an evident attraction for the Republican Brotherhood which is shown in, for example, *Vandaleur's Folly*. It recurs at odd intervals throughout the cycle. Of all the political movements examined, the Brotherhood — which includes sisters — is the only one left unscathed; indeed it is hardly discussed. Yet in the final decision about the Easter Uprising it is given a crucial role. In the end it represents a form of elitism which shrouds politics in a mysterious aura for the uninitiated and which leads to an individualistic view of politics peopled by tragic heroes or heroines. In their updated version of Brecht's words to Hans Eisler's cantata *The Mother* (1984), Arden and D'Arcy do try and relate allegiance to the IRA to the daily problems of existence and resistance of the Catholic community. Yet, leaving aside the aesthetic problem of the project, there is still no explanation of such an allegiance beyond stating it to be the case. While being didactically powerful, no evidence is advanced as to why or how the contemporary parallel to Brecht's Russian Communists in 1905 should be the IRA.

Lying at the heart of the artistic and political problems is the contradiction between the direction and purpose of Arden's and D'Arcy's work and their quest for exclusive control over it — a dilemma not unlike that of John McGrath and 7:84. One can hear the echo of Arden and D'Arcy in the young poet Aneurin in *The Island of the Mighty* as he says: 'The poet without the people is nothing. The people without the poet will still be the people... All that we can do is to make loud and to make clear their own proper voice. They have so much to say...' The difficulty lies in how the poet relates to the people in order to express their proper voice.

It has to be said that both *The Island of the Mighty* and *The Non-Stop Connolly Show* could only be presented by the large subsidized companies or, with much effort and organization, at another such 'one-off' weekend festival of the kind that first produced the Connolly cycle. It would take an extraordinarily committed and resourceful amateur group to attempt either and yet it is with such groups, together with small touring companies of limited resources, that D'Arcy and Arden have chosen to work. Even here, sharp differences can arise that endanger future collaboration, as the experiences of working on *Vandaleur's Folly* with 7:84 shows. It might be perverse to write gigantic works knowing that they cannot be adequately performed except under conditions which would not be accepted by the authors. However, it is not just an idiosyncratic, personal perversity; it also indicates a basic deficiency in the structure of British theatre.

Concentration on the political and theatrical problems of Arden's and D'Arcy's work does it less than justice. They can manipulate the feel, texture and rhythm of language based upon an extraordinary depth of careful research and skilful, vigorous presentation of stories in a way that is unique among contemporary dramatists. No one else is capable of mingling prose, verse and music as they can, and for this reason alone their departure is a monumental loss to British drama. Arden and D'Arcy chose to put their energies elsewhere; they went into exile from a British theatre which could not accommodate them, and by their own efforts they could not create the theatre which was necessary for them or the times they lived in. But theatre cannot be established by an individual alone, however gifted; it requires collective enterprise and in this sense it would seem that Arden and D'Arcy have operated a self-destruct. Nevertheless, it has to be asked whether a theatre apparently incapable of performing such work does not also stand in danger of self-destruction.

CHAPTER NINE

Edward Bond: Pessimism of the Intellect — Optimism of the Will

Edward Bond is a difficult playwright to write *about* because he himself provides so many pointers as to what should be said. He is one of the most prolific of modern playwrights with, to date, well over twenty plays since *The Pope's Wedding* (1962). These include main-house spectacles at the National Theatre, an open-air musical play for the Campaign for Nuclear Disarmament, and plays first performed by amateur groups. They range over a variety of styles from the surreal to formal realism. Bond is also the most publicly articulate of playwrights, accompanying his work with poems, commentaries, asides and justifications which, on occasion, exceed the length of the plays themselves. Not only has Bond increasingly erected a theory of theatre, he has inhabited every corner of his plays, directing them and analysing them to the point where it becomes difficult to approach them by any other route than that laid down.

There are certainly contradictions in Bond's work that derive from the many elements which he is trying to encompass and the changing emphases which he applies. There are political, social and poetic as well as dramatic aspects. Sometimes they fuse but sometimes they pull against each other. One obvious fact is that, despite being a socialist committed to writing political plays, his work is often dense and inaccessible. He appears to have paid little attention to the problem which has vexed most left-wing playwrights — that of writing popular plays for a wide audience.

What distinguishes Bond is the breadth, power and single-mindedness of his dramatic vision and the constant purpose with which he has attacked the central issue of most of his plays — how can things change? At times, as if in despair, he seems to have answered that they cannot; at others he has presented almost mystical responses; and he has openly embraced revolutionary change. But always he emerges in a new direction, exploring some new avenue. This continuous search has kept Bond alive but it has also often led to stresses between intention and execution.

Saved (1965) and *Early Morning* (1968) illustrate the difficulty. Together with plays like John Osborne's *A Patriot for Me* (1965) they provoked a cultural scandal which fuelled the campaign to break the theatrical censorship exercised by the Lord Chamberlain at the time. Banned in the very heartland of theatre's avant-garde elite, every intellectual weapon of that elite was mobilized in order to justify their presentation, with Bond himself in the forefront. The case was easier with *A Patriot for Me.* Legal repression of homosexuality was something worth challenging as a cause in its own right, and the extension of this repression into a stage censorship which refused even to allow the historical existence of homosexuals was an obvious and vulnerable point of attack, particularly after the promised relaxation of the late 1950s. But stoning to death a baby in a pram (in *Saved*) or a lesbian relationship between Queen Victoria and Florence Nightingale (in *Early Morning*) needed, or seemed to need, a justification stretching beyond what was actually seen on the stage. It required a moral purpose which could be said to uplift rather than degrade the audience. Such morality has long been the fabric of the theatre in Britain because it has usually been necessary to demonstrate that more is on offer than idle amusement or, as with *Saved*, a straightforward description of people's lives.

It is this need for a moral justification that marks out a playwright of Bond's generation from those who came a few years later. For the latter the moral bankruptcy of Britain was so manifest as to need no explanation. Interference from something as daft as the Lord Chamberlain's office would have called forth glee rather than moral indignation. (The situation changed somewhat after the immediate post-1968 euphoria when interference came through the courts.)

In the case of *Saved*, which Bond sees as gradually widening its focus to represent society at large, the justification is not that it is an 'Oedipus comedy' or that it is 'almost irresponsibly optimistic' as he suggested in his 1966 playnotes. What Bond has written is a brutal, comic and sad account of life in the type of seedy London streets and parks where he was raised. The violence is sudden, shattering and, of course, a slightly unbelievable dramatic device, with its unreality at a measured distance from the very specific and truthful life which surrounds it. The point is not that babies are habitually stoned to death in London parks and that this is a truth that is kept from us. What Bond is saying is that the defences of human morality in contemporary society are weaker than we might care to acknowledge and that *this* is the truth that is being kept from us. It is statement by implication not analysis and the justification is clearly social rather than aesthetic.

Alongside this assertion it seems rather pointless to analyse the nature of Len, the central though detached character, as being 'naturally good, in spite of his upbringing and environment... But he is not wholly good or easily good because then his goodness would be meaningless, at least for himself.' (Again the words are from Bond's notes.) *Saved* is neither optimistic nor uplifting; it is deeply disturbing. However, the author seems to find it difficult to accept the implications of this because the way the play comes over is at odds with what is intended. Bond wants to see optimism in his society but this is not present in the writing, in spite of what he says in his notes. There is both a poet and reasoning intellectual locked inside Bond's plays, working at times in phase but not always. It seems as if there are both ideological and emotional grids present that sometimes fit together and sometimes move apart.

The acuteness of this contradiction is felt at its keenest in Bond's most complete work, the group of plays which form a thematic trilogy: *Lear* (1971), *Bingo* (1973), *The Fool* (1975). With *The Bundle* (1978), they mark a decisive change in the basis of his writing and together they describe a remarkable curve of development along which, almost uniquely for a modern playwright, one can follow a clear passage of intellectual growth.

Lear, a reworking of the Shakespearean story, was written as the Vietnam War rose to its final genocidal peak. It was not just a war against people but against the physical environment which supports people, against nature itself. The niceties of Peter Brook's *US* (1966), burning butterflies as symbols of pointless violence, were long past. What Bond does in *Lear*, with that extraordinary jump of imagination which marks him as a great playwright, is to return to the kinds of symbols that Shakespeare used to express the shock of great events. Unnatural events in the human world are matched by disturbances in nature; stars burn and animals change their patterns of behaviour. The ghost of the Gravedigger's Boy is gored to death by maddened pigs who suddenly become savage. There is a continuous use of animal images, particularly of animals confined:

> LEAR: ...This is a little cage of bars with an animal in it... Who shut
> that animal in that cage? Let it out. Have you seen its face
> behind the bars? There's a poor animal with blood on its head
> and tears running down its face. Who did that to it? Is it a bird
> or a horse? It's lying in the dust and its wings are broken. Who
> broke its wings? Who cut off its hands so that it can't shake the
> bars?...

The offence against nature is most clearly symbolized in Lear's and then Cordelia's earth wall. It has come to represent all the acts of natural destruction to which society, with its technological control, has become irretrievably bound. Each successive dictatorship has continued with the useless task of building the wall as a defence against enemies, either real or imagined.

Bond seems to *want* the final act of trying to pull down the wall to be invested with considerable significance as his Lear, through violence, blinding and madness, finds a new purpose. He is allowed, at last, to make a real choice. In almost every Bond play this offering of choice is the key dramatic issue. But in the context of *Lear* the act is so random and so futile that it seems an almost meaningless choice except in terms of the individual conscience. It stands as a symbol of optimism in the fight against tyranny but the power of the state and its use of technology is so great in Cordelia's realm that simple moral gestures become pointless. Yet they must be made, if only as a mark of private morality.

Lear is a gigantic play. Its difficulty lies in the weakness of the oppositions that Bond creates; this leads to a circular argument. The wall is the necessary outcome of a technological imperative. Believe in the myth — that its construction is necessary — and all else follows: labour camps, arbitrary laws, the withering away of all other life save that devoted to the norms of wall-construction. There is no weapon that can oppose this, other than the one which Cordelia and the Carpenter take up: physically to fight and destroy the enemy and in the process become corrupted and overtaken by similar obsessions, regardless of differences in ideological position.

In dealing with violence, Bond repeatedly returns to the theme that people are not born with innate aggression or hatred but that it is taught them. The 'natural' or 'innocent' people who live in harmony with their surroundings, for example the Gravedigger's Boy, or Susan and Thomas who take in the dissident Lear, have no aggressive feelings. The humanity of these characters is derived straightforwardly and directly from their poor and humble circumstances, and from the insight gained through living outside 'normal' society. But again and again innocence is overwhelmed by superior forces.

It took more than outrage to write *Lear* in 1971. It took considerable political courage and perception. What Bond suggests was then almost unthinkable on the international Left: that whatever the end to the Vietnam War and whoever took the place of the brutalized government then in power, they could not fail to be brutalized by the experience. (1971 was the time of Ho Chi Minh not Pol Pot and such a view was not widespread.)

Lear is, politically, a perfect protest play. By its nature it is largely symbolic; Lear's final gesture may be a relieving nod towards the continuing existence of a will to resist but it is just that — a gesture.

Bingo is the bleakest of the four plays. It stands morally at the bottom of Bond's curve; the re-creation of an exact historical situation removes even the abstract possibilities of rural retreat in *Lear's* mythical kingdom. The central character, Shakespeare, in the last years of his life, has built himself a garden with orchards and fields surrounded by a wall. This attempt at retreat is disturbed by an historical equivalent of Lear's wall: the desire to enclose land in the name of higher agricultural productivity. The case for this is given with great precision; Bond is too good a playwright to let it slide away as an obvious and unspeakable crime. The good and the bad farmers are said to be mixed together; only by separating their land can the good succeed and make the land more productive. Of course this will mean some temporary hardship amongst the poor farmers and those unfortunate enough to have no written title to their land but that is the price of progress. The case is strong and made stronger by its inevitability; stand out against it and nothing will happen save individual ruin. It is the voice of a siren reality made the more persuasive since, with historical hindsight, it is the voice of a winner — the new rural capitalism.

> COMBE: ...Listen. I've seen suffering, I've even caused some of it —
> and I try to stop it. But I know this: there'll always be real
> suffering, real stupidity and greed and violence. And there can
> be no civilization till you've learned to live with it. I live in the
> real world and try to make it work. There's nothing more moral
> than that. But you live in a world of dreams! Well what happens
> when you have to wake up? You find that real people can't live
> in your dreams. They don't fit, they're not good or sane or noble
> enough. So you turn to common violence and begin to destroy
> them.

Yet from this persuasive view of progress follows all the suffering and violence that flow past Shakespeare's garden: the beggars, the denial of those elementary virtues of charity and kindness to the destitute, the whipping and the hanging which become, in concrete form, exactly the kind of blood-lust which dominates *Lear*.

> BEN JONSON: ...I've been in prison four times. Dark smelly places.
> No gardens. Sorry yours is too big. They kept coming in and
> taking people out to cut bits off them. Their hands. Take off
> their noses. Cut their stomachs open. Rummage around inside
> with a dirty fist and drag everything out. The law. Little men
> going out through the door. White, shaking. Even staggering.

One of the most effective dramatic devices in *Bingo* is Shakespeare's almost total disengagement throughout the first two scenes when he talks only in brief and direct sentences. He never breaks this form of communication with others, being quite unable to express his feelings or having anyone close enough to make it worthwhile. Suddenly, in Scene Three, in a speech which resembles in its animal imagery the caged creature of *Lear*, he releases in one flood the reasons why he deserted London:

> SHAKESPEARE: ...The baited bear. Tied to the stake. Its dirty coat
> needs brushing. Dried mud and spume. Pale dust. Big clumsy

fists. Men bringing dogs through the gate. Leather collars with
spikes. Loose them and fight. The bear wanders round the
stake. It knows it can't get away. Flesh and blood. Strips of skin.
Teeth scraping on bone. The bear will crush one of the skulls.
Big feet slithering in dog's brain. Round the stake. On and on.
The key in the warder's pocket. Howls. Roars. Men baiting
their beast. On and on and on. And later the bear raises its great
arm. The paw with a broken razor. And it looks as if it's making
a gesture — it wasn't: only weariness or pain or the sun or
brushing away the sweat — but it looks as if it's making a
gesture to the crowd. Asking for one sign of grace, one nod.
And the crowd roars, for more blood, more pain, more beasts
huddled together, tearing flesh and treading in living blood.

JUDITH [*Shakespeare's Daughter*]: You don't like sport. Some bears
dance.

SHAKESPEARE: In London they blinded a bear. Called Harry Hunks.
The sport was to bait it with whips. Slash, slash. It couldn't see
but it could hear. It grabbed the whips. Caught some of them.
Broke them. Slashed back at the men. Slash, slash. The men
stood round in a circle slashing at it. It was blind but they still
chained it to the ground. Slash, slash. Then they sent an ape
round on a horse. A thin hairy man or a child. You could see the
pale skin under its arm when it jumped. Its teeth. The dogs tore
it to pieces. The crowd howled. London. The queen cheered
them on in shrill latin. The virgin often watched blood. Her
father baited bears on the Thames. From boat to boat, slash,
slash. They fell in and fought men in the water. He was the man
in a madhouse who says I'm king but he had a country to say it
in.

This is immediately contrasted with the peace of the river:

SHAKESPEARE: ...I watched the fish jump for flies. Then a swan flew
by me up the river. On a straight line just over the water. A
woman in a white dress running along an empty street. Its neck
was rocking like a wave. I heard its breath when it flew by.
Sighing. The white swan and the dark water...

Writing such as this is more than just powerful language for it provides
a sudden illumination of the purpose of the play. Bond provides a
frame of reference which, whilst beyond the audience's immediate
experience, brings them into contact with the world of the play; what is
happening in modern urban life is not that far removed from the
description of Jacobean London. Without any artificial device there is
a shift from the exact work of imagination in recreating Shakespeare's
last days to that of premonition; the shiver which this scene provokes
comes from the sudden understanding that Bond is writing about us.
He is asking: How can *you* cope with the society that surrounds you?
How can you bear its pain?

But the very power of this scene also acts, if not to deny the logical possibility of Bond's general argument, then certainly to diminish its practical significance. What is being described is urban degradation, a mass of undifferentiated hatred and aggression overwhelming everything in its search for blood. It may still be possible to assert that this hatred is not innate, that it is learned. But the apparent ease with which such lessons are acquired makes such observations redundant; bare survival is the only possibility and even that becomes less and less likely. Even as Shakespeare speaks, a letter comes from Ben Jonson to remind him that retreat is impossible, that messengers will always arrive to bring him the news and that, inevitably, the corrosion of the town will find its way to his garden, his symbol of refuge.

It is clear that Bond expects an audience to arrive at *Bingo* with at least an outline understanding of English history; large parts of the play lose their detailed impact without it. It would have been just possible to have seen the first production of Shakespeare's *King Lear* and, in old age, to have witnessed the Putney Debates at the end of the English Revolution. *Bingo*, in its moment of history, is set roughly between these two events, the first of which in one of its dimensions is concerned with the breakdown of an old political order, the second marking the possibility of a new one. The gulf of political change between them is huge, perhaps as great as anything which has occurred in modern European history, and it coincides with a shift of language almost as large as between the poetry of Shakespeare and that of Milton. *Bingo* acknowledges this gulf in a curious fashion by separating out the language of the Old Man's Son from that of the other characters:

> I'll go away — where there's still space. I want t'be free. I cry for that. Sometoime when I'm out in the fields I climb a tall tree an' set stride the top an' cry. Let me be free. Liberty. Where no one stand 'tween me an' my god, no one listen when I raise the song a praise, an' I walk by god's side with curtesy an' fear nothin', as candid loike a child. So us'll go away. Us plans is laid. Us'll take nowt bar bible an' plough…

The language is quite distinct. The other characters tend to speak with modern rhythms. But the archaism is anachronistic. It points forward from the epoch of the play to the speech of the Ranters and ditch preachers of the 1640s, the voices of an authentic popular movement. The Son stands out both in language and declared purpose as the agent of social change opposed to the technocratic capitalism of Combe. He is obviously meant to allow at least a glimpse of what is to come. Yet Bond allows the character to move away in a cloud of ambiguity, making his final statement of Puritan intent at the very moment when Shakespeare is swallowing a handful of pills to kill himself. The possibility of change is opened up and then apparently denied. The Son in his accidental patricide is shown to be no less violent and wanton than his oppressors. Shakespeare at least dies with self-knowledge. The Son departs with his illusions intact, a doomed opponent of the new capitalism. His father was the only one able to evade the responsibility of his time because he was the 'natural', the old man returned to childhood by a wartime injury. He alone had the residual power to relate directly to nature:

> ...I like snow. Yont yo'? Then they rabbits all come t' see. You charm a rabbit by your play. They set theyselfs round in a circle. Heads on one side. I grabs one an' broke his neck for'n...

But his simpleness in the end offers no way out. He is implicated in the death of a young vagrant woman by his pursuit of sexual pleasure and finally shot by his son. This casual event occupies an odd and disturbing place in *Bingo*, picking up Bond's interest in the Oedipus story and his observations on the corrupting aspect of necessary armed rebellion that are found in *Lear*. It is the final closing off of even the most stunted path to survival, that of returning to childhood. It also acts as the symbol of closure for social progress but dramatically it carries very little weight. It is a dreadful act, tossed away on purpose off-stage as something out of focus.

This passage between generations is something which recurs in Bond's work, from *The Pope's Wedding* to *Summer* (1982). It occupies a central place in *The Narrow Road to the Deep North* (1968), *Lear*, and *The Bundle*, as well as in *Bingo*. It is always unresolved, always problematic, and reflects Bond's continuing preoccupation with how society does or does not change. Bond is not concerned with families as such, yet children constantly appear as symbols of the future and representatives of a new society. Family involvement is often seen as an encumbrance — Shakespeare is hounded at the edge of death by his daughter, who is anxious to settle the inheritance. The central point of Bond's concern with children is really how they can differ from their parents and, therefore, how new societies can be created from old. Are they just reproductions or can they change qualitatively? And if so, then how?

Despite this interest in change, Bond's plays up to *The Fool* are notable for their lack of any sense of real social movement, even when describing a moment of great development — Lear's overthrow, or the land enclosures in *Bingo* and *The Fool*, for example. They present society as a treadmill; compare Scopey's retreat to the hermit's hut in *The Pope's Wedding* with Cordelia's assumption of power in *Lear*. Both on quite different scales suggest an inevitable individual and social repetition of past events which scarcely needs explanation. The new generation simply assumes the mantle of the old.

Similarly, Clare's journey from his poor background to the asylum, torn by the tensions between his poetry and the pressures of his public who are his class oppressors, seems to be inexorable. Bond underlines this stationary, if dialectical, view of society by a curious historical elision between *The Fool* and *Bingo*, which are separated by two hundred years yet paired in almost every respect, from the common concern with the artist's withdrawal to the same precipitating mark of technological progress — land enclosure. Bond emphasizes this continuity through the archaic feel of the opening mummers' scene in *The Fool* but at the same time he reflects back on the difference in epoch by making *Bingo* the more dynamic. Clare is a victim, Shakespeare is not, and *The Fool* appears almost as a coda to its predecessor with much less savagery and urgency. However, the two plays contain the same elements of urban cruelty, rural uprising and repression, with death or the retreat into madness as the inevitable fate for the sensitive artist. The only real exception to this in either play (and it forms at best an ambiguous exception) is the character of the Old Man's Son in *Bingo*. Bond's first break with this view comes in the second part of *The Woman* (1978), a play which he began at the same time as *The Fool*. It is his female *Lear* on a world historical scale and it looks forward to *The Bundle*.

The trilogy of plays, *Lear, Bingo, The Fool*, forms the most potent series in postwar British drama. The relentless circularity and hatred of technical progress, with even the vague rural alternatives of *Lear* wiped out in the following plays, brought Bond close to the edge of intellectual repetitiveness, as shown in the uneasy, symbol-ridden libretto *We Come to the River* (1976).

Bond's distinctive virtue is his intellectual progress; and finally in *The Bundle* he managed to write what is still the only one of his plays in which both political and dramatic intent seem to be wholly fused. It is also one of the few postwar British plays to sound a convincing note about the possibilities of social as opposed to individual change rather than its inevitable decline and decay. Using a single symbol, a river, for both the power of nature and the possibilities of human technology, Bond allows the issue of human choice to be an open one in terms of effect as well as of moral virtue. Subtitled *New Narrow Road to the Deep North*, the play takes as its starting point the same incident as in the earlier play, *The Narrow Road to the Deep North:* the 17th-century Japanese poet Basho refusing to take in an abandoned baby and instead setting off on a journey to seek enlightenment.

In *The Bundle* the baby abandoned by its parents on the river bank is adopted by a ferryman. This extra burden on his family proves sufficient to drive them to destitution so severe that he finally sells the half-grown child into slavery. The child, Wang, grows into a man who, when similarly faced with the choice of taking in an abandoned child, takes the other path of moral choice and throws it into the river. By uniting the dispossessed, Wang manages to create an army capable of overthrowing the ruler of the river and to set up a just society — at least to try; that much is left to the future. The Wang of the earlier play becomes a tyrant; this Wang becomes a revolutionary leader, but the price of socially effective action — the death of a child — is high in individual terms. Bond, however, has not just moved from changing an oppressor into a liberator. He takes up the theme of Cordelia and examines it anew. In *Lear* the would-be liberator turns into the new oppressor but in *The Bundle* Bond is not content to take an easy way out and simply reverse the values. The enlightenment of Wang, who faced the same situation of abandoning the child as did Basho, is seen as coming through collective action and is contrasted with the individual and delusory enlightenment of the poet. Wang's journey belongs also to the peasants whose enlightenment comes from working within their technological possiblities to bring social and production relations into line with their moral code. But Wang had to make that choice to organize; he could have suffered the same degradation as Basho.

After the murder of the child, Wang is next seen in a situation of shell shock common to many of Bond's main characters:

> ...I ran through swamps, crying for seven days. I saw the rich prey on the poor. The poor prey on themselves. An old woman. She wore knitted mittens. Her hands were like a squirrel's paws — holding an empty bowl. She knelt by the pilgrims' path and said: 'Give — heaven will bless you.' What heaven would bless such pilgrims when it hadn't blessed her?

He comes out of this despair to lead a revolution, but the stress is not on tactics; the play shows virtually nothing of how the revolution takes place. The focus is again moral, but in terms of its social effect. What will the new world be like? Nobody knows. The river, which is the life of the village, can also be its death, yet under Wang and the new order the flooding is prevented. However, this too costs a life — there is no utopia. Wang's closing remarks seem to sum up the playwright's intention:

> ...We live in a time of great change. It is easy to find monsters — and as easy to find heroes. To judge rightly what is good — to choose between good and evil — that is all it is to be human.

The dramatic excitement of *The Bundle* derives from the finely balanced nature of the choices to which particular characters are exposed and to the specific if unforeseeable consequences of their decisions. The creation of the social revolution requires that a child be saved and that a child be killed — both decisions arrived at with full understanding of the burdens involved. The killing or saving of a child is given its full weight in terms of individual choice. But the necessity to kill or save a child can be given a general symbolic meaning; for the oppressed to adopt an immediate kindness and charity in an unjust society means acquiring all the inertia generated as a means of oppression by the status quo. It is also clear that rejection of such charities exacts a final cost which is the embracing of necessary action, even armed struggle, which will take its penalty of human pain. The play is a learning process in which Bond establishes the impossibility of ever fully knowing the outcome of particular decisions; political actions have to be undertaken with the possibility that they will not work out as expected. The assumption of *Lear* is that nothing righteous can be achieved in the face of overwhelming power beyond ineffective individual moral certainty; the philosophy of *The Bundle* is that individual moral certainty is never possible but that positive social change is an imperative and that social morality may be constructed and tested. Rather than excluding the individual from the problem of balancing choices, it makes those choices the more important to make.

The power of this change in Bond can be seen in the speech when Wang contemplates the abandoned baby, picking it up and putting it down again; the audience does not know whether he will keep the child or kill it. When he finally, suddenly, makes his choice, a powerful dramatic device encapsulates all the potential of the theatre; as he hurls the bundle into the audience he holds on to a corner of the sheet: the strip of white cloth flutters down as a child is killed out of free choice — an act which one understands and with which one may agree or disagree. It is a perfect dramatic moment and a precise and extreme challenge to an audience's own ability to make judgements.

All of Bond's plays up to *The Bundle* mine similar seams — the nature of society and the way its culture shapes human beings, with its violence being passed on to the individual. They consider the oppositions of madness and sanity, of town and country, of nature and nurture, of ruler and ruled. They constantly resort for dramatic effect to mystical elements — looking east for purposes of abstraction, the use of gnomic, clipped language, and of ghosts, naturals, or innocents — yet there is an equally strong sense of material and practical elements of technology causing rather than preventing suffering. There is also a concern in the face of this with the nature of the artist, of myth and of ideology.

These obsessions are refashioned in *Restoration* (1981), 'a pastoral' set in 18th-century England — or (to quote Bond) 'another place at another time' — in which the standard fare of the period drama is turned on its head. It is a new departure for Bond which represents the basic shift that began in *The Woman* and came to fruition in *The Bundle*. The new principle is to put underlying political purpose firmly in charge but it also reveals Bond's often underrated sense of humour.

In *The Woman* the past weighs heavily on the present. Bond undermines the classical substance of our contemporary myths and shows that history is the history of painful struggle. With *The Bundle* this is taken up through communal efforts to break with the past and build for a new future. Here Bond achieves an integrated political aesthetic that he has not been able to repeat as successfully. In *The Worlds* (1979) he moves on to look at tactics. He returns for the first time since *Saved* to contemporary Britain and sets up three areas of life which interact but scarcely meet: the bosses of a factory, its striking workers and a group of left-wing terrorists who use kidnapping as a weapon to force the bosses to settle the strike.

It is clear where Bond's sympathies lie. This is a play about answers and only the workers are allowed any leverage on this front. Yet for all their worthiness and representative class role they are as a group inescapably dull and dramatically static. Bond seems to be unable to find any place to move them intellectually and is concerned not to use any false dramatic way of developing them. The dramatic interest of the play resides in the interaction between the bosses and the terrorists. The crucial problem is that Bond will not allow the workers to denounce the terrorists. They discuss the problem and are allowed differences of opinion but in the end it is the intellectual preference of the playwright that determines their decision. Bond seems to want the workers at least to understand the terrorists. Yet it is clear that, outside the world of the play, workers generally condemn random kidnapping and extortion; the intellectual case Bond makes for the principle of their refusing to do so is threadbare. The 'poetic' and the 'intellectual' seem out of phase this time.

The meaning of the past for the future, and again that persistent theme of the generations, reappears in *Summer* (1982). But this time the use of long speeches to make a point on meaning and perception is not particularly effective. *Summer*, set abstractly in Eastern Europe, though by the sea, seems to have been written to serve a predetermined purpose rather than the investigation of a process. Yet, even in this rather unsatisfactory piece, there is an odd and disquieting moment as though once again the material of the play is spreading out in ways which Bond cannot fully control intellectually. Most of the play is devoted to a generation which passed through the Second World War and who recount and relive that experience through the prism of class and privilege. At the very end the two young lovers, until then subsidiary characters, suddenly emerge in emphasis. All the time the elders are talking of the past, particularly of atrocities in the war, there is, waiting, an obvious dramatic turn — the moment in which the sins of the parents are visited on the children. But it never happens, at least not in any obvious way. The lovers are affectionate but quite distanced from each other. When the woman leaves to have a baby there is no question of the lovers staying together; perhaps they will visit, perhaps not. They are refusing entry to the passions of their parents, even if the price is to have almost no passion at all.

In *The Worlds* Bond allows contemporary youth the response of rage. In *Summer*, as though by an afterthought, he allows them the possibility of cool and measured withdrawal, surviving by keeping society at a distance. It is the first time such an option has entered his plays, like a specific observation of his times which he has to admit dramatically but with which he cannot cope intellectually.

Contemporary reality is both an inspiration and a problem for Bond and the embracing of explicit socialist philosophy becomes curiously contradictory. His political impulse is toward the actual, yet the dramatic realization takes him back inside his head. The workers in *The Worlds* are not convincing as social representatives; the new, possibly socialist, society of *Summer* is vague and even mystical. In his extremely ambitious *The War Plays* (1985) Bond confronts the most dramatic political issue of the age: nuclear destruction. But his view of a devastated future, however powerful poetically, has little connection with the present.

Bond's vision remains universal: the societies we create are our own, distinct from the past but unavoidably shaped by it; our children are both ourselves but also new individuals. These paradoxes of human existence are Bond's chosen themes and they will always escape resolution. That he continues to search for new ways of understanding them and presenting them with such enormous dramatic power is what makes him one of Britain's greatest living playwrights.

CHAPTER TEN

Howard Brenton:
Mad Dogs and Englishmen

Howard Brenton is a playwright whose career was born out of the most decisive break point in postwar British theatre. Up to the mid-1960s, whatever the departure in content or style, the mode of playwriting and the whole production process had not significantly changed. Breaches in this order might have occurred in particular cases, but only Joan Littlewood at Theatre Workshop had tried to break the overall pattern.

Brenton's arrival at the Brighton Combination in 1968 coincided with a turning point in the process of playwriting that had been prepared by Theatre Workshop but which went beyond their work. This was not a moment of his making but one that he used to full advantage. In *Gum and Goo*, to take an early example, an archetypal 'knock-up' play produced in eight days in 1969 for a teachers' conference, there is a point when the actors switch on hand-lamps in a blackout, illuminating their faces from below. It works with a change in the dialogue that shifts the whole nature of the play from children playing together into an unexpected and disturbing area of fantasy. It is a remarkably effective piece of theatre, worked originally on a budget of thirty shillings. Whilst a writer sitting alone could conceive of such an effect, including precise stage-directions, and then have sufficient control over the director to ensure that they were carried through, it is obvious that such a conception comes much more easily from someone who is part of a production team.

When a writer actively participates in play production, not just as a peripheral adviser on hand during rehearsals, but as an integral member of a working group, the nature of the product is changed, particularly in terms of actors' commitment and style of presentation. Much of the work written in this way is not preserved. It serves its immediate purpose of entertainment, education or politicization, and is then discarded. Relatively few such pieces are published as texts. Nevertheless, as a process for developing a writer it opens up important new areas.

Brenton has moved a long way from the workshop style of Brighton

Combination and the touring Portable Theatre (1968-72). Although he continued to collaborate — *Deeds* (1978) with Trevor Griffiths, Ken Campbell and David Hare, *A Short Sharp Shock* (1980) with Tony Howard and *Sleeping Policemen* (1983) with Tunde Ikoli — his main thrust has been to create Shakespearean-sized plays for large, mainstream theatres. His versions of Brecht's *The Life of Galileo* (1980) and Büchner's *Danton's Death* (1982) as well as his original plays — *Weapons of Happiness* (1976), *The Romans in Britain* (1980) and *The Genius* (1983) — all express his own feeling that the alternative dream has faded. His collaboration with David Hare on *Pravda* (1985) is, with a rather double-edged irony, the sharpest expression of this.

Perhaps more than any other playwright who has made a similar progression, Brenton retains in his work the marks of that initial training, not just in certain techniques — fast cutting, the interlocking of scenes, use of sudden shock to create effect — but also in the sensuous nature of the theatre that he creates. He can bring on a dumbshow with Christ and the Grand Inquisitor followed by Stalin; he can call for the interior of the London Planetarium to be represented on stage; and he can produce out of a wedding cake a tap-dancer in strip tassles and red heart motifs.

The strong poetic feel to much of his writing enables him to conjure up the images of entire societies. In *The Churchill Play* (1974), *The Romans in Britain* and, to a lesser extent, *Weapons of Happiness*, the language and the imagery work with the grain of the play to evoke society at large even if presented as a microcosm. In one of his most successfully realized plays, *Epsom Downs* (1977), with its evocative and original image of horses who can talk (played by naked actors), Brenton manages to summon the feel of Derby Day through a range of techniques that evolved from his collaboration with the Joint Stock Company in their visits to Epsom and in their collective use of that experience in rehearsal.

Brenton has an epic, public style that is direct and hard and he has developed it enormously since the early plays. *Christie in Love* (1969), which he wrote for Portable Theatre, opens with a policeman digging. He recites a limerick:

> ...There was a young girl named Heather
> Whose cunt was made out of leather
> She made an odd noise
> For attracting the boys
> By flapping the edges together.

The intention is to shock and to jolt the audience out of its initial composure. But there is little more than that; the play lacks any precise focus for its moral rage.

The language Brenton uses does not always effectively match his purpose. In *Sore Throats* (1979), a play about the break-up of a marriage, the intimacy seems at odds with his epic vein until, late in the second half, the husband returns after an unsuccessful attempt to create a new life in Canada. In a long monologue he describes the birth of his child on the roadside after a car accident. It is a stunning evocation but out of keeping with the rest of the play, and it goes nowhere. The carry-cot, in which the husband says he has his son, turns out to contain only bricks. The symbol is empty and rings hollow against the density of the style.

Brenton's bravery has always involved taking on new areas of investigation but he remains at his best with his main theme — nationality and the concept of Englishness as a historical, emotional and political construction. He has returned again and again to this, from the dislocating styles of the disturbing *Christie in Love* and the sprawling irreverence of *Scott of the Antarctic* (1971) to the ambitious but flawed *The Romans in Britain*. In between, in *Brassneck* (1973), written with David Hare, *The Churchill Play, Epsom Downs* and *Weapons of Happiness*, Brenton continued to explore the nature of the English.

In *Scott of the Antarctic* Brenton uses ridicule. The play was written as part of the Bradford Arts Festival for performance on an ice-rink, with the Bradford Ice-Skating Club taking the parts of various extras. King Edward, tormented by his Victorian (in all senses of the word) childhood, throws a tantrum at the sight of part of the globe that is not coloured red. God, deciding that the British need to be taught a lesson, ordains an expedition. The Scott expedition is played out by a group of actors, without skates, stumbling in knockabout comedy towards the centre of the rink. At the last minute, Amundsen, driven by the Devil on a motorbike, zooms in and plants the Norwegian flag. The British stumble back, go mad and die. It is a relatively slight piece of work, apart from the bravado of the production idea and its alarming prescience. (A biography of Scott written a decade later suggests that the members of the expedition may indeed have gone almost mad due to vitamin deficiency and were certainly organized with a lunatic incompetence.) Yet the play contains most of the seeds of the later work. Its concern is to discover why the English are as they are and to analyse the moral decay that Brenton comes to see as the disease of England. (Brenton, along with David Hare, with whom he shares a concern for the roots of national experience, largely ignores any Scottish, Welsh or other national interest within Britain.)

Brenton's first really large-scale work came with *Brassneck*, written with David Hare. The play follows the progress of a mysterious entrepreneur, Bagley, and his family, as he arrives in a Midlands town and proceeds to tie up all its institutions in a web of interlocking corruption. It is not a fully successful play, mainly because it loses Bagley, its most interesting character, too early, but it is fast, funny and tough and takes on one of the great scandals of British life — its largely unspoken but ingrained corruption. The play's failure is to say, 'This is what it is like' rather than 'This is why it is so'. The all-embracing nature and uniformity of the corruption defies analysis and implies that it is in the nature of all people. Ironically, *Brassneck* is an example of David Hare's point that it is not enough to show that 'Eden was on Benzedrine throughout the Suez crisis' or that 'Tory M.P.s liaise with crooked architects and bent offshore bankers' if the audience replies, 'Well, we do know now; and we don't believe it will ever change. And knowing may well not affect what we think'.*

Both Brenton and Hare were clearly concerned to move beyond the kind of understanding contained in *Brassneck;* Hare moved on with *Plenty* (1978) and Brenton's next piece was *The Churchill Play.* The divergence in style between these is sharp but their original concerns were quite close: how history comes to be shaped, both in the objective sense of the sequence of events and in the more crucial area of subsequent interpretation.

The Churchill Play starts from the premise that in 1945 something was lost in Britain, possibly a chance to create socialism, certainly the opportunity to break away from the old patterns. It assumes that what was perpetrated instead was a gigantic fraud, a society based on myths, one of them being that Churchill was a great war-leader loved and supported by the British people. The play begins with an immediate and characteristic Brenton theatrical coup. We see Churchill's coffin lying in state attended by four guards. Ghoulishly he taps on the inside of the coffin and rises up asking for a light for his cigar. The set is collapsed and is revealed as the staging for a play being rehearsed by the inmates of a British concentration camp some time in the near future. It is a brilliant example of the kind of effect Brenton used with the bicycle-lamps of *Gum and Goo* or the dead murderer Christie rising up from a heap of newspapers at the beginning of *Christie in Love.*

Such effects are more than bravura stagecraft, however. In *The Churchill Play* they establish immediately the idea of a myth which lies behind reality and the feeling that the solid and unpleasant presence of the camp has been moulded by those manufactured images of the past. The opening supplies the unspoken comment that things are like this because this is how people believe their history to have been. Some of that history is real, grim and very much to the point; an army sergeant reminds a liberal army doctor, whom he suspects of being soft on the prisoners, that he was trained in the streets of Belfast and, later, in

---

* From a lecture at King's College, Cambridge, published in *Licking Hitler* (Faber & Faber, 1978).

industrial riots in England. But also there is history as myth — such as
'The Churchill Play' being presented by the inmates for a parliamentary delegation to the camp. This counterpoint between myth and
reality runs through the whole play. The key point is when the two
overlap. One of the inmates rehearses a Londoner cheerily shouting
'We can take it' to Churchill as he tours the bombed capital. The
inmate then says that it was not like that at all. What the man really said
to Churchill was:

> We can take it... But we just might give it back to you one day... And
> in his book on war he wrote it down as... give it 'em back.

The play hangs a little uneasily between its separate intentions: the
immediate pain of the camp is very pressing and the writing contains
some fine imagery, but the ending is arbitrary and implausible. The
inmates' final attempted breakout comes as rather a desperate throw,
doomed to failure.

This unease is the biggest problem with *The Churchill Play*, and one
that runs through many of Brenton's other pieces. He invites a political
understanding but defines it in emotional terms; the underlying perspective remains imprecise. Yet Brenton is clearly on the Left, both in
his own eyes and in those of the world. He has written many plays
dealing with contemporary left-wing politics in which there is no doubt
whose side he takes — *Magnificence* (1973), *Weapons of Happiness, A
Short Sharp Shock, Thirteenth Night* (1981).

While Brenton reflects the flavour of some Left politics, it is difficult
to say exactly what his politics are beyond the umbrella label of
socialist. In *Epsom Downs* he manages to freeze Britain's class society
into a single frame but, however memorable the play's political references, such as the appearance of the ghost of the suffragette Emily
Davison, they represent no more than a simple and assertive radicalism. The politics of *Thirteenth Night* and *Weapons of Happiness* do not
touch life with any of the assurance of *Epsom Downs;* this makes the
criticism of the Left as being too far removed from ordinary people
more a criticism of the plays themselves. The truthfulness of Brenton's
view is limited, for example, by the nature of the Left coup in *Thirteenth Night.* There is no popular pressure behind the takeover and this
places the play in a world of paranoia that inflates and distorts just one
aspect of the Left-Right struggle inside the Labour Party. Calling it a
'dream play' may reflect Brenton's awareness of this. But the tension
between dream and reality is not dramatically resolved. Similarly, in
Weapons of Happiness, which links the experience of a South London
factory occupation with that of central European Stalinism, the young
workers are unconvincing and the comparison falls apart. The banality
of the anti-Thatcher polemic in *A Short Sharp Shock* reveals the basic
weakness of Brenton as a political analyst. His strength lies in the

fictional worlds he creates when they comment on, rather than represent, contemporary life.

Looking at the plays, it seems that Brenton's political views are those
of many whose ideas were shaped by the student upheavals of the
1960s — anti-Stalinist but, deeper than that, predominantly individualistic; militant but romantic. Standing on a chair about to hang
Christie, an inspector bellows to the audience:

> Society cannot allow the fucking of handbags. Pussycats. Dead
> women. What would happen if we all went right ahead, according to
> desire, fucking all? Bleeding anarchy...

In *Weapons of Happiness*, the Londoner Janice, who calls herself,
confusingly, both a Communist and Trotskyite, says to Frank, the old
Communist who escaped the Czech treason trials of 1952:

> JANICE: Well, we're going to change this fucking country.
> FRANK: Nothing will change in England. Decay, yes. Change, no.

Like many of his contemporaries, Brenton tries to combine a commitment to socialism with a more easily grasped libertarianism, and
many of his plays centrally concern the points of conflict between these
two great currents. This is perhaps most clearly articulated in his
adaptation of *Danton's Death*, but the tensions between principle and
realpolitik, between individual desire and collective need, inform all
his work.

His perspective seems to require a break-out from the channels of
traditional political activity to achieve or at least foreshadow an immediate and comprehensive liberation, both personal and political —
as a character in *Thirteenth Night* puts it, 'a politics to end politics'.
Brenton does not attempt to present clear-cut solutions that do not
exist in the real political world but he does on occasion insert heightened moments at the end of his plays to offer a resolution that is
undercut by reality. In *The Churchill Play* it is the disaster of a futile
escape; in *Weapons of Happiness* it is the sentimentality of the fleeing
workers finding a disused farm before sloping back to city life; in
Thirteenth Night it is the burnt-out bunker before snapping out of the
nightmare.

More successful in its ending, though fraught with the same problems when dealing with contemporary politics, is *The Romans in
Britain*. This work goes deeper than *The Churchill Play* (of which it is a
direct descendant) in looking at nationality, and in particular at national myth. Brenton creates an old and forgotten society at the time of
Julius Caesar's incursion into Britain in 55 BC. It is not a particularly
pleasant or prosperous society. The lives of its inhabitants are brutish
and short. Strangers are treated with suspicion and usually killed.
Slaves are taken to perform basic manual labour and are regarded as
sub-human. But there is a pattern of life which is self-regulating and,

within its limits, successful. It can maintain within itself a body of knowledge that defines each group of villages as some kind of integrated wider community of people — a nation if you like. Inside that body of knowledge the nation is secure. It grows food in certain ways, respects kinship and certain kinds of national alliance, kills all strangers except for traders in wine and iron, and conducts negotiations with other nations according to particular rules. It makes war on other nations, also within certain rules, and supports a priesthood. It is the priests who are the custodians of national culture and knowledge and who transcend nations, forming an international elite capable of exerting a form of international supervision. Brenton defines a very full and complete world within which there is considerable security.

Into this world there comes an alien body: the Roman army. This force is described in terms which betray an almost supernatural fear:

> First Envoy: I have seen the Roman army.
> Understand its nature. No you can't, I can't.
> They have come from the other side of the world.
> And they are one. One whole...
> I know your Grandfather hated my Grandfather —
> That he was an invader too. Invader. The word.
> Outsider, outcast, who came on your fields. As that did.
> [*He points to the sacrifice.*]
> But the Romans are different. They are — [*He gestures, trying to find the word. He fails. He tries again.*] A nation. Nation. What? A great family? No. A people? No. They are one, huge thing.

This envoy has come to enlist the help of the tribe. He fails and is turned away. The point, however, is not that he has failed to convince the people about the Romans; it turns out that at least the elders understand full well that he is telling the truth. What is crucial is that it is impossible to *understand* the Romans within the frame of knowledge that the nation possesses; they have to be treated as though they are just another band of cattle-thieves. To understand their nature or, at least, to acknowledge that understanding, spells doom just as surely as ignoring it. There is a beautiful and chilling moment when three men of the tribe meet three Romans. Unafraid, one of the men curses the Romans in stylized ritual, unfolding the nature of the death that he will bring to them. Then, not even comprehending the language let alone knowing the fear that such a curse should bring to them, the Romans casually kill him. The one that they spare is a Druid who speaks a little Latin. He is brought before Caesar, who questions him, then orders him to be turned free in the forest with an image of Venus tied around his neck, knowing that the image alone is enough to defile him. The Druid understands that what he has been touched by is more than a simple force. It is an area of knowledge that will destroy his people as surely as swords, for it is a knowledge that cannot be sustained within their own mythology:

> They've struck a spring in the ground beneath your feet, it will never stop, it will flood everything. The filthy water of Roman ways.
>
> They'll even take away death as you know it. No sweet fields, rich woods beyond the grave. You'll go to a Roman underworld of torture, a black river, rocks of fire.

The play falls apart somewhat in the second half when it becomes concerned with the subject of Ireland, which it hardly explores at all. The Irish characters are barely sketched — they are not even caricatures, just ciphers — whilst the view presented of Ireland's politics is difficult to penetrate. Nor is the character of the English officer, who commits a kind of ritual suicide to expiate the faults of his race, a great deal better. He is not much advanced beyond Captain Scott, an English upper-class eccentric who is mad largely because he is an upper-class English eccentric. The halves of the play hinge around this character and the weakness of his portrayal means that they do not ever quite fit. The officer wants to return to the roots of his race and seems to believe that the contemporary Irish have held on to their own version of those roots. They therefore have to be respected, almost revered. But the crucual point is that those roots are constructed social myths necessary for the survival of a specific social formation. There may be an endlessly revived national sentiment, something recycled in different guises, but it all remains a myth, a disguise for the real functioning mechanism of society. It is also, Brenton suggests, not difficult to create such myths at the right moment of change in a society.

The Churchill Play explores one specific myth, namely the creation of Churchill as the British super-hero. *The Romans in Britain* attempts to broaden the scene to encompass both creation and breakdown. In scenes that interlock with those set in contempory Ireland, we are shown a society breaking down after the withdrawal of the Romans. The old society is gone forever; an old man who tries to recover a statue of a pagan god is killed by his daughter out of a fear at revival of the old customs. Finally there remains a small group of refugees cast adrift with no family and no community, in a world that is falling around their ears. A refugee cook, caught up in the aftermath of the Saxon invasion of post-Roman Britain, decides to change his trade to poet for which, optimistically, it is assumed there is always a demand. He invents a poem about a king:

> 1st Cook: Actually he was a king who never was. His Government was the people of Britain. His peace was as common as rain or sun. His law was as natural as grass growing in a meadow.

And there never was a government, or a peace, or a law like that.

His sister murdered his father. His wife was unfaithful. He died by the treachery of his best friend.

And when he was dead, the King who never was and the Government that never was — were mourned. And remembered. Bitterly.

And thought of as a golden age, lost and yet to come.

MORGANA: What was his name?

1ST COOK: Any old name dear. [*to Second Cook*] What was his name?

2ND COOK: Right. Er — any old name.

Arthur?

Arthur?

The cook's beautiful speech provides an ending that brings together the whole theme of the play and presents it as a single haunting question. Why do we, the English, choose such myths, filled with remorse and failure?

Brenton's plays have always been like grenades tossed over a parapet into the audience. The vivid images and sudden changes of dramatic direction are designed to keep one disturbed and on edge. The effect, though sometimes miscalculated, is never less than bold. Brenton has come a long way from the thirty shilling budget of *Gum and Goo,* and he shows an uncanny ability to cope with the English theatrical system. He is, one expects, a survivor.

CHAPTER ELEVEN

David Hare: 'Plenty' and the Politics of Despair

It is usually artificial to impose on writers the influence of the exact decades in which they write. There is a constant overlapping divergence so that simple categories such as being 'of the 1950s' or of any other arbitrary period are misleading. Nevertheless, even with such a stricture, there was a particular wave of writing which began at the end of the 1960s and which followed a distinct trajectory in the following decade. This was connected with a new sense of purpose within the theatre. Writers were not just putting new wine into old bottles; they were trying to break the old bottles as well. It was a moment of political rupture, of total disillusionment with the existing practices and a sudden enthusiasm for new ones. This shift was reflected not only in the working practices of playwrights; it was also seen in the changing content of plays and in their general moral stance.

Within this context David Hare can be called the specific playwright of the 1970s, from *Slag* (1970) to *Dreams of Leaving* (1980), with this latter play acting as an epitaph to the decade. But beyond chronology there is a particular pattern to his work that marks the passing of that decade, with its growing disengagement, corruption and, finally, bitter nostalgia, in a way that is mirrored in no other contemporary writer.

In 1971 Hare was the trigger for a collaboration with Howard Brenton, Brian Clark, Trevor Griffiths, Stephen Poliakoff, Hugh Stoddart and Snoo Wilson on the play *Lay-By*, a symbolic act of moral disgust that was written to shock and to defy conventional criticism. It was presented by Portable Theatre which Hare had founded with Tony Bicât and which, in 1972, produced another collectively created play of equal savagery: *England's Ireland.* (This was written by Howard Brenton, Tony Bicât, Brian Clark, David Edgar, Francis Fuchs and Snoo Wilson as well as David Hare.) Soon, however, Hare's first major play, *Knuckle* (1974), a critical and commercial success about the corruption and decay of suburban life cast as a neat pastiche of a conventional thriller, was sitting in the West End. The following year Hare helped set up, with David Aukin, William Gaskill and Max

Stafford-Clark, the touring Joint Stock Theatre Company, which was given a radical image by its production of Hare's *Fanshen* (1975). By 1976 he was gracing one of the National Theatre's large stages as director of Howard Brenton's *Weapons of Happiness* and in 1978 he directed his own play, *Plenty*, there. Cast by many critics in the role of prime spokesman for his generation of left-wing playwrights, Hare is nevertheless something of a loner whose plays seem distanced from the social and political forces which he acknowledges as crucial in shaping the world he is writing about.

Despite the shift in social setting and a new-found sophistication — including his appointment as an associate director of the National Theatre, in charge of his own acting company — Hare has stayed true to the underlying vision of *Lay-By*, in which mortuary attendants play sex-games with the body of a drug addict while philosophizing about the starving in India.

> [*The bucket has got blood in it. They wash the body in blood and put it in the sling. They hoist the body up with a pulley and lower it into the bin.*]
> DOUG: Makes you philosophical.
> [*Dick lights a fag.*]
> Take mice.
> DICK: You tell me.
> DOUG: So they put these perfectly normal mice in this cage see? And they leave them. Just feed 'em and leave 'em. And they multiply and die and multiply and some more die. And the number grows. And grows. And there isn't enough room anymore. They can't turn round. Take proper exercise. Tripping over each other's shit. And then it all starts to fall apart. Anarchy, chaos. Total irreversible breakdown. Nothing. Void. The whole thing.
> DICK: We're not animals.
> DOUG: I dunno. I sometimes catch myself sniffing around. If you get my drift.

Even with the fluency and the vigour in the writing it is easy enough to dismiss *Lay-By* as typical university review material in a new role of social anger. Nevertheless, a group of playwrights of great importance in British theatre in the 1970s started the decade by putting their names to a piece that views Britain as a landscape of such brutality and corruption that it is bereft even of small human emotions. In a nearly contemporary play, *Bingo* (1973), Edward Bond asks how it is possible for an artist to live or stay sane in a society of unredeemed violence. The writers of *Lay-By* have no time for this particular dilemma; in such societies as Britain has become even survival is a matter of dehumanized and random processing.

There is a clear gulf existing between this 'generation' of playwrights and those before them, which opens along a moral rather than a political dimension. The social vision of a Bond or Mercer may be bleak but it never completely excludes the possibility of moral choice. Much of the work in the 1960s had the emphasis of such choice as a main feature. For Hare and his collaborators that possibility of choice is excluded; there is no time for working out the subtleties of moral gestures. The hallmark of their contemporary society is corruption, both at the specific material level and, more basically, in the social and moral lives of individuals. This is spelt out in *Brassneck* (1973), written with Howard Brenton. Hare writes about survival in the face of this encroaching corruption. Even the one play that appears to stand out against this pattern, *Fanshen*, which is based on a book about changing life in a Chinese village, has as a major component the ways in which a new revolutionary society tries to shake off the corrupting influence of the old society and the ways in which such influence creeps inexorably back.

As Hare's decade progresses the possibilities of survival become more limited. *Plenty* (1978) is the pivotal play in which all the pieces of individual and social perspective come together, and it forms one of the most ambitious attempts in postwar theatre to show why we are as we are, both as a nation and as individuals. The key scenes of *Plenty* are those that frame it — two episodes in France during and just at the end of the German occupation. One is reality, the other nostalgia. The play is concerned with how the one becomes the other.

A young woman, Susan, is sent to France by the Special Operations Executive in 1943. The network she works for is broken up so when she has to meet an incoming agent, Lazar, there is almost nothing left for him to do. He is, in any case, in the wrong place. She gives a few fragmentary notes on how to survive in a world of great hostility into which British agents are dropped, half-trained, with poor chances of lasting very long or achieving their objectives. Even the French underground is none too friendly. They have to rescue a parachute drop at gun-point from a Frenchman who tells them, 'Nobody ask you. Nobody ask you to come. Vous n'êtes pas les bienvenus ici.' As Susan comments, 'They just expect the English to die. They sit and watch us spitting blood in the streets.'

This episode of messed-up, bloody and inconclusive heroism dominates the rest of her life. In one of the final scenes, set some twenty years later, Susan goes to a cheap Blackpool hotel for one brief and fantasized fuck with Lazar. At this stage of the play fantasy and reality are confused and in the play's final passages we are squarely into the fairy world of nostalgic reminiscence. Susan walks to a hill overlooking the village where a party is being prepared to celebrate the Liberation. She discusses life a little with a caricature rural Frenchman and then announces, 'My friend. There will be days and days and days like this.' Curtain on the sunshine and pastoral beauty, which is a lifetime away from the fearful reality of the opening.

Nostalgia is a great British growth industry and forms one of the major components of its contemporary culture. It has become a minor art form in its own right on television and in films. There is no other country able to reproduce with such exactness not only the physical details of past society but also the precise forms of social class relations. Every year with unfailing regularity there rolls out for worldwide sale another set of meticulous reconstructions either of real historic events or of period fiction. The breadth and detail of this sub-culture of nostalgia is startling, forming a national drug that offers a regular fix of comfort and security. It provides a continual reminder not of anything so specific as economic success or imperial power but of a time when everything was in its place and could be understood as part of a coherent social whole. This can be just as true of left-wing contributions to this cultural flood. Jim Allen's powerful *Days of Hope* (1975), a series produced by Ken Loach and Tony Garnett for television, refers back, almost wistfully, to an uncomplicated time when workers were real workers and the bosses were truly grinding the oppressed.

One of the strongest aspects of *Plenty* is that it shows how the need for such nostalgic meanderings arises within the aimlessness of post-war society and its abiding sense of failure. It also shows just how destructive such sentiment can be. *Plenty* moves through the first years of postwar Britain, noting both breakdown and the failure to make any decisive break. All aspirations burn out within this framework. England is presented as a country that has lived like a camel off the fat in its hump, without making any attempt to regenerate itself.

Susan is shown living through moments of particular symbolic importance: the Festival of Britain, Suez and, rather less specifically focused, the time of the big Aldermaston marches. Throughout, both Brock, the failed diplomat whom Susan marries, and Alice, the failed artist, have simply passed away the time, steadily diminishing themselves. The one character left with any redeeming sense of purpose is, oddly, the relic, the ambassador who finally cannot accept Suez and speaks out against it. For this he is abandoned, his funeral ignored. After the ceremony a 17-year-old taught by Alice cadges money for an abortion of a child she has casually conceived. The cycle of corruption is complete, echoing in contrast Susan's hopeless and desperate attempt a decade before to break out of her situation by having a child with a man she hardly knew. The portrayal of Alice's life is the more striking because it avoids making any crass statement about her. Instead she is shown as still active, still outwardly struggling but with a growing moral void inside her. The causes still exist but the struggle for them seems no more than a gesture.

Plenty is an intensely personal play. The great events that are its backdrop remain as unexplored history. Hare's achievement is that he tries to make historic the personal lives he examines, through their close if indirect links with the passage of Britain as a nation. The cumulative effect of despair and moral corruption is undeniably powerful. The problem lies in the difference in dramatic levels Hare uses to illustrate cause and effect. Boldly and with a serious purpose he refuses to utilize the over-simplified chains of causality for which he has attacked many socialist writers. The effects of empire, of war, of economic stagnation, of racialism are not, he suggests, amenable to any simple class-based descriptions nor are they based simply in economics. Britain is a country that has failed, in various ways, to sustain itself. As a consequence people despair and go mad. This does not happen uniformly or according to any predictable pattern but still they are driven insane.

Hare suggests that the only remaining social sustenance is nostalgia — a readjustment of the past in ways which allow history to provide a security and comfort that the present denies. Even Susan, in the end, is forced to resort to this adjustment so that she can draw strength from her past. In a lecture (printed as an appendix to *Licking Hitler*) Hare says:

> We are living through a great, groaning, yawling festival of change — but *because this is England* [our emphasis] it is not always seen on the streets. In my view it is seen in the extraordinary intensity of people's personal despair, and it is to that despair that as a historical writer I choose to address myself time and time again: in *Teeth 'n' Smiles*, in *Knuckle*, in *Plenty*.

This statement is a positive stand against political simplicity and caricature. But there are problems connected with this view that diminish the dramatic success of such a highly political yet personal play as *Plenty*.

It is an evasion to say that 'because this is England' there is an extraordinary amount of despair in personal lives and to counterpose this to activity 'on the streets'. It may be true for most people, much of the time, but the job of an historical writer is to attempt an explanation — something that Hare only partially carries through. He relies upon the assertion that as a nation the British never really suffered and that only those who have known some pain and loss can hope to regenerate themselves both personally and socially. In the opening scene in Brussels, the English (and it is the English who stand for the decay of Britain) are shown as presiding over the ruins of Europe or taking motor holidays, constrained only by a limited travel allowance.

> BROCK: The misery is contagious, I suppose. You spend the day driving between bomb sites, watching the hungry, the homeless, the bereaved. We think there are thirty million people loose in Europe, who've had to flee across borders, have had to start again. And it is very odd to watch it all from here.

The only ones who can understand are those who have had their own portion of suffering.

> SUSAN: ...Those of us who went through this kind of war, I think we have something in common. It's a kind of impatience, we're rather intolerant, we don't suffer fools. And so we get rather restless back in England, the people who stayed behind seem childish and a little silly. I think that's why Tony needed to get away. If you haven't suffered... well.

Given the dominant complacency, all they can do is more or less quietly go under.

> LAZAR: I don't know what I expected... What I'd hoped for, at the time I returned. Some sort of edge to the life that I lead. Some sort of feeling their death was worthwhile. Some day I must tell you. I don't feel I've done well. I gave in. Always. All along the line. Suburb. Wife. Hell. I work in a corporate bureaucracy as well... I hate, I hate this life that we lead...

Regardless of whether or not this is an accurate portrayal of those who have suffered acute personal pain, it is hardly possible to slide the diagnosis on to entire cultures. There appears to be a simple equation: Britain equals rich but empty and Europe equals poor but fulfilled. It is an equation that is reflected in the irony of the play's title.

The implied position of the play is that the war had massive effects in Europe which, by and large, Britain avoided. The war provided in Britain a momentary arousal of social tension, superimposed upon a long-term decline rather than forming a decisive break point as in many European countries. But the portrayal of personal anguish as the only true antidote to social complacency is false in both dramatic and social terms. The specific description of 'Englishness' presented by *Plenty* is that of a nation that has never suffered and that, within England, those who have suffered as individuals are the only ones aware of the social blockage thus formed. Awareness or non-awareness are the only two stances offered and in the end both positions are passive.

In *A Map of the World* (1982), written at the beginning of a new decade, Hare repeats the problem but on a global scale. Both England and the rest of Europe are now presented as the rich who have not suffered compared to the poor third world. These two worlds confront each other behind the scenes of a UNESCO conference on the role of the writer. Hare's elision is this time even more grandiose and remote than in *Plenty*. A young and vaguely left-wing journalist, Stephen Andrews, stands for the liberal argument of the exploiters, and a reactionary Indian author, Victor Mehta, who lives in luxury in the English countryside, stands for the reality of the exploited. A Mozambique delegate, embroiled in the *realpolitik* of international power blocs, is seen to stand for those who have taken some control of their destinies in a non-capitalist way. However, he is no more than a secondary character; the main debate, which is unashamedly set up as an intellectual and formal joust, is between Andrews and Mehta. The prize, equally unashamedly articulated, is to possess a woman. The main protagonists seem to represent aspects of Hare's own persona, a view given some credence by the 'film within a play' technique that is used to question the nature of perception and how perception is changed into art as record and commentary. Hare gives Mehta the best arguments and melodramatically kills off Andrews, the loser — a symbol perhaps of Hare in the 1980s shaking off his past. In the shape of Andrews, the English are no longer even capable of producing an individual sufferer as they are in *Plenty*; that crucial experience belongs to a foreigner who nevertheless has to leave his country to survive.

What Hare says is that in a decaying society there are particular people who feel that decay acutely and another group who fumble and grope along, either immune to despair or at least in some way able to cope. At the end of *Plenty* it is the failed and corrupted Alice who takes Susan's flat as a home for battered wives; in *Teeth 'n' Smiles* (1975), it is Laura, the rejected and stifled group manager, who has to find the money to get her band home. Yet, in a rather diffuse sense, both are presented as failures; they are people who have dodged the central moral problem of their lives.

Hare produces an elite of sufferers like Susan; they carry the problem of Britain on their shoulders, by virtue of some event in their past lives. (In the case of the rock-singer in *Teeth 'n' Smiles* this may be as nebulous as being born into the wrong country at the wrong time.) The consequence of forcing the burden of suffering so heavily onto an elite is to make their pain, and in some cases their eventual madness, carry an enormous weight in order to preserve the internal dramatic balance of the plays. It is necessary to be totally convinced that those who are suffering are possessed of special insight and deserving of special attention. Otherwise the elite becomes simply a set of rather eccentric or fragile individuals who cannot take the normal stresses of everyday life. It requires great concentration of dramatic intensity to succeed in this aim and in *Plenty* Hare almost achieves it. But in the final scenes of fantasized retreat there is a gap between intention and achievement that robs Hare of his prize.

Hare is one of the few male playwrights of his generation to have persistently presented women as central characters. This points up a boldness as well as an ultimate failure. In fact he moves to another extreme; from his first play, *Slag*, which has only women characters, through *Teeth 'n' Smiles* and *Knuckle* to *Dreams of Leaving*, it is women who possess almost a monopoly of sensitivity to the nature of the society they live in. But he ends up by using the women as dramatic

devices. Essentially Hare does not write about women at all but rather
as blanks on which he can imprint an external, male pressure; and to
such pressure they respond only with pain or madness or, if they are
secondary characters, with baffled dismay. They exist without any
personal form; they have neither history nor any specific individual
comment. They are a formal expression of what Hare sees as the only
human response to the nature of society, an expression of that detachment which seems to be his recipe for survival. Men have to assume
some kind of presence in his plays that alters what they find around
them; the women exist as vacuums. Susan, for example, is given no
history, no social placing at all. The oddity of her being chosen as an
SOE courier when no more than an adolescent is not explained. She
appears to have no family. She is simply in France to receive the one
powerful stimulus which directs the rest of her life and which fashions
her sexuality.

In *Knuckle*, the 'she' is a lonely, isolated woman rather implausibly
working as a night-club manager — though it is an implausibility
which matters very little in a formalized pastiche, a dramatic exercise
in form which makes very effective commentary on abstracts such as
profit. In *Teeth 'n' Smiles* 'she', the rock-singer, is the fragmented
centre of a collapsing world. In *Dreams of Leaving* (which, although
written for television, has to be mentioned as the final implosion in this
phase of Hare's drama) 'she' is the mysterious Caroline who adopts
the logic necessary to Hare's progression: an unexplained, silent and
perverse withdrawal into madness.

Throughout the plays men shout at women 'Why don't you respond?'

> BROCK: ...I've spent fifteen years of my life trying to help you,
> simply trying to be kind, and my great comfort has been that I
> am waiting for some indication from you... some sign that you
> have valued this kindness of mine. Some love perhaps. Insane.
>
> [*Plenty*]

> WILLIAM: Don't you understand, don't you see what I'm saying, it's
> me who sticks up for you, it's me who stays loyal...
> CAROLINE: Yes, yes I see. And you want a reward?
>
> [*Dreams of Leaving*]

But finally it is the women who go mad, give up, seek only immediate
gratification, like the fantasized 'zipless fuck' in *Plenty*:

> LAZAR: Don't take your clothes off whatever you do.
> SUSAN: Of course not.
> LAZAR: That would spoil it hopelessly for me.

Hare, like many other male playwrights, finds it difficult to cope with female sexuality except in the form of women demanding immediate and complete sexual satisfaction. There is a real basis for Hare's observation of women refusing or being unable to communicate their emotions to men. But his response is to assume that its origin is in some kind of mental disturbance. It offers no real explanation rooted in the very feature he sets out to explore — the impact of social life, in particular male dominance, on personal conduct. He fails to acknowledge that often women do not seek to explain themselves to men because to do so is a recognition of domination and to remain silent is self-defence and a weapon.

Maybe Hare does hint at this by the grossness of the prize in *A Map of the World* — the winner of the argument wins the woman as well. But if this is meant to puncture any pomposity that surrounds the debate or undercut its importance as measured against the problems of the real world then the effect is contradictory; it confirms Hare's use of women as ciphers on whom he chooses to imprint his message. There is a subdued anger about this which never surfaces explicitly but underneath one suspects the same man-eating fears that Osborne expressed all those years before. (Despite the obvious differences there are nevertheless a number of similarities between Hare and Osborne.) As Susan says to the man whom she has chosen at random to impregnate her: 'Deep down I'd do the whole damn thing myself. But there we are. You're second best.'

The world remains an alienating force which ultimately prevents any communication and in which each individual is left to work out his or her own existential deal. The characters do not really talk to each other in *Plenty;* they pursue separate and distanced lives. *Dreams of Leaving* is Hare's final comment on a decade's work because it finally abandons history, abandons the project of connecting the levels between individual and social change and offers instead a vision of total non-communication taken as an explanation in itself. The central female character is almost the exact mirror of Maitland in Osborne's *Inadmissible Evidence*; where he offers a flood of diatribe and commentary on his self-obsession, Hare's heroine neither offers nor needs reasons for her retreat into silence and madness. It is sufficient to itself, a symbol of decay that has lost touch with any social force and has become, instead, an abstract pathology.

It is not surprising, therefore, that Hare's writing seems to have lost its way in the 1980s. *A Map of the World,* technically adroit and ambitious, lacks a plausible and coherent centre, whilst *Pravda* (1985), written with Howard Brenton, is little more than an inflated throwback to an earlier era but without the cutting edge. It is a complete expression of the dilemma which Hare raises concerning the inadequacy of merely exposing corruption: 'We have seen. We have known. And we have not changed.'* In *Pravda*, a Fleet Street comedy, press magnates are portrayed as evil despots and journalists as supine doormats. The audience laughs and demands even greater and more malignant caricatures. Brenton's style can survive this; after all, the grenades sometimes fail to explode but he readily moves on. For Hare, however, who has survived as a prisoner of conscience on a more delicate balance, the problem is much closer to the heart. Whilst expanding his channels of communication in other media, he has lost touch with the age in which he lives and has less and less to say.

---

* Lecture at King's College, Cambridge. *op. cit.*

CHAPTER TWELVE

Caryl Churchill:
Women and the Jigsaw of Time

It is an obvious fact that postwar British theatre writing is dominated by a group who are, on the whole, well-educated, white and male. The same is true, of course, of the other key areas of power in the theatre, especially directors, and this preponderance is itself a reflection of society at large.

'Why?' would be easy enough to answer if dealing with the question in terms of ethnic domination, given the barriers to education and to other opportunities that exist systematically for all ethnic minorities in Britain, not to mention the enormous cultural pressures in the British theatre which make it a very strange place for those not imbued with a particular cultural background. But the absence of women playwrights has to be considered in a more complex manner. After all, within those areas of university education which, for better or worse, have produced many modern playwrights, there is virtual equality of numbers between men and women. In many arts degree courses, women are in the majority, and with the novel they have always held a position of importance and, in postwar years, have often dominated. Yet in the theatre women have been almost entirely absent as playwrights. Research shows that women have always played their part in the development of theatre, although more is written about the all-male Greeks or the all-male Elizabethans than about the women in *commedia dell'arte* troupes or the female aristocrats who wrote under Elizabeth I.

A complete explanation for the absence of women would require a close examination of society, of how theatre is organized and of the experience of those women who have tried with varying success to establish themselves. But some general points can be made.

The theatre is dominated by men as directors and senior administrators, who are responsible for major decisions about productions. Despite their apparent liberality, it is clear that many men still hold that women cannot cope with the stresses of directing and cannot write for a general audience. The same decision-makers are of course responsible for the middle-class male-centred ambience of the theatre and the whole process is highly competitive. Most women are accustomed to withdrawing under such conditions; they tend not to compete in the male-dominated world of the theatre any more than they do in any other similarly structured area of society. Those who do take up the challenge are subject to the accusation of aggressiveness — an admirable quality for an ambitious man but regarded as unseemly in a woman. Female performers have their own particular problems: the small number of female parts that are available limits opportunity, whilst the pressures of family commitments and the constant, subtle, norms of physical attractiveness make it much more difficult for a woman to reach her full acting maturity.

It has required a positive and sometimes explosive intervention by women to gain acceptance as playwrights, even with the alternative theatre. They have established their autonomy with women-only or women-dominated collective groups but there are still few signs that the major state companies are prepared to change their directorial and play selection policies. But at least by the 1980s it was no longer a rarity to see a play written or directed by a woman.

Caryl Churchill occupies a very particular position among contemporary women dramatists; she has travelled the furthest and is capable of some of the boldest drama. Churchill has been writing since the early 1960s — as long as Edward Bond and Harold Pinter, though not with the same performed output. Her work until 1972 was written either for lunchtime theatre or for radio, a medium that attracts a high proportion of women writers, probably because it requires less author involvement during production.

Churchill has said that her early radio plays 'tended to be about bourgeois middle-class life and the destruction of it.'* Her decision with her husband, a barrister, to change the way they lived was a turning point for Churchill as a playwright. The element of destruction has remained in her plays but the awareness of personal experience and a gradual deepening analysis of it, both as unique to her but also shared with other women, has been crucial to her development. In 1972 she began writing for television, which she has done ever since, and with the production of *Owners* at the Theatre Upstairs that year, she began her fruitful relationship with the Royal Court where she was the first female Writer in Residence. She has had presented there *Objections to Sex and Violence* (1975, downstairs), *Light Shining in Buckinghamshire* (1976, upstairs), *Traps* (1977, upstairs), *Cloud Nine* (1979, downstairs), *Three More Sleepless Nights* (1980, upstairs, with Soho Poly), *Top Girls* (1982, downstairs) and *Fen* (1983, downstairs).

---

* Quoted in Cathy Itzin: *Stages in the Revolution: Political Theatre in Britain Since 1968* (Methuen, 1980).

The Royal Court association was closely related to her work with the Joint Stock Company, whose collaborative procedures had an important impact on her; it meant the end of her artistic isolation and she learned to refract through personal detail onto a wider social and historical canvas. Her collective work with the feminist group Monstrous Regiment — *Vinegar Tom* (1976) and, as co-author (with Bryony Lavery, Michelene Wandor, David Bradford and the company) *Floorshow* (1977) — was equally important in this respect and it led to a sharpening of her analytical abilities.

In *Light Shining in Buckinghamshire* Churchill presents episodes from the explosive mixture of religion and politics of the English Civil War, summoning up the vigour, rapture and confusion of the period. Some of the verbatim dialogue of the Putney Debates held among the Parliamentary Army leaders is inserted in the centre of the play at the end of Act I. It is matched at the end of Act II by a long scene between certain individuals involved in the Revolution and now tossed aside by it. This scene deals with personal hope and despair rather than with the great public matters of the Putney Debates. (This balance of internal structure between two poles of experience recurs constantly in her work; for example the modern/Victorian halves of *Cloud Nine* or the two sisters in *Top Girls*.) The inclusion of material from the Putney Debates themselves, however, rather reduces the coherence of the play. They are an extraordinary record, a transcript of a classic debate on popular power, but their very force and precision and the lack of any explicit connection between the Leveller leaders and the other characters make the surroundings more inconclusive than they should be. But what the play does show, and in 1976 this had a powerful contemporary parallel, was how underneath the flow of rhetoric associated with times of great social change there is a mass of people who attempt, in their own ways, to pick up pieces of the rhetoric and live them out in their own lives. The consequences for such people conducting their own social experiments may be far more deep-seated and disastrous than for the leaders.

For Churchill *Light Shining in Buckinghamshire* marks the beginning of her use of complex and rather formal dramatic structures to link personal and public experience. Although she does not here use the tricks of time-change that have been a feature of much of her more recent work, the power and imagery of the religious fervour, based upon obscure and unexplained theology, creates the same sense of disorientation. The play throws the audience off-balance and makes it work hard to understand the significance of what is being shown.

Vinegar Tom is in many ways a companion piece to *Light Shining in Buckinghamshire* though it is more personal and firmly focused on women, in particular a group accused of witchcraft. The common feature is not their sorcery but their independence; they are learning to live without men. Their choice is not a particularly conscious political one for they have drifted into independence or been forced into it. One young woman, Susan, goes mad after an abortion; another, Betty, is bled with leeches for refusing to marry the man of her father's choice; another, Alice, is accused by the husband of a hard-hearted neighbour who has refused to help Alice's starving family. His sexual frustration finds an outlet in a witch-hunt, which persecutes such women for being outside society, both economically and sexually. For their independence the women are accused, tortured and finally hanged. They represent a challenge and a threat, and are made into convenient scapegoats.

Monstrous Regiment was committed to the use of music, which throughout *Vinegar Tom* probes its contemporary significance and prevents it becoming lost in its historical setting. The final, savage song points to the male fear that is being confronted across the centuries:

> Do you ever get afraid
> You don't do it right?
> Does your lady demand it
> Three times a night?
> If we don't say you're big
> Do you start to shrink?
> We earn our own money
> And buy our own drink.
>
> Did you learn you were dirty boys, did you learn
> Women were wicked to make you burn?
> Satan's lady, Satan's pride,
> Satan's baby, Satan's bride,
> Witches were wicked and had to burn.
>
> Evil women
> Is that what you want?
> Is that what you want to see?
> In your movie dream
> Do they scream and scream?
> Evil women
> Evil women
> Women.

The appeal of *Vinegar Tom* is direct. It is an accusation: this is what was done to women and this is what continues to be done to women in other ways and in other disguises. The conscious awareness of the audience is vital to the play's structure and impact.

All playwrights, and especially those working with touring groups, have some conception of the audience for whom they are writing, either in commercial or sociological terms. There is a sense in which male writers write for men, but this is normally subconscious. Many women dramatists, and this is clearly true of Churchill, are writing deliberately with women in mind though this is not to say that they are writing exclusively for women. Even as a feminist group, Monstrous Regiment has included men in the company and has played to mixed audiences. But the awareness of writing with women in mind is reflected in the determination with which Churchill moves into certain dramatic areas of great complexity and delicacy that concern sexual politics.

An example of the confidence that Churchill derives from her assumed context is *Cloud Nine.* It uses the dramatic techniques of historical and character inversion that she has made very much her own. The first act is set in a late Victorian colony and the second in contemporary London, though for the characters of the first act only 25 years have passed. Men play the parts of women and vice versa and adults play the parts of children. The Victorian half is a comedy of repression with all kinds of sexual relationships occurring under the facade of Victorian colonial respectability. It is highly stereotyped and written with a deliberate and alienating mockery which is very funny. With Union Jack flying, the head of the household, Clive, presents his entourage far from home in Africa. Betty (played by a man) is 'all I dreamt a wife should be, And everything she is she owes to me.' Joshua (played by a white) is the perfect servant. He 'really has the knack. You'd hardly notice that the fellow's black.' Edward (played by a woman) 'is young. I'm doing all I can To teach him to grow up to be a man.' To which Edward replies: 'What father wants I'd dearly love to be. I find it rather hard as you can see.'

The contemporary half of the play is also full of diverse sexual pairings but they are presented as having gone some way towards challenging repression. There is no lack of problems or of pain for those involved but the overall feeling is one of possibility: perhaps women can love women; perhaps they can even live happily with men; perhaps they can bring up children half-way sane. In the final optimistic movement of the play, Betty, the young wife of the first act, comes out to embrace Betty, the ageing mother of the second who has accepted that her son and daughter are both gay and has herself begun a timid process of sexual adventure. The cast sing *Cloud Nine*, celebrating liberation from the expectations of sexual role-playing: 'It'll be fine when you reach Cloud 9... Upside down when you reach Cloud 9.' Whatever the contortions and personal chaos, the ending is one of hope that the bungled and haphazard personal liberation of the 1960s and 1970s (indirectly observed in *Light Shining in Buckinghamshire*) could lead to something positive. Nevertheless, this section is not written with such assuredness as the first and, in comparison, tends to underscore the hope as tentative and romantic. Perhaps Churchill's belief in the possibility was less firm than she could admit at that time.

There is a gap of only three years between *Cloud Nine* and *Top Girls* but an emotional chasm exists between them; what emerges as hope in the former has been changed into fear, pain and something close to degeneration in the latter, as if Churchill were acknowledging the reality after the illusion. *Top Girls* takes the historical intercutting of *Cloud Nine* one stage further. A dinner party assembles at a smart restaurant. The host is a contemporary career woman, Marlene; the guests are women from a real or fictional history — Joan, the legendary woman pope; a 19th-century explorer, Bird; a Japanese Emperor's courtesan; a character from a Chaucer story, Patient Griselda; Dull Gret from a Brueghel painting of women expelling devils from Hell. They talk in fast and overlapping conversation which eventually lapses into drunken uproar. The apparent babble is difficult to follow. Intentionally there is no attempt at formal exposition; each woman talks to her neighbour, interrupts and responds to interruptions. It is in fact a highly structured text with every question and interruption being answered, but the audience is left to pick out key points from this apparently absurd context. It is a bold dramatic device achieving an almost complete disorientation and sense of historical chaos while at the same time spanning history to embrace its continuity through certain aspects of women's experience.

The play demands a degree of rapport or commitment between audience and subject. What pulls the threads together is children — the conflict for women between rearing children and independence, and the problem of living a full and caring life without children in a male-dominated, competitive society. It is a child who finally becomes the focus of the play at the moment when she is becoming a woman. Only Dull Gret, who is almost inarticulate throughout, stands apart from the others. She is the bottom line, a woman who has done nothing but bear children, scrape for food, and avoid death until finally pushed down into Hell:

> ...But most of us is fighting the devils. There's lots of little devils, our size, and we get them down all right and give them a beating. There's lots of funny creatures round your feet, you don't like to look, like rats and lizards, and nasty things, a bum with a face, and fish with legs, and faces on things that don't have faces on. But they don't hurt, you just keep going. Well we'd had worse, you see, we'd had the Spanish. We'd all had family killed. Men on wheels. Babies on swords. I'd had enough, I was mad, I hate the bastards.

All the women are telling their life-stories and in the process telling about the role of women in history. The strain of disentangling the threads is emphasized by the lack of an explanation of the nature of the gathering. The women seem perfectly at home, ordering Waldorf salad and cannelloni in between talk of the 13th-century Japanese court or 9th-century Rome. It is not suggested that the gathering is a constructed fantasy of Marlene, though it might be. The party simply exists as a given fact: women meet, complain about men, tell stories and get drunk. It is another example of the disorientation that Churchill invokes by various dramatic devices in most of her work. The audience is forced to struggle to understand at a deeper level than the apparently bizarre reality being presented. In effect she uses dramatic structure as a symbol for the point she is trying to make. *Top Girls* is partly an intellectual puzzle. The necessary clues are all presented to find the solution, except that the solution is itself a puzzle. How can women survive, with children or childless, in the kind of society we have?

The rapid and unexplained set-piece is completely removed once it has served its purpose. Abruptly the scene changes to a London West End employment agency where Marlene has just won promotion over a man to become 'Top Girl'. The structure of these scenes is much simpler than that of the opening chaos in the restaurant. Yet the same pattern recurs, as the women who work in the agency and those who come to find jobs tell of their struggle for some kind of independence or self-realization. They describe the bulldozing careerism, the nervous breakdowns, heavy drinking or loneliness, or the years of grudging 'spinsterhood' in an office. Yet the women who do not work fare little better. One young woman dreams of speeding up motorways in a Porsche, eating fillet steak and mushrooms in posh hotels. In real life she is unemployed. The wife of the man passed over for promotion by Marlene is presented as obsessed with her husband's career; bitter and afraid she has no world outside the failure or success of her man.

The third area shown is that of the adolescent, Angie, being brought up in East Anglia by Marlene's sister, Joyce, who is seen as tightlipped and hard pressed. The child is wild and spiteful, resenting Joyce, and playing fantasy games with her one friend. (Both of the children were played by adults in the original production.) The fantasies are very rich and usually violent, and they counterpoint the hectic yet shallow lives of the adults at the agency. Angie's talk with her friend is full of death, destruction, sex, war, menstrual blood and of a fearful fascination with the mysterious world of adults that is going to solve all her problems. This hope is focused on Marlene in London. However, when Angie takes a brave step and visits the agency on her own, she is written off by Marlene as 'a bit thick', unsuited for anything but being 'a packer in Tesco'.

The dramatic resolution of the piece is very simple, though a little too rushed. Marlene turns out to be Angie's biological mother, having left her with Joyce when she was seventeen. In the final scene, set before Angie's trip to London, Marlene visits East Anglia; the sisters quarrel with the practised resignation of those who are both very close and also far apart. Neither is condemned for her own particular way of surviving. In the closing moment, Angie wakes from a nightmare and is comforted by Marlene:

> MARLENE: Did you have a bad dream? What happened in it? Well
> you're awake now, aren't you pet?
> ANGIE: Frightening.

It is a depressing conclusion, which the audience knows to be justified from the chronologically later but dramatically earlier scene in the agency when Marlene is dismissive of the adoring Angie, asleep in her office.

There is an underlying ambiguity in *Top Girls* that recognizes the conflicting impulses for women in male society between self-fulfilment and responsibilities which stem from their biological uniqueness. The successful but empty Marlene emerges as a crude Thatcherite while Joyce is the one who has kept faith in her working-class politics. There is a sense in which Joyce has also kept faith by raising her sister's abandoned daughter — a moral balance which is overweighted by the discovery that Joyce lost her own child because she was too tired and busy bringing up Angie. Although this does not represent the simplistic elision between sexuality and politics of, for instance, *Objections to Sex and Violence*, the left/right contrast does appear to be tacked on to the rest of the play rather unconvincingly.

The deliberate and caricatured barrenness of Marlene's life is too harsh a contrast with the extraordinary lives of the chosen historical characters. Churchill on purpose has not made Marlene an engineer, a doctor or a barrister, for example, a choice which would have altered the balance of the play decisively. Perhaps the roots of her need to be independent are more important? But they are only sketched in and are presented as little more than a dislike of her home life. The need for Marlene to be free may be as basic as that of the explorer Isabella, but the play denies her the possibility of Isabella's transient but intense joy. Whether that is Marlene's fault or the lack of any corresponding possibility in our society to Isabella's exotic experiences is never made clear.

Independence is explored again in *Fen*, which is in many ways a companion play to *Top Girls*, set in the harsh countryside of Angie's home — the flat Fens of East Anglia. Here a group of women pick their way through their repressed lives, hounded by the farm owners who employ them and hedged in by the demands of family, especially their children.

There is little or nothing of comfort in *Fen;* the chill of the landscape spreads into an emotional coldness. There is little of the humour which pervades *Cloud Nine* and even *Top Girls*. Its bleakest feature is the emphasis Churchill places on the harm women do to themselves, regarding themselves as rubbish, or to others as a reflection of their own self-hatred. In particular they turn on the only two women in the play who attempt an independent life. One leaves her family for a lover and, after being torn apart emotionally, is killed by him as the only resolution to her dilemma. The other simply lives alone. She is radical and assertive in her attitudes to the farm owners and for this she is taunted by the children and regarded as eccentric by the adult women.

In *Vinegar Tom* the independent women are tortured and hanged, but by men. Between themselves they preserve a certain common trust and solidarity. In *Fen* it is women who fail to support each other and allow no room for independence. The play lacks the complexity of internal structure and balance of *Cloud Nine* or *Top Girls* and falls uneasily between an imaginative, poetic style and a naturalistic one. This is a common tension in Churchill's plays that expresses itself in her experiment with form and with stage time. This is most coherently achieved in *Traps* (written just before *Light Shining in Buckinghamshire* though performed later); different moments in time co-exist on stage, as do the different relationships among a group of people in a country cottage at those moments. Their only reality is the one conferred by the play; there is no resolution to the conflicts of their lives save that they all happen and can be encompassed within the play.

Although Churchill's other plays are not as esoteric as *Traps*, they are also driven by intellectual concerns, and have the brittle quality of determined but tentative exploration. Churchill does not write at full throat, as does, for example, Pam Gems. She has not commanded the big stage either at the national companies or in the West End, nor aimed at a popular audience. She would not describe herself as a political playwright — nor is she — just as she would not accept the label 'feminist' without qualification.

In terms of subject, Churchill's most political play — in the traditional sense — is *The Legion Hall Bombing* (1978). It is a dramatized version for television of the trial of Willie Gallagher who was sentenced to twelve years' imprisonment on bombing charges in Northern Ireland. At the time of the broadcast Gallagher was on hunger strike, protesting his innocence. Churchill took her name off the credits because the BBC cut the epilogue and re-wrote the prologue in which she had indicted the anti-democratic Diplock court system used by the British in Northern Ireland whereby evidence obtained under force is admitted and a judge sits alone without a jury.

In *Softcops* (1984) — a departure for Churchill in its reliance on images, though characteristically juxtaposed without regard to chronology or traditional narrative — she takes again the theme of law and order to explore how authority breeds its own opposites. Cops need robbers as society uses increasingly sophisticated techniques to isolate illegal acts. In this way, methods of control, whether in school or hospital or social work, help to depoliticize resistance and win conformity.

Churchill's sexual politics are more sharply focused than her other political leanings, which, broadly speaking, are critical of the values of capitalist society. However, her recurring theme of sexual relations and independence of women often has a political corollary: Marion, the childless property developer in *Owners;* Marlene, the Thatcherite in *Top Girls* who abandons her child; the coincidence of the sexual and political repression in *Objections to Sex and Violence.* Churchill's awareness of gender is more highly mobilized than her awareness of class, and at the centre of this preoccupation she places — uniquely in the theatre — one of the most basic of social activities: rearing children. Having, or not having, a child is a thread that runs throughout her work.

Her final position remains ambiguous, moving from a celebration of sexual liberation to suspicion of its neutralizing effects on women. There is a hint of a kind of biological reduction hanging over this, for, despite her appreciation of the role of material conditions in *Light Shining in Buckinghamshire*, her view of female independence largely ignores the role of money in determining the ways in which women approach child-rearing. The distinction made is often between women who have children and face their responsibility and those who do not. But Churchill never comes to a dogmatic conclusion.

This line of development may be due to her isolation from the left-wing movements and culture of the late 1960s and early 1970s in which her male counterparts were involved, and her emergence from this isolation with the strengthening of the women's movement. She came to feminism through an analysis of her own experiences and a scepticism about all given ideas and social roles. Her plays reflect this journey. They do not argue a position; they examine contending philosophies within what could very loosely be called a feminist-socialist perspective. There is a close link between the intellectual content of her work and the dramatic structure and language of each play. In that sense she is like Edward Bond in whose work one can also trace a continuing thread of intellectual change. But, unlike Bond, it is the fusion between intellect and effect that is the driving force and largely determines the ultimate success of each play.

It is easy enough to find flaws precisely because any gap between content and effect shows up in the complex structure and language that Churchill devises, and because she develops her thoughts constantly. However, she has broken through barriers and taboos both in form and content and, to a point, in acceptance. That she has achieved this, and that other women playwrights are building on their experiences in similar ways, is an optimistic sign for British drama.

Select Bibliography

The best introduction to the playwrights is the plays themselves. Virtually all those referred to have been published. There is a mass of secondary literature on individual writers, ranging from major studies to countless magazine or newspaper articles. In a few cases, writers have also published autobiographies.

The following offer a general background to postwar British playwrights or commentary on important aspects of the period:

Ansorge, Peter. Disrupting the Spectacle: Five Years of Experimental and Fringe Theatre in Britain (Pitman, 1975). *Spirited survey of the alternative theatre's pioneers. Good on the libertarian influence.*

Arden, John. To Present the Pretence: Essays on the Theatre and its Public (Methuen, 1977). *Major, radical, statement on role, meaning and practice of drama.*

Beauman, Sally. The Royal Shakespeare Company: A History of Ten Decades (Oxford University Press, 1982). *Full account of background to and first 20 years of a key, nationally subsidized company. Less critical the nearer the author comes to the present.*

Bentley, Eric (editor). The Theory of the Modern Stage: An Introduction to Modern Theatre and Drama (Penguin, 1968). *Primer of practitioners whose ideas shaped postwar drama, such as Artaud, Brecht, Gordon Craig, Stanislavski.*

Bradby, David and **McCormack, John.** People's Theatre (Croom Helm, 1978). *Outline of attempts to broaden the content and appeal of theatre in Europe and America.*

Brook, Peter. The Empty Space (MacGibbon and Kee, 1968). *Manifesto of rediscovery and renewal.*

Browne, Terry. Playwrights' Theatre: The English Stage Company at the Royal Court (Pitman, 1975). *First 20 years of crucial company in which it presented the work of more than 150 writers. List of plays and interesting financial tables.*

Chambers, Colin. Other Spaces: New Theatre and the RSC (Methuen, 1980). *Summary of how the RSC was renewed through the influence of the alternative theatre and the work of Buzz Goodbody.*

Craig, Sandy (editor). Dreams and Deconstructions: Alternative Theatre in Britain (Amber Lane, 1980). *Informative essays covering the spectrum of post-1968 activities.*

Elsom, John. Post-War British Drama (Routledge and Kegan Paul, 1976). *Lectures-turned-essays on selected trends.*

Elsom, John and **Tomalin, Nicholas.** The History of the National Theatre (Cape, 1978). *Saga of establishing Britain's most publicly-funded theatrical resource.*

Findlater, Richard (editor). At the Royal Court: 25 Years of the English Stage Company (Amber Lane, 1981). *Illustrated compendium of reminiscences with list of productions and their casts, and financial tables for each year.*

Gooch, Steve. All Together Now: Alternative View of Theatre and the Community (Methuen, 1984). *Insider's view of undervalued theatre work and links with its audiences.*

Goorney, Howard. The Theatre Workshop Story (Methuen, 1981). *Rare book on this outstanding company, by one of its members. Anecdotal, warm-hearted, with list of productions.*

Itzin, Cathy. Stages in the Revolution: Political Theatre in Britain since 1968 (Methuen, 1980). *Brisk, chronological reportage of key figures and groups, making much use of interviews. List of productions and their venues.*

Marowitz, Charles, Milne, Tom and **Hale, Owen** (editors). New Theatre Voices of the Fifties and Sixties: Selections from Encore Magazine 1956–1963 (Methuen, 1965). *Reports from the front line as theatre underwent its first major postwar change.*

McGrath, John. A Good Night Out — Popular Theatre: Audience, Class and Form (Methuen, 1981). *Polemical lectures based on experience of leading socialist touring company.*

Rowell, George and **Jackson, Anthony.** The Repertory Movement: A History of Regional Theatre in Britain (Cambridge University Press, 1984). *Origins and development of new voices outside London, with a chronology, sample repertory programmes, audience attendance figures and comparative funding statistics.*

Taylor, John Russell. Anger and After: A Guide to the New British Drama (Methuen, 1962). *Immediate response to the 1956 watershed, taking in television as well as the Royal Court, Theatre Workshop, the regional upsurge and the Arts Theatre.*

Trussler, Simon (editor). New Theatre Voices of the Seventies: Sixteen interviews from Theatre Quarterly 1970–1980 (Methuen, 1981). *Views of major figures including Barker, Bond, Brenton, Edgar, Griffiths, Hare, McGrath, Mercer and Wesker.*

Tynan, Kenneth. A View of the English Stage 1944–1965 (Paladin, 1975). *Selection of reviews charting course of theatre with flair and wit.*

Wandor, Michelene. Understudies: Theatre and Sexual Politics (Methuen, 1981). *Introduction to women's and gay liberation in the theatre.*

Wardle, Irving. The Theatres of George Devine (Cape, 1978). *Illuminating account of a man and his colleagues at the centre of theatrical innovation.*

Willett, John (editor and translator). Brecht on Theatre: The Development of an Aesthetic (Methuen, 1978). *Chronologically ordered translation of Brecht's major theoretical writings. Should be read alongside the plays.*

Index